THE SOUL OF A TRAINER

THE SOUL OF A TRAINER

You Were Born to Change the World

Thomas Plummer

Foreword
Dan John

On Target Publications
Aptos, California

The Soul of a Trainer—You Were Born to Change the World

Thomas Plummer

Foreword: Dan John

Photographs by Thomas Plummer

ISBN-13: 978-1-931046-46-6
First printing June 2018

On Target Publications
P O Box 1335
Aptos, California 95001 USA
OTPbooks.com

Library of Congress Cataloging-in-Publication Data

Names: Plummer, Thomas, author.
Title: The soul of a trainer : you were born to change the world / Thomas
    Plummer ; foreword Dan John.
Description: Aptos, California : On Target Publications, 2018.
Identifiers: LCCN 2018005497 (print) | LCCN 2018016270 (ebook) | ISBN
    9781931046459 (epub) | ISBN 9781931046466 (pbk.)
Subjects: LCSH: Personal trainers--Miscellanea.
Classification: LCC GV428.7 (ebook) | LCC GV428.7 .P58 2018 (print) | DDC
    613.71--dc23
LC record available at https://lccn.loc.gov/2018005497

DEDICATION

Always to Susan

You are, and always will be,

The best thing in my life

CONTENTS

FOREWORD

It's easy to enjoy Thom Plummer. I enjoy his workshops; I enjoy his company, and I enjoy his writing.

I always feel like Thom is talking to me. Even if I am sitting in a room with 500 other people, Thom seems to be talking right to me. When he talks about the crazies, the lazies, and the daisies who inhabit the gyms and fitness clubs, I swear he is talking about Crazy Jerry and the other nut jobs at my old gym.

When he leans in and whispers to us in his prose poetry style about living a full and balanced life, I can feel his arm around my shoulders.

I found great joy in this little story:

"I remember lost nights drinking wine around a table with friends until asked to leave (we have been kicked out of better places than this, we insist yet again), grabbing more wine and then talking, laughing, and giggling until we were out of wine or too tired to go on."

As I read this, I wondered out loud: "Wasn't that with me?"

And, more to the point, we ran out of wine?

Thom has done wonders for those of us in the fitness industry. He reminds us, constantly, that those of us who coach and train don't have to be martyrs or monks when it comes to being fairly compensated.

Moreover, he firmly believes we should live in a balance. In this volume, you will find a wonderful give and take with some hero on social media:

The reader took offense with Thom's focus on making a living as a trainer. In what might be my favorite part of the book, Thom valiantly and brilliantly points out the reader's folly by explaining that compensation is both earned and expected...and that living with Mom might not be the way to go through life.

Thom, unlike our modern social media gurus, freely admits and accepts mistakes. I find this both refreshing and real. It also makes for honest, laugh-out-loud reading. Be careful reading this on an airplane as you will need to explain yourself to your neighbors and flight attendants.

He gives us an uncommon wisdom: Peace will come to you when you stop giving a damn about what others think of you. Thom isn't a 14-year-old girl crying over the lack of "likes" on her Facebook page. He doesn't need a thumbs up. Thom is here to tell you some things about life.

I'm thinking that my gravestone may have to be changed to this line from Thom:

"I don't want to be perfect, but I am totally happy being wonderful."

And, for the record, I will not quote Thom on this one, but I will give him full credit for the single best insight in the history of fitness:

> *Number Nine on the Worst Ideas in Fitness:*
> *The guy who first invented moderation.*

Moderation sucks.

Drink good wine and just do more pushups.

But, this is why we love him. Right after he rails against moderation, he reminds us of this:

- *Sit quietly and read.*

- *Respect every human the same.*

- *Change the world around you for the better today.*

I spent much of my life teaching theology and religious studies and I'm not sure I can summarize our brief dance on Planet Earth any better...certainly not any clearer.

If all you read is his *Unwritten Rules of Fitness,* you will be a better spouse, parent, coach, trainer, and human person. Let Thom tell us this universal truth:

"If you always do the right thing with your clients, do your best to get results, and concentrate on charging a fair price for what you know, you will win. No one goes broke doing the right thing."

Thom Plummer. I feel better about humanity just saying his name.

Dan John

PREFACE

My life has been spent on the road.

This over 40–year career has resulted in more than three million miles in the air, uncountable and often nasty hotels, airport bars only a raging alcoholic could remember, and an average of over 40 weeks a year on the road since the 1980s.

I wouldn't change a thing, not one second, not one miserable night sleeping on the floor in an airport during a snow storm drinking Jack Daniels with the road manager from Jefferson Starship, not one canceled flight, not one low-rent, end-of-the-day, one-star hotel, not one hangover, not one pint, and not one "stay up until 4:00 and then catch the 7:00 in the morning" flight home.

Why?

Because there have been over 300,000 people who have shown up to my workshops and they expected me to be there, to be alive, and help them get better in business and in their lives. These people have bought a few hundred thousand books, faithfully followed me on social media, and have trusted me over my entire career to always do the right thing for them in their businesses and, as I aged through the years, as a personal coach in their lives.

These loyal supporters had faith I could change their success, fix the major problems and issues in business and life, and simply be there as needed to make sure they didn't fail. This trust had to be met and has resulted in a long run. Every second was worth the adventure because almost all of them succeeded and made our industry a better place to work as we chase our passion.

This book is a collection of posts that became a way to laugh at what we do, to make a quick business point, or to teach a life lesson after a call with a particularly stressed-out client. The coaching business is one of the most important ways to make a living. You change lives; you do it every day, and now you can make some serious money doing it. Until just the last few years, coaching was mostly a labor of love because there sure as hell was no money in the profession in the early days.

I created the modern training business in the mid-90s. It was more accident than power of the mind, but it worked as a business concept. The days in the early era of the training business, where you could work your ass off and maybe do $300,000 a year in your little gym—if you were really good—became a place today where some of the best, and sometimes not the best, can do over two million dollars in the same spaces.

The business model has evolved through the years, but fundamentally it still works. Today there are successful gyms in over 30 countries using the business platform I created and teach in our workshops. Coaches are living their dreams because their businesses make enough money to create a living for those who choose to dedicate their lives to changing the world.

Thank you to every single student who ever attended a workshop or purchased a book.

Your faith and trust kept me going for longer than I ever planned or believed I could.

I hope you enjoy this book as much as I did creating it.

Thomas Plummer
January 2018

INTRODUCTION

You were born to change the world.

Few people in your life will have the right perspective to tell you this, because few will ever be in a situation to touch as many people as you will.

Most of your friends and your support group would laugh you out of the room if you had the nerve to openly admit this is what you believe about yourself, that you are passionate about a career few others understand and many mock. It is hard for them to grasp that you are living your dream and wearing funny clothes every day, while they toil away in an office or driving a truck, doing work that matters little to them or to the universe.

Your mother might say she believes you were born to change the world, but she is also the one who still cries in the closet because you never became a famous doctor and secretly wonders why you only own one nice outfit, yet you have 50 tee shirts. Someday, she hopes, you will grow up, get a real job, and be like your older brother, who hates his career and envies your willingness to live your dream.

The reality is no one but you has to believe you were born to change lives. If you believe being a fitness professional is your life's work, then you were born to change the world by making those around you healthier, happier, and more functional in life because of your help, guidance, and willingness to care.

In our business, we often get so busy, we mentally lose sight of what we are getting done in the world. Your day starts at dawn; you slap down food as best you can, standing at the kitchen counter while the rest of your house is asleep, and then you're off to work starting with your first client before most of the city is awake.

Most of you will still be standing in the same gym smiling and sweating at 9:00 o'clock that night. One-on-ones, small groups, teams of 20, athletes, wannabe athletes, old people, professionals, spoiled housewives, and even the occasional superstar are all part of a coach's day, but this endless stream often dulls the perspective that you have the strength and talent to make whomever is in your face for that session a better person.

Because a trainer cared, an older lady was able to pick up and hug her granddaughter.

Because a trainer cared, a guy got promoted when he gained confidence in his body.

Because a trainer cared, a couple had sex for the first time in a long time and felt good about taking off their clothes in the light.

Because a trainer cared, a woman rode a bike with her daughter for a half an hour, wearing a bigger smile than the kid.

When you are tired, hungry, and have had enough of your clients this week, remember that because a trainer cared, the world is a much better place, and because you care, you are helping change the world one client at a time. Make it a good week and take pride in giving a damn about what you do and whom you touch.

You exist to change lives. That is the soul of a trainer, and that is the mission of a professional coach.

You are not here to build wealth, although if you are a true master coach, that will happen. You are not here as a simple employee paying your dues while learning your craft, although this is where many of you will begin. If you're a true professional, you are not there wasting a few years of your life waiting to grow up and get a real job, although sadly, too many coaches with immense potential leave the industry too soon because they never figured out what it takes to survive such a tough business. You are there every day to change the lives of those around you; this is a heavy responsibility few others can understand.

We often think of other careers as the ones that matter, but few have the potential to affect so many lives as deeply as a master coach. Schoolteachers do noble work, but only touch a small handful of children a year. Police and firemen are dedicated professionals doing often dangerous work with little respect, yet they too only touch relatively few people. Perhaps medical professionals are the only ones who reach as many people as a coach can during a typical week. We may dress funny, and we can certainly take credit for inventing the meal eaten standing up and served in plastic bowls, yet the world is a better place because people like you choose to help others live better lives.

You cannot reach your potential as a master coach without understanding the foundational fact that what you do matters, and what you do makes a difference in the world around us. If you understand this, you are on the right path to build a long and profitable career as a true fitness professional.

It takes years to become a master coach, and while many new trainers often use the term, few have earned the title because reaching that elite status takes more work than most are willing to put into their careers. "Master coach" has many definitions, but perhaps one of the strongest is when you finally reach the point when you understand you don't know everything, and never will.

Becoming a master coach is about the journey, and never about arriving at a single destination. There are master coaches in the field, such as Dan John, Mike Boyle, Gray Cook, Greg Rose, Alwyn Cosgrove, or Janet Alexander, and the next-generation masters, such as Charlie Weingroff, Justin Grinnell, Rick Mayo, and Ali Gilbert, who just seem to get better with age. They never fail to amaze those around them with their never-ending search to be better, learn more, and keep growing.

Your goal is not to worry about the title, but to concentrate on becoming the best you can be over time. It's an adventure that will not end as long as you choose to grow and progress.

This long process toward becoming a master coach is about lifelong learning and studying the lessons from those who have gone before you.

This book is about those lessons, but you probably won't find these anywhere else in your search. There aren't any training tips here, no ideal workouts, or ways to coach a better swing.

The ideas and concepts in this book are about how to create a fulfilling career, sustainable over time, doing work that matters, and being able to make a decent living in the process.

Being a fitness professional is one of those rare careers where if you have the passion and want the dream badly enough, you can make it happen. You can be the coach who, at the end of his days, looks back and says, "I made a difference, and my clients and those around me are better today. I did my job as a true professional."

Working in fitness used to be something you did until you moved on and got a real job. The average fit pro usually lasted less than eight years and was gone. But that is changing. People now realize fitness can be a life's work, and they can spend the rest of a working career doing what they love. The day you declare to yourself and everyone in your life that this is it, this is my choice, and this is what I am going to do until you pry that last kettlebell out of my cold dead fingers will be the best day of your life.

The challenge is to keep moving forward and up so there will be enough money to pay for your family and your life. Increasing your business skill set, advancing your knowledge, and trying different aspects of the fitness world all combine to keep you funded and mentally growing, which is vital to stay alive in this field.

Many people waste their entire lives searching for a perfect place in life. Maybe you have already found yours, but you just haven't yet told the world you are exactly where the universe thinks you should be.

Knowing what you want, who you are, and where you are going makes for a very happy person in life. I hope that is you living a life in fitness.

Thomas Plummer

FITNESS PROFESSIONALS ONLY HAVE TWO SPEEDS

FITNESS PROFESSIONALS ONLY HAVE TWO SPEEDS

Fitness professionals only have two speeds in their internal motors: full on, flat out and all in, or destroyed on the couch, drooling like an old bulldog, and often not smelling much better.

Fitness professionals, as well as many other driven people attempting to create a career and a life, are always worn out physically, and most importantly mentally, because they never learn how to rest both body and soul.

Working 60 hours or more a week, slamming down a few beers on Saturday night, and then lying in a heap on the couch all of Sunday, hoping it's raining so the kids will nap with you all day is not rest. That is just not working. Knowing the difference will improve your life.

There is no true rest for your weary soul and body without combining mindlessness and mindfulness into your disciplined routines of life.

"Mindless" means to disengage completely from your life for a few hours at a time. No phones, no work all week then do a race all weekend, no clients, no marketing books, no "Let me check my email," no texts...just a few hours out of sight and out of mind.

"Mindfulness" means to rest with intensity focused on where you are and what you are doing. If you take the kids to the park, you are all about them for a few hours. You play, run, hide and seek, roll in the grass, and never once try to parent with a phone in your hand, not-so-secretly trying to check your messages.

"Mindfulness" means you are present in your life, committed to the moment at hand, without the need to let your mind attempt to be in many places at once, such as responding to an endless stream of texts constantly taking you away from where you are in the moment.

Think about being mindful this way:

You are holding your child, who is slumped in your lap enjoying the nearness of you.

These moments are gone in a few brief years, never to be recaptured.

During those moments, ones that may make up your last thoughts 50 years from now as you lie dying, is there any text in the world more important?

Is there really any call that should interrupt a walk on the beach with the one you love, the one you committed to for life, and with whom because you have so few moments of togetherness, your relationship is strained?

You and your significant person, you and the kids, you and friends, or just you, mindfully aware of the hike, the café, the view, or just sitting with a cup a tea, focused on nothing but simply enjoying a few focused minutes outside of yourself, letting mind and soul heal.

You are tired because you never learned that planning rest is as important as planning work. Resting your body and soul isn't something you do after you have completely torn apart each one; mindless and mindful rest is something you do to prevent you from destroying yourself at an early age.

We used to think there was something noble in life and business to work ourselves to death building a career. Then a generation of "successful" people woke up and realized they now had money, but little else of their lives was left. Chasing the dream over time ended up killing the dreams that are important.

Can you have it all?

Can you chase endless dreams at the expense of all other things in life?

Yes...and probably no.

Balance is an outdated concept, at least the way the term was defined by too many people who probably never created anything of value. "Balance" was defined as everything in life being equal at all times.

Your family, your job, your commitment to the community, and your faith all lived in balance with the idea that if you put too much energy into one, you would damage or lose the others. Everything equal every day.

There is nothing of value in the world that was not created by someone who pushed the edges, challenged how things were done, and went all in to change the world. It's hard to change the world around you unless you are focused to the point where you just can't breathe another day without finishing the dream.

Going all in—surging—can be coupled with backing off and creating a life that matters. Surging means all in. Backing off means to take the time to heal and rest. Surging means telling the family that for a few weeks, "I am going to go completely insane. I am going to 'surge' and I can only carry you, a friend or two, and hold my job if I want to get this done. I have to give up most everything else.

"After the surge, I will return to normal, or as best I can to appear that way, and we will take that vacation, resume the beach time, go to a few parties, and have a life again. But not for these weeks when I am going to give everything I have to write that book, or create that new company, or somehow figure out what it takes to move my life forward in a big leap."

Surging means nothing more than total concentration, followed by a period of normal existence in a crazy world. Surging means that for an extended time, you force yourself out of balance into a mindset where getting it done is the most important thing for a defined period of time.

When we are not in a full-on surge, we taper work with rest. We find mindless things to clear our minds, but we stay mindful of the moment we are in, knowing that moment may never come again.

Working hard in life is a good thing. Resting hard is a better thing.

Done together, you can own the world, but no one needs yet another tired, worn-out, cranky, recently divorced person who never learned that a little planned soul preservation might have saved a marriage, business, and family.

WHY DID YOU BECOME A COACH?

Simple question, hard answer.

You most likely started down one of several paths. You might have been a former athlete and this is your life. You love fitness and always wanted to be part of it, or you are motivated by the need to help people and this is your vehicle.

The reality in this profession is that it doesn't matter how you got in—it only matters that you find a reason to keep doing what you are doing.

We get in for a variety of reasons, but we only stay for one. If you don't commit to changing the world around you each day, you will fail. There are better ways to make money. There are endless jobs with better hours. There are jobs that are more respected than what we do.

But there are very few jobs where the potential to change lives is greater.

If you stay, you stay to change lives.

If you are smart, you can make a lot of money doing this. But the essence of what you do every day is to get up, lead clients to a better life than they would have without you, and then go home, quietly happy knowing that what you do matters to a lot of people and not many do it better than you.

At the end of your days, it won't matter why you chose this profession.

It deeply matters why you stay. Remember why you do what you do.

The world is a much better place because you are a professional coach.

WE FORGET THE POWER OF A SOFT WHISPER

You sit in a bar listening to a friend, offering words of advice late at night over a quiet glass. Twenty years later, he thanks you for setting him on course...and you never even knew he really listened.

You spend five minutes talking your kid through a failure he feels is going to destroy his young life and you become his role model. Twenty years from now, at a family event, he thanks you and quotes back your exact words.

You smile at the kid in the coffee shop, use his name, and say "Thank you," and turn a stressed-out employee into a newly energized person ready for another 100 customers.

The old homeless guy on the corner just sits and stares. He no longer has the strength to even ask for money. You slip him a five-dollar bill and a sandwich and whisper, "Here, sir, I hope this helps." You walk away and don't notice he has tears in his eyes, because for just a little while you have given him hope.

Your boss goes ballistic. Projects are behind; people didn't show for work, and everything seems out of control. You whisper privately, "I can get this done, boss, don't worry about it." A year later, you get a promotion you didn't know was available because that whisper set you aside from everyone else on the team.

Your spouse is melting down from "too much kid" and you quietly whisper, "Go sit outside and have a glass of wine. I will take them for ice cream." Later that night, your person falls asleep in your arms and you have no idea what the heck just happened, but you cuddle and smile.

There is power in every word you speak.

Think carefully about what you say and take ownership of everything you speak. Words, and the tone in which they are delivered, are remembered forever.

Your words can change a life, can heal a wound, can turn a bad day into a smile, and can define how you are viewed by others.

You are your words. Your personal strength is always determined by your willingness to speak the truth, and your willingness to lend that strength to others.

There is power in a soft whisper.

THE MORE CONNECTED YOU BECOME, THE MORE ISOLATED YOU CAN END UP

We seek to become more connected, but the reality is, you can have thousands of "friends" and not really know anyone.

In our jobs, we have hundreds of contacts and clients, but if we needed to borrow $100, we are down to that small circle of friends who could fill a booth at a favorite bar.

We know everyone, but are close to so few.

We get insecure when we post on social media and no one responds, so we desperately test our friends by asking them to give us a connecting word or post an emoji in the hope they are still there.

We don't understand Facebook is content-driven and if our content sucks, very few of our friends or followers will see our posts. Insecurity and the constant need to connect drives the almost drug-addicted sensation of an "I need instant likes or I am worthless" response.

Ten years ago, taking your own picture would have been considered an act of pure ego. We are now overwhelmed by an endless stream of selfies, ranging from a good time with friends at an event to "check out my ass, don't you think it's beautiful?"

If we can't get validation within, we seek it from without, through posting pictures to an open public and hoping someone thinks you look hot posing naked in front of a mirror.

We are now trained to respond so instantly to the beep of a device that we ignore our kids, our friends, and our family.

We can't turn it off for an hour to eat dinner.

We can't go to bed without having our little friend within reach.

We can't have a face-to-face conversation with anyone, because when the damn phone beeps, whoever is on the other end becomes more important than the live human in front of us.

We have also lost our ability to make good decisions.

Phone calls to discuss problems are now reduced to texts.

What took thought to answer now takes a quick thumb and a few characters.

It beeped, and the beeping device always demands an answer.

We sacrificed almost everything good in life to become the most connected generation, and we have lost our friends, our ability to think, our ability to communicate, and our ability to validate ourselves from within.

We are more connected than ever and have nothing much but an increased sense of loneliness to show for it.

FIVE MISTAKES EVERY PROFESSIONAL MAKES
AT LEAST ONCE IN A CAREER

Number One—You think lowering your price will attract more clients.

Lowering your price just lowers your credibility.

Every single money person in the world knows it is impossible to be the cheapest and be the best at the same time.

Number Two—Your training methodology overcomes your common sense.

Hurting people by pushing them through a workout designed for an athlete because you aren't smart enough to understand not everyone wants to compete at a national level is bad business and bad coaching.

Number Three—You go through that pure period in your life when even your own mother hates for you to come to dinner. Lead by example, quietly believing in your lifestyle, but leave the preaching to the television evangelists.

Number Four—You become one-dimensional, where you know or care about nothing beside fitness and training. It is okay to have a life; your goal should always be to become a fully functional, well-rounded human being.

Number Five—In your heart, you want to be involved in fitness for life, but you give up your dream to take a job in the "real world" because someone else believes it is time for you to grow up. Being a coach and helping people become better because they work with you is a noble thing. You can do forever if you believe in your passion.

We all make these mistakes.

Knowing you can overcome them is the power you need to succeed.

TODAY, I ONLY SEE BEAUTIFUL

Today, I only see beautiful.

I refuse to see petty and mean.

I will not get caught up in your political madness.

I will not judge and will not be mean.

Your "my way or you are wrong" obsession won't bother me.

Today, I will be at peace in the knowledge that being me is enough,
and your effort to dominate my life won't affect a single moment of my existence.

Today, I experienced personal freedom for the first time in my life.

Today, I only see beautiful.

And there isn't a damn thing you can do about it.

YOU ARE NEVER WHERE YOU ARE SUPPOSED TO BE

You are sitting at your desk, thinking about your next workout.

You are at the gym, thinking about what you left on your desk.

You are with your kids, checking your phone for texts.

You are out with friends, checking the pictures your kids sent.

You go to dinner with your spouse and talk about how little time you have together, wasting the entire evening of being together.

You go to a race over the weekend, but you are so busy taking and posting pictures of the race, you forget to enjoy the experience.

You rent a movie, but don't see what you are watching, because you are face down on your phone or arguing with your spouse about not spending time together.

You never have time to call old friends because you are too busy at work, thinking about your workout and texting acquaintances.

You are everywhere you should be...but never anywhere you could be.

You waste your life outside the moment because you never learned how to focus your energy on where you are and what you are doing.

Just once this week, try being where you are, focused on what you are doing... with the distraction of your phone off for a few hours.

You have a wonderful life, with good friends and the perfect family.

Too bad you are never there to enjoy any of it.

BEACHSIDE, MELBOURNE, FLORIDA
Never another winter, just days near the water and sand

LIFE IS NEVER
ABOUT WHAT YOU OWN

FIRST, THERE IS LIFE

First, there is life. Then there is stuff, and then you find life again.

When you were a little kid, it was all about moving and experiencing.

As a kid, life was a series of never-ending adventures beginning when your eyes opened and ending when you were face down on your blanket next to the dog at the end of the day.

You ran, played, kicked stuff, crawled, and hung out with your friends. Life was an ever-changing experience that was different every day, and added up to a rich life.

Now the kid sits.
And sits.
And sits.

We replaced the experiences of life with stuff.

Kids sit and stare at phones, TVs and iPads, and binge watch Netflix. The only adventures they have are those they watch other people have. Our kids went from experiencing life to its fullest to having no life at all.

We get older; we are now trained to collect stuff.

We are in our 20s and can't live without $300 sunglasses.

We have the trendiest car, the right clothes, live in a place we can't afford, and are buried under the need to collect stuff we can't afford and will take years to pay off.

Stuff often overwhelms us for most of our best years.

We give too much to our kids when we are in our 30s, buy too much house that keeps us sitting at home in it all year, and we collect all the trappings of life, preventing us from actually having a life.

But it will change.

Everyone, at some point, heads home.

As we age, we realize a smaller house and bigger adventures are what we now want.

We realize nothing will ever replace a few hours talking with our kids on a trail walk.

We realize that when our parents pass, we would give
almost everything we have to have just one more day.

Stuff matters less; the experiences and adventures of life matter the most.

We go full circle.

We start as adventurous souls with friends exploring the world around us, get distracted
for a bit and become addicted to the collection of meaningless stuff, but always return to
what is important, which is the enjoyment of life.

Why not just skip the "stuff" stage?

Why not live simply and collect the experiences of life,
 instead of yet another piece of crap your kids will sell cheap when you are dead?

Find the kid you used to be.

Find the one who thought running down the trail screaming was the biggest thing in life.

Find the kid within you who savored the minutes of the day
and never cared about owning much of anything.

Find your life again.

THERE IS NEVER A DAY

There is never a day in your life when someone isn't demanding leadership.

The staff needs you to lead. Your clients pay you to take charge and make good decisions that benefit them. Your family looks to you to stand up and make the decisions that keep everyone safe, financially secure, and together through the good and bad times.

If you work for a boss, you are judged every day by your leadership ability.

Working with a client and getting results is leadership.

Managing the business on your own is leadership.

Getting stuff done with your staff that benefits the business is leadership.

You can't lead if you aren't worth following.

Who you are as a person is always exposed by who you are as a leader.

You cannot demand respect; respect is earned each day by your actions.
It doesn't matter if the staff likes you—it matters if you are respected.

Many young leaders are so insecure, they keep their teams dumb. This type of leader likes it that way. Any new idea or thinking he didn't come up with makes him mad; free thinkers and people seeking to grow are eliminated.

The real test of leadership is this: Can you leave your business for a few days and can it continue successfully without you? If not, you have no team; your business is all about you, which limits the potential the business might have had.

Every leadership book ever written comes down to this: Are you trustworthy, do you know what you are doing, and does your staff believe in you?

You are a role model, whether you want to be or not.

People who are honest, consistent, have high integrity,
and are morally upright end up leading people who value those traits.

People who lie, cheat, and manage by fear lose their best people,
and eventually their businesses too.

Leadership is simple: Be someone others want to follow.

I THINK OF LOST DAYS
SPENT WALKING IN THE SUN ALONE

I remember lost nights drinking wine around a table with friends until asked to leave (we have been kicked out of better places than this, we insist yet again), grabbing more wine and then talking, laughing, and giggling until we were out of wine or too tired to go on.

There have been sunrise runs in the mountains I will remember until an hour after I die. There were campfires in the snow, holding hands with the one I loved or was at least trying to love that night, stolen kisses, intense discussions on what life might really mean, and alcohol-infused midnight calls for no other reason than to hear an old friend answer.

There have been magic minutes hugging a child I wish would last for all eternity.

There have been tears over failures, toasts to a win, celebrations of happiness, and celebrations of a death that could never be mourned because the lost person had been so full of life that mourning would never honor his soul.

There are failures that try our souls, rebounds in love that save us from bad relationships we thought would kill us, and lost years of hiding from the very life we seek.

And there have been nights of shear agony waiting for the ones we love and might lose before dawn.

There have been weeks at work where a few beers with the staff on Friday is the only way to celebrate. And there have been times where only good wine out of the bottle would work, sipped alone while cowering under the desk, loudly praying for a merciful universe to burn down that piece of dog-crap facility.

I miss hugging my mother, drinking beer with my dad, and driving too fast down a California two-lane on a Friday on the way to the wine country.

There are friends, gone too early, whom I still give a silent nod to over a glass, afternoons spent with the one I love just staring at the water. There are days when I just need to be with an old friend talking about endless things that only matter to us, and where the old stories of "back in the day" still make us laugh.

Yet, I don't regret a single day of my life.

Our journey defines our lives.

We make horrible mistakes, lose our way, cringe in embarrassment at how stupid we were when we were young, and miss the ones we love.

Yet all woven together, this is who we are—why would we want to be anyone else?

We are all flawed, perfectly weird in our own ways, and destined to live lives we create ourselves.

I wouldn't change a single damn thing.

JUST WALK!

Get up, get out, and just walk.

No headphones, no phones, no step counting devices beeping on your wrist—just you walking along a nice street or wooded trail, being present in your life.

Try it for an hour. Today, you don't need to carry anything heavy, worry about intensity or pace or the calorie count; just walk and enjoy the moment lost in your own thoughts.

Just walk, and use the time as quiet meditation, or think about your next big change in life, or just reflect on everything good in life. Use the walk as a quiet time for prayer if you are that person. No music, no distractions—just you thinking about life for an hour and moving gently along the road.

We sometimes make exercise too much of a big thing, when just an hour walk may do more to heal the body and especially repair the soul. Just walk, and let the world fade away as you let your mind get in tune with the energy around you.

Even a dog knows to walk along quietly, sniff the world, and enjoy the time. When did our dogs get smarter than us? Just walk, and get over the need to make every workout a stress-filled day chasing personal records, crazy new exercises, and competing with every other person in the gym.

Exercise can just be a walk, with no goal other than to keep putting one foot in front of the other and enjoying our own thoughts.

Just go for walk and let the world heal you.

Just walk, for no other reason than you are healthy enough to get up and enjoy what so many people voluntarily give up in their lives: the simple joy of movement.

Just walk, for the simple reason that you can.

Just walk!

SANTA MONICA, CALIFORNIA
One free day on the way to Australia

I AM OKAY

I AM OKAY, ALTHOUGH A LITTLE MESSED UP

I am okay because I go through life slightly messed up.

Even a bad day walking on the beach is better
than the best day I ever had wearing a tie.

If you can't spend time alone, you are not yet an adult.

How do you heal and grow if you don't ever have time to think?

I always believe people are good until proven otherwise,
but when proven otherwise I have no time for idiots.

It's hard to even take care of my own life at times.
I can't understand why anyone would obsess about how others live,
who they marry, who they sleep with, or the color of their skin.

Never saw the need to chase being perfect, always thought being a slightly messed-up good
person was a much better goal in life.

Is my family safe and happy?
Am I safe and happy?
Yes?
Then screw everything else.

It is just money and stuff, and I can always make more money and buy new stuff,
but I can't ever replace the really important things in life.

There are friends who are always there with you.

And there are other friends you seldom see,
but who still cherish your friendship and have never let you go.

Both are pretty cool friends to have.

I would rather be poor than spend even 10 minutes doing something I hate.

Look back 10 years. Did time pass in about 30 seconds?

Any journey so brief but so wondrous should never be wasted doing work you don't like
or living with someone you like even less.

If you have over $5 in your pocket and you have eaten today,
you need to give some money away and change someone else's life.

You can have it all in life, if you first learn to give away your time and money.

Being present with the one you are with is more important than waiting for the phone to
buzz. Turning off the phone and being present with those you are with or being totally
involved in what you are doing is a better way to savor your life.

Turning off the phone is nothing more than gaining control over your life
and respecting those you are with today.

Living life slightly messed up should be your dream.
Normal people are boring.

Messed-up people are the only ones worth hanging out with in life.
Be messed up...and be proud of it.

THERE IS BONE WEARY

There is bone-weary, dragging-ass tired,
the kind of tired that overwhelms everyone
who works hard for what they want in life.

Then there is soul tired,
where you work beyond the human capacity to function
and end up with the intellectual ability of a drunken monkey
and the personality of a steroidal wife beater.

People who love what they do are usually willing to work harder to chase their dreams than others, but at some point, you pass the point of "tired" and enter "soul tired," where your decision process suffers, people around you begin to notice you are becoming somewhat of an ass, and you find yourself yelling at the counter person at the coffee shop because she misspelled your name on a paper cup.

We all need time to heal, yet it is a badge of honor in our industry to work to the point you start losing what you worked so hard to achieve.

Plan some time to heal your mind, soul, and body.

Sit quietly, heal quietly, walk gently, and disconnect yourself from the world.

Even you, whom the world can't live without,
will find a way to survive for a few days while you heal that damaged soul.

DOING WHAT YOU ARE DOING

Doing what you are doing got you what you got.

If you don't like what you got, doing what you're doing isn't doing it for you.

If what you got isn't what you want, the only way to get what you want is to stop doing what you're doing and start doing something different.

But doing something different means you have to admit that what you are doing isn't working and you are wrong, which is more painful to most people than not getting what they want from doing what they are doing.

Doing what you need to do requires admitting you never really knew what you were doing in the first place.

Which is more important to you, doing what you're doing and failing, or doing what you should be doing and admitting that maybe you were wrong?

Set your ego aside and start doing what needs to be done, so what you get is what you always dreamed of from life.

If the ego diminishes, the world will grow for you.

COME, GROW OLD WITH ME!

Walk with me on the beach for years to come,
until we become those funny old people in the big hats.

Dance with me in the kitchen
while our grandkids laugh and cheer.

Hug me because you still want to be in my arms,
not just because we have been together so long.

Sip wine with me by the fire
and be the love of my life forever, and then just one more day.

Kiss me like you did the first hour we were together
and remember that startling feeling that we might be falling in love.

Hold my hand and never let go
as we sit quietly and watch the world pass.

Make me laugh like you did when we were just getting started in life
when children, houses, and life were things yet to be discovered.

Make me cry by telling me the old stories of our love and passion
when we were young and living through the journey that made us fall in love forever.

Cuddle me at night so the world seems safe
and that nothing can ever separate us.

Stand with me late in the night, staring at the Christmas tree,
remembering the love that has defined our lives together.

Come, grow old with me.
The best years of our life are yet to come.

ALARM AT 4:15 A.M.

Ugh, I overslept again. Just closed my eyes for 30 seconds and lost 20 minutes.

Coffee standing up; coffee is my friend.
Strong, nasty coffee that is the fuel of life.
Would I trade a child for coffee at 4:00 a.m.?
I hope I never have to find out how weak I might be, but of course, it would depend on the blend.

No clean tee shirt.
Smell yesterday's entry—not too bad.
A little wrinkled, but more sweat should take care of that.
Extra deodorant just in case.
Hair? Glad funky hair is in, because I have absolutely no choice today.

Kiss the spouse, who is still in bed.
Spouse smells good.
Covers up to the ears.
Tempting to crawl back in, back to sleep, and go out and get a real job tomorrow.
Peek in on the kids.
Cute when sleeping.
Out of control when awake.
Cute is good this early.
Out the door.

More coffee on the way in.
Mr. Starbucks, you have my undying love.
Is it bad they know my name and automatically reach for my usual order?
How much caffeine is too much?
Need to look that up because I am sure I am over any known daily limit.

Client shows up at 5:00 in a foul mood.
Up too late, ate too much, and is whiny.
Smile, smile, smile, or I might say something bad, such as, "Try going to bed a little earlier, turn off your damn TV, and maybe give up the big bowl of ice cream at midnight."

Client complains about lack of progress.
We have the "You can't out-train a bad diet" talk yet again.
Client listens (again), but I can see it in her eyes she thinks
I am the one secretly sneaking in at night adding all that weight to her butt.
One glass of wine a night my ass!
Or should I say one bottle of wine a night…her ass?

Next client is early and impatient, then the next one, and the next one.
If I am lucky, I might get to poop at about 2:00 p.m.
I need to train myself to poop at 4:00 in the morning.
That would make the day easier, but would it cut into my coffee time?

Do my own workout.
Already been up for eight hours.
Under-caloried, over-caffeinated, stressed, and not focused,
but an hour later it is done and could be the highlight of my day.
The worst workout I have ever had is better than none.

Call the spouse.
The kids are still alive.
The house hasn't burned down yet.
Good until 9:30 p.m. at least.

Spouse is having a bad day at work. Listen while eating a snack. Thankful it isn't crunchy.

Who doesn't love split shifts?
Run a few errands, eat too quickly, get my workout in, and then here comes Mrs. Johnson.
Five years, three times per week, hates to sweat
and I think she is here just to get me to stretch her in that special way.
Mrs. Johnson has issues, but she pays well.

Team training at 6:00 p.m.—let the energy begin.

Scream, yell, and motivate 20 people who just want a collective butt whooping and I love every second. One-on-one is boring after so many years, but team training keeps me young.

Meal 1,246 out of a plastic bowl, eaten standing up in the break room.
Did I remember to poop today?
More deodorant? Hey, dude, do I smell bad?
Yeah, same shirt as yesterday. What, your same shirt for three days?
I guess I'm good then.

Out the door at 9:00 p.m.
On the couch drinking wine, hoping to kill the jittery coffee hangover.
Spouse proves undying love by having a meal ready.
Cuddle the kids and realize I could have it much worse.
Spouse is in the shower.
Consider the sex thing. Fall asleep scrolling.
Hope I can get lucky before work tomorrow, if I can only get the spouse up at 4:00 a.m.
There is always Sunday.

Maybe my mom will take the kids Saturday night.
An adult dinner with the spouse in adult clothes in an adult restaurant without the kids.
Do I even have adult clothes?
Promise the spouse not to fall asleep at the table after two glasses of wine.

Repeat until rich or dead...I will take rich, please.
The good thing about all of this?
If I am good, I just might make the world around me a little better today.
Might change a life or two,
and might do something my kids can respect as they get older.

Weird way to make a living...but I couldn't imagine doing anything else in life.

A SIGN DOESN'T MAKE YOU A PROFESSIONAL

A sign on a building doesn't make you a professional coach.

A one-day certification doesn't make you a qualified trainer.

Personal records and selfies only illustrate that you are in shape;
neither of those means you can get anyone else in shape.

Business cards stating you are for hire as a "master personal trainer" only mean you can afford to buy business cards and do not prove you are a trainer or a master at anything.

Writing a 16-exercise "perfect" workout plan usually means you were up late last night watching YouTube. Writing this plan does not certify you as a real coach.

Even having people paying you to train them doesn't make you a true professional; it just means the clients may not understand the difference between you and a real coach.

What makes you "real" in the gym business?

Someone trusts you, pays you, and you get that person the desired results. You are on your way.

Add some ethics where you always value the client over your own gain,
and you might have a chance.

Throw in some professionalism showing you realize how you charge, how you dress and act affects all the rest of the trainers around you...and you are showing signs of promise.

Most importantly, it is about respect for the client and understanding that being a professional coach is always about trust. Someone who has issues, challenges, goals, and dreams came to you for help. That person made a decision to trust you with money, time, and life.

When you understand all coaching is about living up to that trust—on that day and only that day, you might be able to look in the mirror and tell yourself you are finally a professional coach.

NOTHING TO WRITE ABOUT

Nothing to write about, so I am writing about nothing.

Nothing, such as spending an entire day with your family doing nothing together and it is the best day ever.

Nothing, with your mates and several hours later...and maybe after a few drinks, doing nothing became great conversation among old friends.

Or stopping by the parents' house for no reason at all and then sitting doing nothing and hearing the old stories one more time.

And maybe sitting on the floor with a good client at the end of the session, talking about nothing and realizing this client is one of the best people you know.

Even just getting in your car and driving with no particular place in mind. Just driving and doing nothing and letting the day and your thoughts lead the way.

Many of you are obsessive planners and anal idiots who need every second planned. Sometimes the best thing you can plan in life is nothing and just let the day unfold.

It's the weekend. Gather your family or friends, or just take off by yourself and spend the entire day doing absolutely nothing, letting life lead the way.

Doing nothing might be the start of something big you'll remember forever.

YOU WILL HIT BOTTOM IN LIFE AT LEAST ONCE

The wave of pain will wash over you.

And you will wish it would end so you can breathe again.

And it will end.

And then you realize the worst the universe has wasn't enough to kill your soul.

And you will come crawling out the other side with a severe case of "fuck you, if this is all you have, then bring it" attitude the world has ever seen.

Now you are stronger than ever.

Now your life will begin, because you found your strength.

Then you will live.

Then, and only then, can you become who you were meant to be.

STUFF THAT SHOULD BE HANGING ON YOUR MIRROR

Stuff that should be hanging on your bathroom mirror so you have to read it every day:

I will not let any mistake I might have made in the past screw up today.

If I am not hurt and if my family isn't hurt, I will let nothing petty bother me again.

What others think of me is their problem, not mine. There is a very small group of people whose opinions I care about, and beyond that group, what anyone else thinks just doesn't matter.

There will be really bad days in my life, but this isn't going to be one of them.

Take five minutes today and call someone who needs a little support.
If you want friends, be a friend. Call, don't text.

One small random act of kindness today means little to me, but could change someone's life.

Have I kissed everyone and told them all I love them before I leave this house?

What am I going to do today to make some money and further my career?

One meal at a time makes for a fit human being.

The other guy may be better looking, smarter, luckier, richer, and further ahead, but there isn't a single human being on this planet who can outwork my motivated butt.

If I am a miserable ass, everyone around me will reflect that negative crap...and I just won't let that happen.

I am changing lives.

I deserve every dollar I make for the work I do.

Let the rest of the world be miserable if they want.
I will be happy and polite just to piss them off.

Damn I am good... now let's get on with this day.

THE CLIENT WAS A MISERABLE HUMAN BEING

The client was such a miserable human being he had to be fired,
and that put a smile on my face for the entire week.

He set a call every month.

We developed a new list of things for him to do every month.

And he did nothing every month...nothing but complain, moan, blame his staff,
blame his wife, blame his dog, and mostly hate the universe.

So, I fired him.

No more calls, no more miserable excuses, and no more complaining to myself, "Man,
I really can't stand this guy; I just don't need the money that badly to take this beating."

And then he didn't call the next month and life was good.

My attitude improved. I didn't dread his call days ahead of the scheduled time,
and I was able to focus more on the clients I enjoyed working with.

I was happy, and the darkness in my life lifted.

You have this client.

These black-hole people suck the light and energy out of everyone in their lives. They
will never be happy, never be successful, never get in shape, or probably never have a
good day, simply because their misery is more important to them than any change in
their lives or relationships could be.

They blame the universe for the situation, and they often blame you too.

His failure is never his failure, but a combined conspiracy by everyone around him to
hold him back—as if anyone cared enough about the jerk to form a group to stop him
from being successful.

Fire this client, and fire any client you can't stand to see walking through the door
and who makes you miserable in your own business.

That will be a good day. That, indeed, will be a very good day, and you will thank me.

PROVINCETOWN, MASSACHUSETTS
A peaceful birthday at the end of the world

PLEASE,
LET ME BE FOUR AGAIN

I WANT TO BE FOUR YEARS OLD AGAIN

This Christmas, I want to be four years old again.

I want to sit on my parent's lap, snuggled in with a cup of hot chocolate,
my dad reading *The Night before Christmas* with Mom holding my hand.

I want to sit on the floor and stare up at a giant tree that sparkles, twinkles,
and dances in the light.

I want to stare at candles that only got put out that time of year
and smelled of everything Christmas and everything that was good in the world.

I want to believe in the magic of Christmas, where Santa Claus is coming tonight,
where the house is filled with love, and where my parents spent time with me with no
phone or any other parent-distracting device in sight.

I miss Christmas music playing from a radio, and I miss when the house was the
perfect temperature to bury myself in a pile of blankets, cuddled with the family dog,
sipping on the biggest cup of hot chocolate a kid had ever seen, with marshmallows
melting in the steam.

I want my grandparents back for just one more Christmas. I want their laughter to fill
a room, and I want to be surrounded by nieces and nephews, all wired up from too
many Christmas cookies and too much Christmas spirit.

I want the scent of pine, the wafting smells of wondrous things baking created from
scratch from recipes 50 years old, and the crackle of the fireplace.

I want people now gone to be alive for just a few hours and bring back the certainty of
a child that no one ages and I will be four forever.

I want to sit mesmerized in front of the TV, caught up in the adventures of Frosty and
Rudolph, believing those magical places exist for me to visit someday.

Most of all, I want to go to bed knowing Santa will be here tonight, and I want to still believe that no matter how good or bad I was, there will be presents for me. Tomorrow when I get up, the world will be perfect for a few hours.

I miss my parents at this time of year.

I miss the magic of believing in something too good to be true.

I miss children gathered in a living room, believing this magic was theirs alone and adults really didn't understand.

If you have children of a Christmas age where everything is possible through magic, cookies, and hot chocolate, don't forget you were once that child.

A four-year-old, protected by parents, cuddled in a blanket in front of the fireplace listening to a story is a memory for a lifetime.

Be present this year at Christmas.

Be peaceful toward the ones you love. Be committed to creating magic with children who will remember those hours until the day they die, and then for an eternity.

Bring back the magic this Christmas. Give your children the most precious gift there is in life: your time, your devotion, and your undivided attention for a few hours.

Maybe the magic you believed in so long ago is still possible, but only you can make it happen for your children...and maybe for yourself.

GOT UP TODAY AND TRIED TO SAVE THE WORLD

Got up today and quietly decided to change the world.

Tired of mean and petty people and the endless ugliness in the world.

Decided to wander around the airport and commit a stream of random acts of kindness to see if my piss-poor attitude toward the universe would change.

Held a baby while a stressed-out mother ate.

Bought lunch for an impossibly young service guy in uniform, pushed a wheelchair between a few gates for an overloaded mother, carried a bag off one plane for an old couple, over-tipped a young girl at the Starbucks counter who works two jobs and gets up at 3:00 in the morning, and held up a short kid so he could pee (really short kid).

Weird morning in the airport, but I am all better now.

Didn't change the whole world, but made a serious attempt to change my little part, and change my foul but temporary attitude.

Any time you get caught up in your own madness, maybe the best thing you can do is to go on a serious rage to help the world and get past your silly self.

Could have sat in the bar being miserable and stared at a glass.

But maybe just attempting to help put a smile on someone else's face is enough to save my soul.

I WAS SO BUSY BEING BUSY

I was so busy being busy, I became too busy to pay attention…and I lost everything.

I was so busy creating a life for my kids that they grew up without me and now are gone.

I was so busy telling my spouse about the big future we would have some day that she left me for a person who was there for her every single day, when she most needed his hand in hers.

My business kept me so busy, it slowly declined because I became trapped by everyday routines. I never took the time to step back and work on what I owned, instead of filling my days doing the work of employees I should have hired.

I was so busy, stressed, and overloaded that time spent at home was spent flat on my back, staring mindlessly at a small screen that entertained me until I passed out from exhaustion.

Workouts became obsessive because I hated to miss a single one. My chase for perfect health cost me my health due to injuries, stress, and the failure to rest.

Food became obsessive because I was too tired to eat any other way.

Life became obsessive because I had no life, and never knew the difference.

You need time to heal.

You need days away with those you love to rest your dog-tired soul.

You need to be effective in life, not just consumed by being too busy to breathe.

"Busy" is usually just busy and destroys the very life you seek.

Relax, take a breath, and maybe understand that you are losing everything you love… simply because you never understood "busy" is often just another excuse to avoid what is most important in life.

IF YOU WEAR THE SUIT

If you wear the suit, you have to be the man.

Superheroes don't sit home watching TV, drinking a beer and saying, "No, I really don't feel like saving the world today. Man, when is that pizza getting here?"

Superheroes get the call, and then they do the job.

You wear the suit; you are the man or the woman who has to save the world.

If you represent yourself as the coach, the guru, or a mentor, you are wearing the suit.

You put it on by choice.

You made the decision to be that hero.

If you take someone's money to present, help, guide, or be the one who claims to change lives, every day you have to be the person you represent.

You wear the suit, everything counts.

You have to take one more call; you have to answer the same question 400 times when you just want a cold beer. You have to be patient with that client who just doesn't get it; you have to live your life as a role model and, most importantly, you have to live up to the expectations you created when you put on the suit and took the money.

Wearing the suit is a responsibility too many accept,
yet fail to live up to what they wanted so badly.

Being the coach, being the mentor, being the guru means you willingly and knowingly understand those who look up and follow you hope and expect you to be the leader they need in their lives.

You want to be a superhero some day?

Make sure you understand there will never be a day when someone doesn't need you to be the hero we all need so badly in our lives, and today, that hero is you.

WHEN YOU ARE YOUNG

When you are young, you have many friends, but as you age you realize your time is so valuable, you only want to spend those precious minutes with the few you still care about in life.

A friend can be someone you haven't seen in a while,
and you start talking right where you left off.

A friend is also someone who calls with an outrageously fucked-up idea and you say, "Man, that sounds like fun. I will be there in 10 minutes."

Friends are also the people who keep you up late drinking one more glass
and talking about life as it should be lived.

You also realize your closest friends drink too much, swear too much,
make inappropriate comments about people walking by,
and that you are the same person.

Friends define your life.

You will always only be as good as the people you choose to have in your life. Friends don't have to even be close, just people you would fly a thousand miles to have lunch with some day.

A person who is a true friend will push for your success and hold you accountable for using your talent and gifts. Real friends don't give a damn about who you live with, how messed-up you were this week, or if you just had your ass kicked.

That friend will listen, buy the next round, point out the stupidity of your plan,
and then support you no matter how jacked-up your life is today.

Real friends are as rare as an honest politician, but the few you choose to keep close are as rock solid as the shaved head of a stupid trainer.

Honor your friends.

Be choosy whom you let in your life.

Celebrate the uniqueness of having someone who cares whether you live or die, but would be the first one to dance at your funeral in remembrance of how you lived.

Today is the perfect day to call someone and say, "I love you; you are one of the best parts of my life."

Today is the day you learn to appreciate those few people who make your life worth living even when you have doubts about yourself.

Celebrate your life and celebrate the gift of friends.

YOU SLEEP

You wander 20 feet from the bedroom to the kitchen and sit.

You eat a giant bowl of kid food with milk and sugar, pretending you are healthy.

You are eating crap from a box.

You carry coffee another 20 feet to your car in the garage.
You sit in this car drinking coffee with sugar during your hour commute.

You arrive at work, go to your desk, and sit for nine hours.
You eat lunch at your desk, thinking you are more productive.

You drive home for another hour camped on your butt.

You walk into the gym and yell at the manager
because you had to park so far away, and then you work out, again sitting on your butt.

Your workout is textbook 1995.
You sit on your butt with a big card telling you what to do next,
and move from machine to machine parked on your ever-expanding backside.

You go home and sit for four hours watching mindless TV and snacking.

Then you lie down again.

Eating too much is bad for you.
Drinking too much is bad for you.
Smoking is stupid and bad for you.

Sitting is just as bad as all those other nasty things.

The last thing you need to do in a gym is sit.
The last thing you need is a circuit-training program older than your grandkids,
but is still sold in every $10 gym, old-school nonprofit, or bad fitness chain since 1967.

Good gyms offer upright, holistic workouts.
Good gyms have coaches skilled in getting you upright and off your butt.
Good gyms are about *movement.*

Get off your butt, people, and find a good gym.

MELBOURNE, AUSTRALIA
Midnight walk

FITNESS IS A CELEBRATION OF THE RESPECT YOU HAVE FOR LIFE

GOING TO THE GYM ISN'T A PUNISHMENT

Going to the gym isn't a punishment for what you ate or how much you sit.

Fitness is a celebration of the fact you are alive and can move.

Fitness isn't something you only do at a gym. Fitness for life means you either approach your body and mind with respect, or you disrespect the gift of your life. One day, everything that defines a healthy human being, such as the ability to pick up a grandchild or to walk on the beach, is taken away from you.

Getting in shape isn't something you only do for a wedding or for the newly divorced. Fitness is a personal choice where you decide to live your life at the highest level you can possibly achieve, because if you are fit and healthy, anything in life seems possible.

What would you give for an extra 10 years of quality life?

If you are 30, this doesn't seem relevant, but if you are in your 40s, overweight, and don't move, you made a decision. That decision was to end your life earlier than others who realize what you do today in fitness determines how you will live 20 years from now...if indeed you do live that long.

You, and only you, can determine the quality, and in many cases, the length of your life.

The mindset for fitness isn't about being perfect or trying to recapture who you were "back in the day," but rather, becoming the best you can be today.

There is no perfect you, but there is a you within who can overflow with happiness, vibrant health, and crazy energy. You now understand you don't *do* fitness; you *are* fitness.

Mindset is everything in the pursuit of personal health, but you have to enter the arena with the understanding that fitness isn't another hobby you only do when you have time. Fitness is the very essence of how you live 24 hours a day...how you think and who you are.

You choose to be healthy; you chose life.

You choose to ignore your fitness; you made a choice...and you will pay for that choice someday. When you can't get out of a chair without help, play with a child, or hold the hand of the one you love on a walk through the woods, what will you pay for just one hour of healthy life?

The sad thing is, you could have had it all along.

BE COMFORTABLE BEING CRAZY

Many people make the mistake of trying to define rules for fit pros,
but the only consistent rule that applies is simple:
Celebrate your uniqueness in the world.

There is no "normal" in the training world,
no single set of rules that applies to everyone,
nor is there one definition of what training has to be.

Being different is normal in this insanity,
but being crazy never has to mean you are not professional.

The industry has attracted serious master trainers, skinny little people half the size of
their clients, people of all colors and shapes, the occasional six-foot lesbian, short little
trainer chicks, tattooed monsters in full body art, old retired guys escaping from real
life, self-created gurus, trainer tech geeks, power freaks, ex-runway models, and the
occasional leftover bodybuilder who still believes in 1995.

And that is a short list of people who call being a fit pro their career.

Celebrate your weirdness. Be proud of not fitting into real-world jobs.

But always remember that in the end,
being a life-changing professional is the only thing that will define you.

BALANCE IN LIFE SUCKS

Everything in life that matters was created by an obsessed person.

There is only rest...and then there is surge, a time where you go all in with all the intensity you can bring to focus on creating the life you want.

Surges can last a few months, or a surge can last up to a year.

When you surge, you focus, create, and change your world.

Surging is about committing with all the intensity you possess to something important in your life for a short period of time, with the goal to master it or create something new.

This is when you start a new business, master an aspect of coaching, write a book, or make a strong personal change in your life.

There is no moderation in life. There is either intensity or rest.

You didn't get fat through moderation and you cannot get healthy through moderation.

You commit to change and then go all in.

The question in life isn't about staying in balance.
The question is, are you willing to plan to be completely out of balance and go all in?

In a surge, you protect family and keep your ability to make money.
Everything else that would hold you back is eliminated.

A rich and full life is about getting things done.

Surge, and change the world.

Surge, and change your world.

And then, rest and plan what comes next.

ASS ANCHORS

Many fitness professionals become immensely strong
because they go through life carrying around so many ass anchors.

Have that client who just wears out your ass by being so needy and demanding?

That is an ass anchor.

Have an employee who is almost good, but secretly fights every change or new thing you try to do in your business? That, my friends, is an ass anchor.

Have that friend who resents your fitness and career because he is worthless and unwilling to take the risk you did, and over every beer, he lets you know how big you are going to fail, how stupid you are for trying, and how much you have changed and become greedy?

He is yet another ass anchor, spending life holding back the good and hard working.

Of course, there is your family, who hates you working in fitness, and wishes you would grow up and become an accountant like Uncle Ed, who died of stress when he was 58 and looked like a 90-year-old pile of mold when he died.

And the sad thing is that person lying next to you in the morning might be working very hard to keep you from chasing your dreams. A mate who doesn't have personal dreams might greatly resent that you do.

Ass anchors are why many fit pros can leap onto large stacks of boxes in a single bolt. Carrying around that baggage makes you an incredibly strong person if it doesn't wreck your soul first.

People who love and support you, however, are like feathers.
You can stuff 50 of them in your backpack and run miles without a sweat.

Your task is to reach down, unclasp those hands wrapped around your muscular ass, and run like hell on fire into your own future.

The year ahead is going to be your year and your time,
but ass anchors aweigh first, my friends, and then run with the wind.

IF YOU SEE A POST YOU DON'T LIKE

If you see a post you don't like, mutter a few swear words and then scroll on.

There is an anger—a meanness on social media—that is so ridiculously childish, it is hard to comprehend there is really an adult at the other end of the madness.

If you don't like a post, don't read the damn thing.

If you don't like a post, scroll past it and get on to the kitten videos. The post isn't a personal attack against you; it wasn't written directly to you, and if any post upsets you that much, ignore it and move on.

You can also join the debate, but you can't hate someone simply for not agreeing with you.

Are you really that petty and asinine you believe anyone who has a different opinion needs to be corrected, taught a lesson, have his butt handed to him, or that you attempt to embarrass a person by calling him stupid?

Are you so insecure in what you believe that you have to attempt to tear down what anyone else believes? Is any post you find by just random scrolling so harmful to you that you have to castigate the writer and attempt to be that one person where everyone says, "Wow, he really put him in his place!"? In fact, the world believes you are the loser because your comments and anger is misplaced and out of proportion.

If you want to debate, maybe start with, "I noticed your post, but have you ever considered...?" Do not start with, "You are a flaming idiot and only a disgusting moron would believe what you just wrote."

Social media gives you a sense of being anonymous. You sit up in the middle of the night, drink and type, and fire off your "I'll show you, you stupid bugger" witty trashing. You smirk smugly to yourself since you don't have to face the recipient in person.

In this case, anonymous is the same as ignorant, where hiding makes you brave enough to attack someone over something so meaningless it dies within 24 hours, which is the life span of a good post.

It is just a post you are reading. A post does not represent the whole person, although that is sometimes hard to grasp after almost any political election. A post is merely a few words strung together to express a thought of the day. If you don't agree with that thought, why, oh why, would you ever take something so simple so personally?

Whoever writes a post has an opinion. You have your own opinion.
Just because you disagree does not make the other person
wrong, disgusting, a lesser human being, or stupid.

Disagreeing just means you disagree on an issue.
Consider the other viewpoint, maybe debate with class, and then just keep moving.

If you are so politically correct that Facebook fires up your butt,
get off social media and don't come back until you are an adult.

If someone writing a post angers you to the point where you have to go after that person with a vicious attack, you are too immature to leave your house and may need professional anger management.

If you hate a post so much, man up, write your own post
and see what the world thinks of your opinion.

And if you are getting angry reading this, you are proving my point.

YOU THINK IT WILL NEVER END

It ends. It all ends.
Your life is today and is only as good as you are willing to let it be.

There is no guarantee of even another hour of you.

Never go to bed mad at anyone.
This ruins your sleep, your life, and your chance to get lucky.

Always leave the house with a kiss and words of love...
you may not be back and the last words are those remembered.

Never get on a plane without a call to your most important person.

Never drop a kid off at school angry.
Kids are too young to understand why a parent hates them at that moment.

Never lose a friend over petty anger that could be laughed at over a pint.
True friends sit and talk.
He isn't a friend if there isn't a pint.

Never let a client ruin your day.
It is better to let the client go away than to
ever suffer one who makes you mad in your own business.

The bad times will pass...and so will the best of times.

You won't be young and beautiful forever,
but you can be old and wonderful, and that might have to do.

Parents will make you bat-crap crazy.
You ignored them when you were a teenager and you can do it again, but never be angry.

Take a surprise day off, gather the ones you love, and just start driving.
You will find something to do, and it will be special.

Be a seeker.
You may doubt, you may deny,
but you should at least look, study, think, and explore all options.

There will be a last day.

You have no idea when it will come.
Every day has to be the best day of your life.

You think it will never end.

It ends. It all ends.

RIGHT AT THIS MOMENT

Right at this moment there is a woman sitting at home vowing to herself
that the new year will be her year physically.

This will be the year she changes her body, accepts her limitations,
and makes feeling good and moving often a part of her daily life.

Here is what every woman should know before she commits to fitness:

Strong women are beautiful women.

You will never become the best you can be
by chaining yourself to a treadmill and walking for hours.

You might lose weight, but even those losses will stop soon.

The structure you see and admire in other women is muscle.

Most of the diseases of aging are self-inflicted.

You can control your physical future by knowing your body,
working with a knowledgeable coach, and educating yourself.

Never chase your former self. We were all somebody back in the day.
Chasing an unrealistic idea of trying to recapture your glory days isn't going to work.

Yes, you might have been the prom queen or a national class soccer player.
But today you should just focus on being the best you can be today,
and stop chasing the woman you can never be again.

The lies you believe will harm your future.

Many women fade after 50, becoming lesser versions of themselves because they have
always believed one inherent lie: If you lift weights you will get big.

That is like saying don't take up golf,
because you are afraid of making all that money on the women's tour.

If you only could go to the gym one day a week, lift weights with a good coach.

If you only can go twice a week, lift weights with a good coach.
Beyond that, you have to adapt your goals to your lifestyle, but you should still embrace what strength training can do for the next 40 years of your life.

Be afraid of the biggest lie ever told.

Your support group will often let you down. When you take control of your life and your body and those around you are still trapped in yesterday, they will often work against your success.

Someone doing nothing hates to be reminded that a friend is seriously working on a better life, and is taking control of how she feels and how she looks. As you change, make sure you are hanging with friends chasing the same goals and dreams.

And your significant other may be your biggest road block.

You might live longer as a woman than any woman has ever lived in the past.
The workouts you do today will determine the quality of life you have in the future.
You can't wait until you are in a wheelchair to change your life. Then it is too late.

The single biggest lie in fitness is dieting.
Diets do not work and never will.

Adapting healthy eating—based upon you as an individual and with the guidance of someone with practical experience—is the only way to keep your weight under control.

Nothing changes until you do.

Being the best you can be is there for anyone chasing that dream,
but no one other than you can set you on that path.

And let me mention this just one more time, find a good coach you trust.

WHEN YOU ARE OUT OF CHOICES

When you are out of choices is when you often make the best choice in your life.

Change is possible in almost any human being, but the willingness to let yourself change is one of the rarest elements in the universe.

Bad choices repeated often lead you to a crossroads.

When you get beaten badly enough by the universe, you finally realize your ego—combined with your unwillingness to admit what you are doing is killing you—has almost destroyed your life and those in it.

Or you sit quietly, cry for a few hours, and then stand up and understand you are you because of every choice you made up through last night.

Good or bad, you built every inch of you, yourself.

Few people will let the ego go long enough to choose a road to personal redemption.

Admitting that who you are today is not who you have to be in the future is, for many, the hardest step forward they will take in life.

This is where the life you always dreamed about
and the person you always wanted to be begins.

BALTIMORE, MARYLAND
Evening walk on the inner harbor

SOMEWHERE
A COACH GOT UP AND
CHANGED THE WORLD

SOMEWHERE IN THE WORLD

Somewhere in the world today, a coach got up and went to work.

Quietly, humbly, she did her job starting at 5:00 in the morning,
fueled by coffee and a whole lot of "today we kick some butt" attitude.

The gym had 100 client visits today.
The coaches got it done with a smile, some intensity,
a lot of good-natured screaming, and solid professionalism.

Each client brought a unique issue to the pile, but every client left a little happier,
perhaps a little more tired, and a lot more inspired.

Our coach is still hanging around at 8:00 at night, slightly beaten, and hoping to get a
decent meal before bed. She got her workout in at noon, between clients, and food is
looking good now.

She heads home, puts the kids to bed, sits quietly for a few minutes,
recovering from a long day of pushing the world around her to be better.

She crawls into bed, and not too many hours later, she is back at it,
ready for one more chance to change the world.

Our coach changes her world every day.
Because she cares, the people around her are better.

Every day, she makes her little slice of earth a better place,
and she never even thinks about what it means to change the world.

Her family thinks she should quit and get a "real" job.

Her friends from school laugh that she is still hanging out at a gym.

And the hours make her question her sanity now and then.

She should remember there are few jobs in the world that change more lives, help
more people, or make more of a difference than being a professional coach.

This coach gets up every day and cares that everyone she reaches finds the motivation
and strength to live a better life...and maybe there is nothing more to be said about this
than, "Thank you."

EVERYTHING YOU DO IN LIFE MATTERS

The touch on the shoulder and smile turned a client's bad day into a good one.

Coming back into the house for one last hug left your spouse
with a quiet love savored for the entire day.

That late-night phone call with a struggling friend meant nothing to you,
but changed that life forever by offering hope and support.

The day you spent with your kids just walking and talking was just another good day for you, but when you are old, that day will be one of the strongest memories in your children's lives. They will repay you by still wanting to hold your hand and spend time with you.

The smile and a thank you at the coffee shop, politely using a server's name, the dollar you gave the guy on the street, and the phone call just to say hello didn't take a lot of time or cost you much, but all of these combined changed the world around you for the better.

What you do each day matters.
Be conscious and be aware you have the power to change
your little slice of the universe with every gesture or word.

You could also choose to be petty, mean, and angry most of your life, and all the potential good is erased, replaced by someone who casts an ugly shadow everywhere. It's your choice every single day.

There are no meaningless acts of kindness.
There are no acts in your day without effect.
There is nothing you do that does not matter.

Be aware that every word to a child, every show of love for a spouse, every kind offer of help to a friend, and every single attitude shown toward a client matters more than you could ever imagine. What is just part of your choice trying to live life at a higher level may be the best part of their day, and maybe even change a life for the better.

There is no stronger power on this earth to change the world than you.

ARE YOU OKAY?

Are you harmed in any way? No?

Is your family okay? Are they harmed in any way? No?

So neither you nor your family are hurt?

Then how could you possibly be upset over anything petty or meaningless in life? Why would you be a total bastard or a drooling, raving bitch over anything that can't and didn't hurt you?

I am tired of petty people yelling at waiters.
I am tired of stupid people demeaning flight attendants.
I am tired of bullies in the coffee shop.
I am tired of people being outraged over the simple inconveniences of life.

If you are hurt or your family is hurt, then kick some ass.

But if you aren't touched and you find yourself getting upset over a common, every-day bump in the road, you need to walk away. Sit quietly and ask why you have let your life slip so low, you are now one of the mean ones who ruin everyone else's day over nothing...absolutely nothing that hurt you.

Are you hurt? No? Is your family hurt? No?

Then to hell with it; it doesn't matter.
Your life is much too valuable to waste being mad at things that just don't affect you.

AN OLD CLIENT AND HIS SON

A client from years gone by asked me to have lunch with his 22-year-old son, who was struggling in school, on edge with everyone in his life and was presenting himself as a constantly miserable human being.

Three hours later, we might have had a breakthrough. The talk changed from a sulking child defending his life to a young man seeking solutions to his misery, and finished with me explaining the rules of being an adult.

This is what I told him, and wish I could share with everyone that age who struggles with the big questions they face in life:

Number One—Promise less, but do what you promise. People believe you when you tell them you are going to do something. They stop believing you forever when you fail to do what you said or change your mind about what you committed to on their behalf. This is especially true for anyone with kids; they never forget a promise that wasn't met...ever.

Number Two—Respect others even if they are different or don't agree with you. Different positions doesn't mean the other guy is bad—the discussion just means he doesn't agree with you on the matter.

Number Three—Live an honest life by always being who you are, and never waste your life trying to be what others want you to be. Start working on what you want, and give up being what your mother wanted you to be when you were her baby. No, you probably aren't going to be a famous doctor and she needs to get over it, and yes, it is okay to wear funny workout clothes until you are 60.

Number Four—At some point, you have to man or woman up and stop blaming the world because you are worthless. You are your own fault and your screwed-up life belongs to you. It's not your mama's fault you are angry or having trouble at work, and it is your fault you make your remaining friends mad after just one beer with you. It is all you, and will always be all you.

Number Five—You don't have to know what you are going to do the rest of your life, but you better damn sure know what you are going to do tomorrow. Worry about the next step and stop obsessing about the last step. You will get there fast enough.

IF YOU DREAD A CLIENT

If you dread working with a client and the thought of the next session with that person makes you irritated, fire that client.

If you have a client who is a pain in the ass to work with, fire that client.

If you have a chronically late client, fire that client.

If you have a sexual harasser client—the groper, the creepy hugger—fire that client.

If you have repeated trouble collecting money from a client, fire that client.

If the client is disrespectful to your team, fire that client.

If the client won't stop bad mouthing other clients, fire that client.

When you dread going into your own business because you fear dealing with "that client," you already know the answer...fire the client.

Your personal integrity and the integrity of your business is worth more than any pain-in-the-ass, always late, always wanting special treatment, bad-mouthing client will ever be.

WE GET STUCK IN THE BAD TIMES OF LIFE

We get so stuck in the bad times of life, we miss the good times.

Bad times happen to everyday regular people, people such as you.

Businesses struggle, marriages end, people die, you make stupid mistakes,
and then you get up tomorrow and there is life and life goes on, with or without you.

When bad times happen, you can become buried by life,
and the burden becomes so heavy you can no longer breathe.

But then the burden is lifted; now what do you do?

Do you seek the light, or remain shaking under the bed in the dark?

Bad times do not last, nor do the good times.

Your life is defined by knowing when to fight, and knowing when to live hard.

When the bad times are upon you, fight with everything you possess to never lose your
spirit or sense of who you are and who you can be.

When the good times are yours, run hard and savor every day and every second
because the good times will also fade away.

The problem is, we often lose everything to the bad stretches in life, becoming trapped
by a sense we will never see the light again. We miss the best of our lives living in darkness we won't allow to end.

Bad times are merely tests of your soul.

Everyone gets a chance for the universe to hand your overly muscular butts on a plate,
but how you take that beating often defines the rest of your life. Deal with it, mess with
it, fight it, and then move on.

You were made strong for a reason and there are many ways
to test the strength of a man or woman.

Life is a beautiful thing, but you don't want to miss the best of your life—being alive
today—because you can't let go of a past you cannot change.

LIVING WITHIN YOURSELF

Few people live centered within themselves. Most people's motivation comes from someone else and isn't internally generated. Living by external motivation is almost always the path to a life wasted and much sadness by a person existing to live someone else's dream or way of life.

The question to ask is, are you doing the work you love? Or are you doing what you feel obligated to do because someone told you to, or perhaps used guilt to force you into believing that this is what you "should" be doing in your life?

There is a young female manager I worked with over the years. She is talented in business, has a training background, and currently manages a small chain of big box gyms that do well financially. Her conflict, however, comes from her support group. Support groups are always a mixed conglomeration of spouses, family, old friends, and often mere acquaintances who feel obligated to voice an opinion as to how you should live your life.

This manager works hard at her job, raises a couple of kids, and loves the challenge of running a company with a few hundred employees doing millions of dollars in revenue. The battle begins for her with a spouse who thinks she should work less and that money isn't everything, and a sister who is a stay-at-home mother who constantly berates her into believing she is neglecting her children and husband by having a career.

There is a basic rule of life here: The more successful you are, the more your old support group will work against you. Few people in your life really want you to be successful because your success forces them to deal with their lack of achievement. The more you rise, the more people you will find hanging on to the seat of your pants to keep you down where the low and slow live.

Living within yourself merely states that spouses come and go and need to live their lives, not yours. Friends enter your life and leave, and family mostly care little about your success when compared to driving their personal agendas that often have nothing to do with you and usually reflect their own inadequacies.

Living within yourself is just another way of saying the only thing you will ever truly own in your life is what is between your ears. Talent and ability is rare and resented by many, but these are the tools that define your life. Pushing to the end of your abilities is what creates a life worth living, and no one should ever stand in the way of people chasing their own dreams.

Do what is best for you and live life on your own terms.

Avoid the words and phrases "should," "you have to," and the classic, "no one does that around here." There is nothing you have to do in your life except live it every day as you want to live it.

Follow your dreams and no one else's.

Do what you want, and never let anyone tell you what you should be doing with your life. Rise to your own talent and realize those with less talent or ability will always conspire to keep you down at their level of comfort, which is often just a mediocre life lived in quiet desperation.

Most importantly, live within yourself.

Eliminate those who fight to keep you down.

Make your life's decisions based on an internal motivation no one can ever take from you.

THERE WILL BE TIMES

There will be times through the years when you do not know what you want to do with your life, but there should never be a time you do not know about the type of person you want to be.

We set goals for our careers, for money, and for our kids, but we seldom sit quietly and think about the type of person we want to become as we age.

Think about these things when you are alone and have a few minutes:

How do I feel others should be treated in life?

What are my limits in relationships? Am I caring and supporting, but do I have limits for people who take everything in life but do not give?

Am I consistent in my behavior to others?

Am I a constant complainer?

Or am I the one who changes lives each day through patience and trust?

Is my personal word good?
Do I do what I promise?
Am I there when I say I will be there?
Do I stand by my friends?
Am I ethical in personal relationships?

In business, am I an employee someone can count on, or am I someone just holding onto a job, doing as little as it takes to get through the day?

Do I give high value for what I am paid?

Do I continually strive to educate myself and make myself more valuable to others?

If I own my own business, do I value the customers and give more than they pay for in our relationships? Am I ethical with my clients? Do I only give them what they need, or do I talk clients into things that benefit only me?

How do I want the world to perceive me? Am I professional, am I well spoken, am I decently dressed, am I someone you would trust with your money, or as a friend?

Have I grown through the years and become an ever-better person, or am I just the same old pain-in-that-overdeveloped-glute-area I was at the beginning?
Am I doing the things that make me happy?

Or am I living someone else's dream?
Am I chasing my goals in life, or just living day by day?

Are my personal values consistent, deep and solid,
not just situational ethics that change by the day?

Jobs change, people in your life come and go, but who you are in life, the values you hold, and the type of person you want to be should be as solid as the biggest kettlebell in the gym.

WHAT I KNOW NOW I WISH I KNEW THEN

Experience is the most brutal of teachers. In life, you often learn by being humbled in front of others, losing money in businesses and bad job choices, and losing relationships either you should have never been in or that were valuable and could have been saved if only you had the experience and maturity to handle things differently.

In my case, there were no mentors in my life until I finally became wise enough to seek them out. Having someone there in my teens and college days and in my early work years could have eased the pain and stupidity of learning everything in the most difficult ways possible. It is said you are the accumulation of all the things you failed at in life, and if that is the case, I now exist as nothing more than a giant ball of wound-up ass kicking.

I always wonder if I had guidance and a friend who had the experience to offer direction in my life, would I have been smart enough to take that help, or would I have been too arrogant and simply continued on my path of try, get beaten, learn, and try again. The arrogance often won, and I now realize there is a fine line between being the rock that sticks to what he believes no matter the pounding and the person who has to do it his way just to prove he can.

Now life is reversed, and I am often the mentor trying to save the seekers from the damage an unexamined life can cause. The question these seekers ask most often in my mentoring sessions is usually direct: "What would you do if you were me?" I always ask what they think first. Then I realize these people are seeking the help I never had, and it is up to me to supply answers based on thousands of clients and a creative life.

Here are the things I wish someone had taught me during my lost years—the things that reflect what I know now, but didn't know then.

*Never waste a day caring about what anyone thinks of you...*unless you are seeking that opinion. We spend too much time wondering if our clothes are appropriate, if we will be accepted by others, or if we are pleasing someone else. There should be a core of people you love and trust, whose advice you respect—although there is no law you ever have to do what anyone suggests or take anyone's advice once you hear it. Stop worrying about your shirt, pants, car, house, or choice of spouse. If what you do makes you happy, then keep on keeping on.

Do a random act of kindness every day. There was a woman standing in the parking lot where I was getting groceries. She was panicked and crying. She had hitchhiked and was trying to get to her kids in the next town. I was going the opposite direction and had a time commitment. There was a young couple in the parking lot. I gave them $20 to drive her to the kids and I smiled all the way home. It was just $20, but it felt like a million. Do something truly random for someone today and get that million-dollar smile on your face.

Respect everyone; be intimidated by no one. Someone will always have more money than you, and many more will have less. Arrogant people who accumulate money and treat everyone badly, from the guy at the coffee shop to the waitress at the local restaurant, are not better than you; they just have more money...maybe. Money intimidated me early in life, and I equated money people with being superior human beings. Then I started to consult with money people and realized that often money was nothing more than an indication of a troubled and wretched human in nice clothes.

The mistake I made was that I couldn't tell the difference between class and money; one is not an indication of the other. Money people can be hurtful, insensitive to others less fortunate, and in general, world-class asses. On the other hand, people without a lot of cash can be truly classy, carry themselves well, and contribute beautifully to the universe.

The lesson here is to learn how to carry yourself well. Anyone can learn how to dress, demonstrate manners, and be classy. Classy is a state of mind, not an entry in a check-book. Truly show respect and courtesy to every human being you meet, no matter what color, sex, sexual orientation, religion, or political party. There is no room for hatred in your life. If I don't like you, I will ignore you, but I will always show you respect.

Always be the professional. It does not matter what job you hold. It does not matter what you do for a living. It does not matter if you make $8 an hour, or millions a year. It matters that you are always a professional. This means bringing full, conscious effort to your work. Work harder than those around you, dress better than those in the same line of work, study harder, and master what you do, even if you are the clerk at the local convenience store.

I find it sad so many people in the fitness industry demonstrate so little professionalism once they enter the field. Being a professional is an internal thing, a state of mind you enter once you dedicate yourself to whatever job you take on. There are no jobs beneath you; you can elevate every job to a professional status simply by refusing to be anything but the best you can be.

Always do the right thing. Sooner or later, you have to go to sleep, and when you do, there should never be any doubt in your mind that every decision you made that day was based on doing the right thing morally, ethically, and professionally.

They say everyone has a number, and anyone will sell out for the right number. Whether you are religious or not, what price do you put on your soul, defined as the one thing no one in the world should ever be able to take away from you?

You might slip, stumble, and find yourself somewhere making a decision that wasn't the right thing, but that was one day and one day only. Now what are you going to do for the rest of your life?

Knowing the right thing may be the hardest part for some people, especially those out of practice and who have spent so many years trying to do the wrong things to so many people. There is a point of no return, where a life led constantly harming others becomes your life's work and you can't find your way back.

I have seen this in old gym owners who have made a career of ripping off every client who set foot in their businesses, and I have seen it in others who can no longer tell the difference between a life of honor, and a life of living off the bones of others.

Start today; the world needs another good human being.

Money and emotions don't mix. Money is easy. You can read about it, take lessons on it, learn to earn more of it, and ultimately you will come to understand money only exists for one purpose. It allows you to live life on your own terms, held hostage by no person, or by a job or career you hate.

But emotion ruins money sense. Emotional responses to money, such as arrogance, greed, keeping up with others, and the need to show off are the things preventing many people from gathering any of the world's common tender. Money isn't hard, but separating money from emotion might be one of the hardest things in the world.

Save 20 percent of everything you make. Living within your means is a learned behavior. It starts by mastering the discipline of saving some of what you make. Spending every dollar you make, racking up credit cards, and living without savings is just plain stupid. If you are just getting started, go with five percent and then raise it by five percent every month until you get to 20 percent.

You expect your clients to live with discipline, yet you can't even save a chunk of your check. Money in the bank is freedom and this freedom has to be earned.

There is no perfect. There is no perfect job, spouse, house, town, friend, relative, project, or life. There is a drive for many people to achieve perfect, and this is what causes procrastination and self-inflicted stress. Don't waste your life chasing perfect, but instead dedicate your life to doing the things the best you can do them, and that will be good enough.

Find someone you respect and ask for help. Most successful people want to give back. Answering a few hundred questions is very little when it to contributes to someone's future.

If you wear the suit, you have to be the man. Can you imagine Superman sitting home watching television, wearing his cool suit and refusing to go help someone?

I was traveling with Greg Rose, cofounder of the Titleist Performance Institute and someone whom I have had on my most respected list since about an hour after I met him. He had been on the road overseas for three weeks and I was coming off a two-week stint. We had just finished a difficult two days doing a very draining and intensive speaker's workshop. As we finished and I am thinking about the cold beverage coming my way in about 15 minutes, a class participant asked Greg to do some video for his clients. Greg jumped right in like he was the freshest thing on the planet and spent another 15 minutes with the guy demonstrating some exercises.

I asked him about it on the way back to the hotel. His response was, "I wouldn't exist if they didn't believe in me and ask for help. If you're the guy, you have to take the time to show respect for those you lead."

I haven't been the same since, and I will stand there until the last person leaves any workshop I am leading. If you wear the suit and claim to be the hero, you have to be the man behind the suit.

Be grateful. Say thank you to whoever helped you get on the path. Be thankful for every dime, every friend, every opportunity, and everything you have. Work your ass off, but realize you are part of something bigger. It is always good to say thank you to those who lend you a helping hand or support your business.

Life in balance is a myth. You can't live a life in balance and ever achieve anything worth a damn.

The key is learning to live in short bursts of imbalance, where you lose your mind for a few months to get that new job going, that new business open, or to finish that book project, and then you go back to a focus on those you left behind.

No one can handle more than three big things in life at once. If you want a great career, go for it and take your family along, but don't expect to be part of the community, a weekend coach, and a dozen other things badly done because you believe doing it all represents a balance in your life.

Focus on the two or three things that define your life and put your energy there. When those are done or fade, find two or three more. Fewer things done better is a much better way to define your life.

Master one thing. This is advice I got and took. Learn more about one thing and you will never be out of work.

For me it was easy; the one thing was to learn more about the fitness business than any other human being on the planet. What is your one thing? Can you define it in one sentence? Can you still say that after 40 years, the passion is still there to share that one thing?

Never waste a single day doing anything you are not passionate about in your life.

Be healthy. There is no reason on this earth to not put your personal health at the top of the list in life's to-do pile. The reality is, we often trade health for short-term gain. We eat stress for breakfast, live on stupid hours, drink too much on the weekends, and end up sacrificing our health for a lifestyle we couldn't enjoy if we lost that health. The struggle may be constant and there are days that don't lend themselves to chasing fitness, but it is a rule of life that they can't bury you if you are still moving.

Move a little more, lose those five pounds, turn off the television, put down the phone, and take the kids for a walk. Fitness is motion, and motion is life.

Explore the nature of faith. Believing in something is worth the effort. Spend time exploring everything about the nature of faith. The values we often respect in others come from man's attempt to understand a higher power. It doesn't matter what you believe in as long as you spend a lot of your life looking. Faith in higher powers arrives at different times in your life. Too many people make the judgment about faith based on what others say and not by exploring for themselves. There is no one way, one religion, or one approach to finding out what makes the universe a place worth living in.

Look, explore, ask, and think and you will end up where you need to be in life.

Life is too short to hang out with idiots. Surround yourself with people who inspire you and eliminate the toxic people in your life. This includes old friends, spouses, nasty family, and anyone who spews a path of toxic negativity every time they are around you.

If it is worth doing, it is worth overdoing. Pick fewer friends, but be the best friend ever. Going to a party? Be the last one out and do it right. Going on a trip? Explore every alley of every country in the world. Going to be in the fitness business? Be the best owner or trainer who ever lived. Mediocrity is for losers. If it is worth doing, it is worth giving it your undivided effort and passion.

Finally, live for today. The time between 21 and 60 is about four weeks. There is no tomorrow; there is only today lived well with passion and intensity.

You should always plan for your future, and you should spend a great deal of time projecting your life ahead, but for some of us, there is no tomorrow and you will only have today. People die young, get sick, or lose their lives in horrible ways that reflect the finicky nature of the universe.

You might not have tomorrow, but you always have today.

THE WEST COAST OF IRELAND
One of the most beautiful places on earth

SHE EXPLAINED TO THE DOG
WHY SHE WAS TIRED
AND COULDN'T TAKE HIM
FOR A WALK.
HE GAVE HER THE PAW AND
TOOK HIMSELF OUT.

SHE TRIED TO TALK TO THE DOG

She tried to talk to the dog about how she was tired and didn't feel like going for a walk, but the dog didn't care and just gave her a paw and took herself for a walk.

She tried talking to the kids about why she didn't want to go to the park with them, but she didn't know how to talk to the top of heads. They turned 10 and she never sees their faces unless their phones break, and besides, the story was the same old thing about no time to play or hang with them. They went outside and left her sitting in the kitchen.

She called her best friend, who said she was on the way to the gym without her and would call her back.

She didn't call back.

Her husband came home and wanted to go for a long walk before dinner. She made some poor excuse, and he went without her...again.

She picked up a cookie off the counter and headed to her room.

She looked in the mirror and realized she was getting older, heavier, more tired, and had less enthusiasm for life. Then she understood no one cares about the "why not;" they only care about getting it done.

Fitness isn't some crazy lifestyle requiring hundreds of hours in a gym, extremes in food, or special equipment costing thousands of dollars.

Fitness is a hundred simple daily choices we have to make anyway.

Walk the dog around the block, or sit on the couch?
Throw the ball around with the kids, or scroll a small screen?
Eat an apple, or eat a cookie? Those veggie things might just catch on!

Drop into the gym a few times per week with a friend, or make the lame excuse about time and skip it again, then sit on the couch watching mindless TV?

Fitness is easy. You simply do the stuff you have to do anyway, every day, a little differently.

You have to eat, so eat some good food instead of crap.
If the dog is fat, there is a good chance you are too.
Do both of you a favor and take a walk.

The kids will do what you do.
If you move, they move.
If you sit, they sit.
At least move for the kids.

And spouses have to choose together to live a higher quality life through movement. If you like the person enough to live together, you should at least want to get a few more quality years together.

Those years come from the simple act of moving.

Fitness is easy. Just move every day until you can't.

And if you move every day, you will most likely have many more days
in your life to irritate people.

JUST SHOW UP

Stop over-thinking everything, and just show up.

Stop worrying about what might happen, and just show up.

Stop stressing that it might not be a perfect workout,
you don't feel up to it, or you are too tired.
Just show up, and it will be worth it.

Just ask.
Ask for what you want, and never be afraid to ask for what you need in life.
Ask that person out, ask for the job, ask for the time, ask for a meal.
Just ask.

Just say "no."
Say "no" to helping everyone, every time anyone asks.
The more you give, the more some people want.
Say "no" more often and "yes" to your own life.

Just say "thank you."
Remember where you came from and who helped you get here,
and say "thank you" often.

Just say "yes."
Say "yes" to new experiences, risk, change, and life.
If it makes you uncomfortable, it might be the best thing you ever did.

Just help one person a day.
Every day you pass people who need your help.
Just help one a day until you die and you will change the world.

Just let it go.
You can't change the past; the past can't touch you.
Stop obsessing about the mistakes every human makes, and get on with it.
You aren't perfect; you messed up—get on with your life.
Just let it go.

Just refuse to be the one who hates everything in life.
Petty, angry people are a waste.

Just refuse to ever waste a day being someone the world hates
and being a prick or the bitch from hell—doesn't do you any good anyway.

Just be you.

No matter what people have said to keep you down, keep you under control,
to manipulate you into doing what they want you to do, just be you and ignore them all.

You are enough, and you are perfect,
even if your ex-spouse tells the world differently.

Just be you.

That is enough to create a wonderful life.

JUST FOR ONE DAY

Just for one day, believe in your own talent.

Just for today, understand you can choose to be a better person.

Today, remember what you do matters and you change lives.

Just for today, know who you are is enough,
no matter what anyone else in your life has ever told you.

Just today, live your own life without trying to carry everyone else's baggage
and the failed dreams they throw on you.

Today, understand there is not a damn thing in the past that can touch you, that there is no mistake made years ago that matters, and there is nothing behind you that can change who you are today.

There is just today.

Just today, just during this short 24-hour time on earth, rise to be the person your significant other, your kids, your friends, and your family know you really are.

Just today, reach out and help someone who can benefit from your strength, money, and faith in them.

Just today, remember not to be petty and to ignore the small irritants in life that simply do not matter but can define how you go through life.

Just today, work out for the sheer pleasure of the movement, the sweat, the fun, and the friendship. Do not obsess about keeping score or trying for the perfect workout.

Just today, stand up for yourself and understand you have the power to make your dreams come true, and today you give yourself permission to chase your own future.

And then tomorrow, do all of this again...and maybe the day after that too.

JUST BECAUSE WE DISAGREE

Just because we disagree doesn't make you wrong
or me a miserable person whom you should hate.

Current culture states that if we disagree, you are a miserable smudge of something stuck to the backside of a hairy dog and I am the loser, unreasonable ass who isn't worthy of your opinion.

And if you feel or act this way, you might be the most childish adult on the planet.

Are you really so right about everything that anyone who disagrees is wrong?

Emotionally secure adults agree to disagree.

We discuss, state our positions, discuss again, and agree to disagree if we have different opinions. Yes, we can have great arguments, wild discussions, and too many beers while making a case, but in the end, it should still be you and me as friends.

Just because you disagree with me doesn't make you wrong.

Just because I disagree with you doesn't make me a pathetic loser.

Disagreeing just means we disagree.

In the age of, "if you disagree, you are against me" mentality, it is difficult to separate the person from the position. You having a opinion on something does not define who you are, but is simply what you are thinking today.

The opinion is not the person.

Sadly, we see politicians who hate each other over positions; we see family members who cease talking because of religious beliefs. We see friends who never speak after disagreeing about things such as a person's choice of sexuality, and we see people who end up hating each other simply because they see two different sides of a simple discussion.

The next time you are angry or feel like writing something toxic on social media because someone dared to disagree with you, think about how childish it is to get angry because someone might have a different opinion than you.

If you disagree with this, it is okay.

I still respect you as a person.

JANUARY IS THE TIME OF YEAR

January is the time of year when the world is full of born-again fitness people.

Oh, the things we would like to tell them.

You paid $9 for a membership.
You got what you paid for, so little money.
Now shut up, and get in line to park to get into that dirty, overcrowded fake gym.

It is all about the food. Big butts are built by big meals, by bad food,
combined with meaningless calories in giant cups.

No trainer on earth can help you get in shape if you don't stop eating the damn crap food.

Any movement is good movement, but 10 minutes of walking the dog to the beer store
does not offset five hours of TV.

No, that string tee from 1995 is not coming back in style,
and I doubt that nasty gray chest hair and crazy pants are either.

Dude, you're wearing a fanny pack. Where is your time machine parked?

No, ma'am, we don't have a 30-minute old-lady circuit,
nor do we have a giant timer that tells you when to move.

Yes, you do need a trainer.

You tried your own nutrition plan and workout for the last 10 years
and you are a pathetic mess.

Maybe that magazine article, written by a guy with three months of experience, was
wrong after all.

Yes, I know that workout made you beautiful in high school,
but that was 25 years ago and maybe your body has changed a little.

If you are wearing it, you ate it.

All that jiggly stuff didn't just jump on your butt when you weren't looking.

Oh, the pain of January in the fitness business.

ONE DAY YOU WILL WAKE UP

One day you will wake up from your very sheltered life and there won't be any more time to chase the dreams that kept you awake at night.

One day will be the last time you hug those you love. Maybe today is the day you realize we go through life one goodbye at a time until it is really goodbye.

And one day will be the last time your child cuddles in your lap for a read and a hug. Years later you wonder why you never savored that moment.

One day you won't physically be able to do what you take for granted today and your life will change forever. You now understand you won't be this "you" forever, but who you are becoming might be just perfect.

One day you will wake up and realize you really did have it all,
but wasted it by chasing more.

One day you will find out what it takes to be a good person
and that will be the best hour of your life.

One day you will realize you exist for only one reason
and that is to leave the world around you a better place because you were there.

One day you stumble and die a little, yet you survive. Then you realize the best days in your life are only possible because of the bad days when you suffered.

One day you will realize you are good enough and anyone who told you differently was wrong. You are not just good enough, you are enough, and that is a powerful realization.

One day you will realize the power you have to change lives, and you will then spend the rest of your life trying to live up to that realization.

One day you will be the best you will ever be.

Why not today?
Why not you?
Why not now?

There is nothing more powerful than realizing your own strength as a person, but if not today, then when?

WHERE WILL YOU BE IN LIFE
10 YEARS FROM NOW?

When asked, "What did it mean to be you?" how will you answer?

Did you make a difference in the world around you?

Did you change lives?

Did you take care of your family and create enough wealth
to take care of them and yourself?

Did you grow and challenge yourself during those 10 years?

Did you care enough to inspire others?

Did you give more than you took from the world?

Did you experience the world, or just collect meaningless stuff
that lost its value and luster days after you bought it?

Is the world a better place because you are in it?

Or are you just 10 years older? Did nothing, changed nothing, inspired nothing,
and just took up space on an already-crowded planet?

It's never too late to change your path.

Get started today.

Ten years will pass in a second, and then it is too late.

THERE ARE FAR FEWER WOMEN OWNERS

There are far fewer women owners than men in the gym business,
but these women often make more effective owners.

Many male owners remind me of owning a big male golden retriever. You take your
big dog to the park, let him out of the truck, and he has to piss on everything to make
it his territory.

In business, this big male dog has to pee on everything to mark his own territory before he even tries the idea. Hey, he woofs, this is a great idea, but I will change it before
I even try it, which is big dog, but bad business.

The female owner will try the plan exactly as prescribed, only changing the idea and
arguing with you later, once she validates whether it worked for her.

Male owners are often more concerned about ego and being right,
while female owners are often more concerned about being effective
and making money.

All you big dogs out there, try not messing with a concept
until you give a new idea at least three months.

Stop pissing on everything at least until you try it.

Female owners, we need more of you in this business.

Open your own gyms and get in the game.

ONE OF THE HARDEST QUESTIONS
I HAVE EVER BEEN ASKED

One of the hardest questions anyone has ever asked me is "Why do you always seem to be at peace with your life…and why do I always feel that what I am doing and who I am isn't quite right?"

Here are some simple truths to help you reach that stage of quiet confidence we all seek:

Number One—Stop caring what others think of you and start caring about what you think of yourself. Accepting yourself with limitations, boogers, and glitches is harder than it sounds. There is no perfect; there is just you and that is pretty damn good.

Number Two—Only seek and do work you love. It's hard to live in peace doing work you hate doing for 40 hours a week, and then find yourself still hating it for another 40 at home.

Number Three—Love and commit to the one you are with, or leave. If you can't be a brilliant life partner, run, and stop bringing down the other person too. If your significant other isn't your best friend, you will find it hard to ever be at peace, even for a moment.

Number Four—Understand there is no one but you to blame for who you are and how you will live in the future. If you are a success, it is your fault; if you are a failure, it is your fault. There will never be peace in your life until you stop blaming the world for who you are.

Number Five—Carrying anger drains your soul. Stop being mad at a universe that doesn't care about your petty stupidity. Going through life angry at every small inconvenience destroys your life, but more importantly, destroys everyone around you too.

Number Six—Helping others have better lives allows you to sleep at night. Givers sleep, but takers are never satisfied, because they can't live without wanting more.

Finally, realize this too will end—the bad times and the good are all just fleeting stages in life. Learn to savor the beautiful moments in your life today, instead of obsessing about a past you can't change, and a future you may not have.

THE BITCHING AND MOANING HAS TO STOP

The bitching, the moaning, the complaining, the blaming, the excuses,
all in the first 20 minutes of the conversation…

"I am sorry, but I just can't work with you anymore."

"Why? I need help."

"Because my life is too short to put up with your endless misery."

"But I need help."

"No, you thrive on being miserable. You thrive on blaming others. You live to make others
suffer. You are a professional victim and I won't work with you again. You live to take, and
even if you are given everything you want, you still find a reason to blame others for your
failure. I could give you a gold brick and you would bitch it is too heavy. Go away."

A day in the life, but learn from this:
You are not strong enough to save people who live to be victims.

It doesn't matter if this is an employee, a significant other, an old friend, a client, or family, there are people in your life who live for the sole purpose of draining the life out of
everyone around them. They are energy vampires who live to drain. Run and run now.

You are better than that.
You are smarter than that.

You must understand that helping just enables the taking to never end.

Choose: you, or the drainer of life. No one is strong enough to carry that big of a load…
and no matter how much you give, it won't change a damn thing anyway.

THE ALARM GOES OFF AT 6:00 A.M.

Tap...snooze.
Tap...snooze.
Now run!

You stay in the shower an extra 10 minutes, leaning against the wall, letting the hot water stream down your back—anything to avoid getting to work.

Breakfast is eaten standing up, the shirt is the same one from yesterday, and you realize you have a serious case of "don't give a damn."

You head to work knowing the only possible way to get there on time is if someone from a science fiction movie beams you there, and even then you would still be late.

As you walk through the door 20 minutes late, you mumble something about the traffic or a wreck.

Your day is about avoiding work, checking your phone every three minutes, and staring at the clock on the wall.

Your shift is over at 5:00. Let the universe protect any small child standing in the doorway as the clock strikes the hour, because you will be running through it as fast as you can move to make your escape.

The day is spent making money for someone you don't respect, but who tells you it is a privilege to work there.

Your talent slowly erodes, because every day is spent avoiding responsibility, refusing to accept any new challenge, or rising up to your own ability.

Your life slowly slips away, and you find yourself older, angry, resentful of anyone who has done anything in life, and bitter that you could have been someone, if only someone had given you a chance.

You got everything you deserve.

This is about respect.

Do you have enough respect for yourself to seek a good job,
work for someone you respect,
and stand up for your own talent?
Do you have enough self-respect to get every drop out of the talent you have, and then work so hard you find there is a hidden reserve that will carry you and that can only be uncovered by sweat?

All you have at the end of life is the knowledge you lived life on your terms, gave it everything you possessed, and either succeeded or failed because of your energy and courage.

You are who you are because that is who you chose to be,
and if life isn't good, make better decisions.

This is really about you.

CENTRAL LONDON

*There is no place I would rather
be walking on a Saturday afternoon*

I AM DYING.
WHAT DO I DO?

"I AM DYING. WHAT DO I DO?"

This was the start of a call from a gym owner three years ago.

"I have cancer. I am 32. It is Stage 4. What do I do with my business? How do I protect my family? I am scared, and the only people I talk to pat me on the shoulder and cry. How do I get through this? I am terrified beyond belief and can't see a way forward."

"I think you are wrong. I do not think you will die. We have enough time to protect your family and business. Here is what we are going to do to make sure your family survives this, even if you don't."

But he was wrong. He did make it, but being alive is not the same as living.

"I've been thinking," says my young client.

"Not unusual for a guy who has been lying on the floor puking for a year, waiting to see if he would live or die. What have you been thinking about?"

"That I am out of time. That I have never had a life. That I started a career, a family, and a business when I was young and that I was at the beginning of everything, but now I would never have a chance to be there at the end.

"I put off everything I wanted in life in order to build a business that would take care of my family in the future, a family I neglected, promising them someday we would have the good times and I would be there for them...and then I was told there would be no future, that I would die and never see my girls past the age of seven.

"My life was lying on the floor praying for life,
but feeling so bad that death wouldn't have mattered."

"You are not going to die.
You are past that now and you need to get on with your life."

"But I don't know how to live. I sit and cry,
thinking there will never be enough time to get my life back."

"You are right, my friend, there will never be enough time…there never is for anyone to waste. But there is enough time to live."

"How do I start?"

"Where are you now?"

"Coffee shop."

"Go home. Tell your wife you are madly in love with her. Hug your kids until you cry. Call your parents and let them know you are through the dark days, and you have decided to live for a while so they don't throw all of your old crap out of your room.

"And then go to work, change the world one client at a time, and then repeat all this again tomorrow, and then again, and then again until you understand there is today, and it is your day. Figure out how to live in this day and not worry too much about a future none of us are guaranteed."

Time is an illusion.

We always assume we have enough time to get the important things in life done, but that is wrong thinking.

Planning for tomorrow is smart; you just might get there.
Living fully today is smarter, because you might not.

BEING A COACH MUST BE
THE EASIEST JOB IN THE WORLD

I mean really, you get to work out whenever you want,
every client is always in a good mood,
and you get to wear fun clothes and live casual.

But what about...

Twenty years of crazy clients expecting you to change a decade of self-abuse into a ripped work of art in about four days.

Twelve years of running your own gym...broke for 10 years and on fire for the last two, which gives you hope for another 10.

Sixty hours or more each week changing the world...just three Saturdays off all last year, vacations are beach, eat, sleep, drink, sleep, beach, sleep, food, sleep, and beach.

On any given Saturday night, you would consider trading the entire gym for three pints and a bottle of good wine.

Or just the pints if it was one of those weeks that can make a grown coach cry like a baby.

Hundreds of meals out of plastic bowls eaten standing up in a storeroom.

Who knew you could drive, text, eat, talk to the kids in their seats in the back, and plan workouts all at the same time?

Coffee, hallowed be thy name.
Coffee, there would be no gym business without your magic power.
Coffee, if there was one shrine that needs to be built that signifies life as a coach in this crazy business, it would be to you, coffee, and your ability to turn the darkest morning into sunshine.

There would never, anywhere in the world, be a 5:00 a.m. workout without the strength of a large coffee to go.

You know your day is long when you hope your 10 o'clock is five minutes late
or you won't get to poop until 4:00 in the afternoon.

Early morning workout before dawn or no workout at all.

Fighting hard for your two kids who are growing up fairly normal, despite the hours and having a professional coach as a parent.

Both kids spent their first three years sleeping under your desk in the gym office, and they turned out fine, except for that one incident with the kettlebell that you never mentioned to the spouse.

Your favorite uncle died and you had to borrow a tie and a coat, and buy dress pants, have someone show you how to tie your new tie, and borrow shoes from your accountant brother.

Still in love with the person of your dreams after so many years fighting for your dream. If there was a Saint of the Gym, your person would be the first nominated.

You always wonder why she never ran away with a person who had a real job, real hours, and weekends off.

Defied all odds and stayed in a business where so many others failed. You wonder why you made it and not them, but then you realize you simply out-worked every other human being in the gym business, and that was enough.

You could love and respect a person like this, one who has never quit chasing a hard and challenging life.

The world needs more people with this strength, who are dedicated to doing the right thing and willing to pay the long dues it takes to be so good at something so difficult.

Really, being a coach has to be the easiest job in the world.

Just ask anyone who has never coached for a living and who will tell you how easy it is.

SOMETIMES I DON'T HAVE TO BE PERFECT

Sometimes I don't have to leave it all in the gym, obsess about the perfect workout, agonize over bad golf, or do everything as hard and as perfectly as I can.

Sometimes it is fun to go for a mediocre bike ride, walk slowly in the sun, play bad golf, and concentrate on enjoying the experience of the moment instead of obsessing how well I am doing it, or how hard, or how many calories I just burned.

It is okay for those around you not to have to live up to your standard of perfect for one day.

Let your kid fail doing something he is perfectly horrible at, just because he enjoys it.

Let your spouse do her own thing without complying with your "perfect" nonsense.

And remember, the client doesn't always need to be perfect;
on some days just showing up is a major win.

Have two beers and don't obsess about a perfect diet day.

Sometimes, life is just about being—not about being perfect in everything, every day.

HERE IS WHAT I THINK

I won't let you make me feel guilty because of your inability to find happiness in your life. Change is scary, but regretting not even trying will ruin your soul.

People who don't read and grow scare the hell out of me.

Many people start down the right path in life,
but few have the heart and pain-in-the-ass persistence to finish things.

Normal people bore me. Weird people make life worth living.

I want to be the dumbest person in the room and never believe I am the brightest
so I am forced to think new things.

You were born with the hardwiring in place. The best parents can do is guide you for a while, then let you realize your predetermined destiny.

Mean and petty people have a special room in the darkest corner of hell
with their names on the door.

I love people who are willing to chase their passion no matter what anyone tells them.

Never let anyone who hasn't done a damn thing tell you not to try.

At least once a week, sit with the one you love, hold hands, drink a good glass,
and stare at the water while talking about your dreams.

A few hours disconnected from the world may be
the best thing you did for yourself this week.

Yes, this might qualify as a rant.

SITTING IN AN AIRPORT

Sitting in an airport on a Monday, watching an overweight mother, followed by an overweight dad, dragging an overweight kid with Mickey ears, and carrying a fat dog.

If only I could scream, "Stop complaining you don't know what to eat!"

If you are so challenged that you can't tell the difference between that donut in your hand and an apple, how can you find your own kid in Disney?

If your life is like this in your 30s, how are your 40s going to be?

Stop eating like a nine-year-old, and stop feeding your kid crap for breakfast. Does anyone really need to explain that anything served from a giant cardboard box, covered with sugar, and eaten out of huge bowl is bad for your health?

You spend four hours a day scratching on a small screen, sit at work on your ever-widening backside all day, and then come home and sit in front of another screen. You do zero exercise, but whine to your friends you can't understand why you can't lose weight.

No, you are not big boned, one of the one percent who has medical issues, or one of those who don't have access to real food.

You, my friend, are part of the 69% who are overweight or obese and you did it to yourself.

Diet soft drinks and light beer are marketing games and have nothing to do with weight loss. You drink a 12-pack of light beer a day for a year, you will not be light, and you can kiss goodbye the chance of ever looking down and seeing your pee pee again.

If everyone in your family is overweight, even the damn dog,
find a good training gym and get some professional help.

Blah! I hate airports and traveling on Monday sucks.

And another thing...

SO YOU WANT TO JOIN A GYM?

Gyms that merely rent you space on equipment are not worth the money, even if the money is less than the cost of a pizza. It is only $10 per month, and not even worth that small pittance to join.

If you don't change your food, no number of workouts will cover a bad diet. Do not ever diet; simply start slowly replacing bad food with higher quality foods. Eating healthy is not dieting.

Be realistic about your age and current condition. Work to be the best version of who you are now and let that old in-shape you from "back in the day" stay in the past.

Get a coach. You have a doctor, an attorney, an accountant, and a score of other professionals supporting your life, so why would you believe you know enough about fitness to be your own coach? Get help, even if all you can afford is a once a month sit-down for a program design to carry you through on your own, but get help.

Accept the current you, and then change. When a coach mentions your extra baggage, it is not body shaming; that talk is the first step in accessing where you are and where you need to go. The current trend is to just go for healthy no matter the weight, but extra weight is the cause of many other health issues.

You do not have to be perfect, but you can always be better.
Your weight is your weight.
Lighter is usually healthier for most people.

Just show up. Even one day a week at a good gym with a coach is far better than doing nothing. Fitness isn't trying for perfect attendance like we did in grade school; fitness is trying to get in shape wrapped around a full and busy life. Just try—just show up, and if you get there about three times per week, you are as perfect as you need to be.

Understand you will fail. There will be crazy weekends that block your fitness endeavor for a few days. There will be new jobs, new babies, divorces, and every other crazy thing setting you back.

So what? Get over it, and get back to the gym.
We all slip, but that doesn't mean we have to slide away.

Lift weights. There are a lot of ways to work out, but most of the world needs a couple days a week picking up heavy things and putting them overhead a few times. Muscle is the structure you like so much when you see a picture of a fit person and that doesn't come from mindless cardio walking slowly and staring at a small TV.

Cardio-only fitness just does not get it done. You need muscle, and muscle needs a little weight training a few times per week.

Anyone can get in better shape. Anyone, no matter what kind of shape you are in now, ranging from, "I still sort of have it, but I just can't find it," to, "my dog even thinks I am pathetic," can benefit from a good coach and nice gym.

Join a gym. Get in shape. Enjoy the feeling of better health.

Move, people, your life depends on it.

WHEN YOU UNDERSTAND TIME, YOU WILL UNDERSTAND LIFE

The big lie about time is there is always tomorrow, which leads you to waste today.

Time is not handed out equally to everyone. Some of you will have time lasting until you are 100, while too many of you will be robbed of your time early, leaving your life, and you, undone and unfinished.

Perception of time changes, but too late for most people.

When you are in your 20s or 30s, there is always time to get everything done in life. When you are in your 40s, the pounding of the clock is louder as you realize you will never get it all done and then, for the first time, you begin to admit you cannot reach every dream.

Time has its way of forcing us as we age to focus on only what is most important. We realize as we get older that we can only finish what is truly important; we have to choose what we really want from life since at some point we are out of time.

Time is also the first thing many people try to steal from you, because they, not you, realize time is the most valuable thing you own. You can replace a car or house if lost, but you can never replace your time. Other people who live to drain your time away from you understand this better than you.

Honor time.

Be reluctant to waste your time on people who give nothing back. Say "no" more often to things that enhance or carry others, but that don't benefit you. Savor the time you have, however fleeting, with those you love. Be a miser who hordes your time, unwilling to share it with people unless they are truly important in your life.

The trick to time is to master it where you can get it to slow down. We do this by focusing on where we are and who we are with, understanding this moment could well be the last we will ever have. Focusing your love on a child for 30 minutes stops the clock, but we waste this time by scrolling on a device developed to rob us of the best moments of our lives by taking us away from what is important.

Understand time and you will understand life…but I have to go now;
I am simply out of time.

YOU ARE WHO YOU ARE TODAY

You are who you are today because of the choices you made in life through last night.

You create your own life one choice at a time.
You choose, every single day, how you will live your life.

And there is always a choice, an option,
or a way to change your life if you aren't happy.

The pushback on all of this is always,
"But I don't know what choice to make, so I don't make any."

You know the choices to make that will change your life, but people who believe themselves to be trapped by life don't want to make the decisions that are hard or painful.

You are trapped in a job you hate,
but won't do the work to change who you are so you can move on.

You are trapped in a relationship that is killing both of you, but blame others for your inability to make a decision that could ultimately lead to a better life for all of you.

No matter what the circumstances, it always comes back to you and your ability to choose life or to choose a lesser version of who you can be and how you live each day.

Some decisions are more difficult than others, but every decision comes down to your choice, your life, and how you want to lead it, no matter what you tell yourself or others.

Every decision counts and every decision leads to what kind of life you want to live.

Ten years from now, if someone asks you, "What did it mean to be you?" will you be able to answer that you lived life on your terms, or will you simply be 10 years older and still afraid of making the decisions that could set you free?

SWEARING YOU WILL GET INTO SHAPE

Swearing you will get in shape is one of the dumbest New Year's resolutions ever.

Getting in shape isn't something you "do." When you scream to the world this is the year you will change your life, you will fail...unless you understand getting in shape isn't something that is done, but how you live.

Health is a journey, not a destination.

Resolution people fail, because they believe working out cancels out all the bad in their lives that led to getting out of shape. You cannot out-train a destructive lifestyle. There is no workout that can overcome too little sleep, too many beers, too much crap food, and a lifestyle dedicated to a butt firmly planted on a couch 10 hours a day juggling electronic devices as your sole source of exercise.

Joining a gym, dropping by a few times a week, walking slowly on a treadmill but changing nothing else in your life is why most gyms should only be gyms during the first month of the year and then turn into bars for the next 11 months.

You join a gym with good intentions, but those intentions fade quickly if nothing else changes, and then you retreat to the destructive life you never really left.

If you want change, change everything, because there is no change that matters in life without total commitment.

If you are in, then get naked, stand on the cliff, and dive for the very deep water.

Fitness isn't wading in the shallow end. It is a lifestyle progression that day by day leads to a life of quality, fulfillment, energy, and passion that can only be achieved by leaping off the cliff with no Plan B.

If you want to get in shape this year, commit your soul, because you are worth it.

No one on this planet can get you in shape unless you are all in and ready to seek a healthier and happier lifestyle that goes along with true fitness.

Get naked and jump off the cliff, or don't pretend this is your year for fitness. All in or stay home is the only way anything worth doing is ever done.

It would be easier with a good coach holding your hand, but I have said that before.

THE HARDEST CLIENT TO HAVE

The hardest client to have is the one who refuses to take responsibility for his own life.

The hardest friend to have is the one who quietly sabotages everything you are doing, being jealous of your attempt to move forward in life.

The hardest relative is the one who insists on killing herself through bad life choices, and there is nothing you can do but watch.

The hardest spouses are the ones who demand you live their dream and give up yours.

The hardest kid is the one just like you, and you know how the story is going to end.

The hardest job is the one where you stay in the shower too long, avoiding going to work at a place you hate, working for a boss you don't respect, and doing mediocre work, because you simply don't give a damn about the place.

The hardest decisions are usually those we ignore, hoping they'll go away.
Yet those are the ones that need to be dealt with today
if you want a better life tomorrow.

The hardest things in life are sometimes out of our control
and there is nothing we can do,
but there are others we can control.

Knowing the difference is a powerful part of who you will be in the future.

If you can control it, own the situation and change it now.
If you can't control it, walk away and let it be.

You can't change the client.
You can't change the friend.

You can own your own life,
if you are willing to own the hard decisions that define the quality of your life.

PERSONAL PRIDE
IS PERSONAL BELIEF IN YOURSELF

The most successful people take pride in everything they do or touch.

If you own a business, you should have deep pride in what you own, how you run it, how the staff treats others, and how clean it is.

If you work for someone, you should always bring a deep pride to the job,
which is reflected in your refusal to do anything but the best work you are capable of.

People who do less than they are capable of lack pride in themselves and value themselves poorly. Who at the end of the day can take pride in work far below your potential, and how can you think so little of yourself, you don't even care how you are judged by that work?

Pride is the driver behind personal growth.

Pride is the driver behind personal achievement,
and pride is what separates the average from the great.

If you are not accomplishing what you want in life,
maybe you just don't care enough to take pride in who you are and what you do.

Don't worry about what others think about you;
care more about what you think of yourself.

NOTHING CHANGES UNTIL YOU GET PISSED

No weight is ever lost until you get mad enough at who you are to force a change.

Unless you are mad, you are accepting. Nothing changes when you constantly give yourself permission to be a lesser version of who you could be.

No failing business ever changes until you get mad enough and scared enough to ask for help.

The biggest lie you tell yourself in a failing business is someone other than you is responsible for what is happening.

If it isn't working, get mad at the idiot in the mirror and fix it.
Any business can be fixed; it is the damn owners who are so hard to change.

No bad relationship will take a different course until one of the partners says, "Enough, we can't keep living this way."

Quietly wasting your life being miserable and accepting it is unacceptable.

You never get wasted years back, but you made the choice to stay miserable.
That was a bad choice.

No bad habit ends until you get so pissed off and disgusted at yourself
that change is the only option left.

You own the bad habits that negate a wonderful life;
these habits won't change until you get mad enough at yourself to force a change.

Compare yourself to no one else.
The question is, "Are you the best version of who you can be?"

If the answer is "no," then change.

But that only happens when you get pissed off enough to accept nothing
but a higher standard of your life.

YOU WERE A COMPLETE AND UTTER FAILURE

You were a complete and utter failure, and that failure was such a beautiful thing to see.

You completely destroyed yourself, and the destruction was magic.

The smoke and stink from your total destruction set the world on fire,
and we are still dancing in your honor.

You sit in the dark drinking and crying, feeling sorry for yourself while the world
celebrates you.

What you lost sight of was that your failure was your biggest success.

You stood up and tried when so many others sit on the porch,
barking loudly like scruffy old poodles at the big dogs in life.

You crashed and were miserable, but we cheered because your attempt to live was at a
higher level than the old poodles even dream about in their forever-cautious lives.

You tried, and failed, and lived, while others hide away, only attempting the small,
the meaningless, the inconsequential in life. Compared to your life on fire, they are the
living dead.

Nothing of meaning is created without failure.
Nothing beautiful is achieved without a crash and burn.

Your failure, a wound of honor in a world too scared to believe in themselves,
is your strength.

Stand up and try again.

The rest of us need to live through your failure,
so we may celebrate your great successes yet to come.

PROVIDENCE, RHODE ISLAND
Total blizzard, yet it was still a packed workshop

STOP OBSESSING ABOUT WHAT YOU ARE GOING TO DO WITH THE REST OF YOUR LIFE

PLEASE, STOP OBSESSING

Please, stop obsessing about what you are going to do with the rest of your life.

We get so overly worried about the last step of our lives, we end up not having a life at all.

Statistically, most of you under 50 could live well into your 90s and beyond.

Do you really think a 30-year-old person has to know now, today,
what he wants to do for the next 60 years of his life?

Do you think anyone who has 60 years in front of her has to stick with one career, one business, one place to live, and according to the numbers, will stick with one person, since people getting married in their 20s have an over-50-percent chance of changing the significant person?

Stop worrying about the last step in life.
Stop worrying about what you are going to do with your life.
Stop going crazy agonizing on why you are here
and what you are supposed to be doing.
Simply go out and live.

Don't obsess about the last step; focus everything on the next step.

How do you want to spend the next three to five years of your life?

You want to start a business?

Then start one and sell it in a few years to make enough money for five years of traveling. A business isn't forever.

Opening a business is just a step to move your life ahead and give you a chance to learn and grow, doing something new while creating wealth.

Want to change careers? Do something new for a while and give it a chance. A new job or career isn't forever. New beginnings can just be a short two- or three-year bus ride until you get off at the next destination.

Whatever you are doing now, never get trapped by the "forever" trap.
Life is a series of steps forward. The steps do not have to be sequential.
The steps do not have to make sense to your parents or friends.
What you are doing next does not have to be forever and, realistically, seldom is.

The goal of a life well lived is kicking back on the front porch when you are 90, telling the grandkids, "Yeah, I tried that too, and it was a crazy time in my life. Never thought I would take a year off and just ride the trains of Europe, but it just seemed like the right thing to do at that time."

Life is about experiences, adventures,
pushing your limits into something new and exciting,
and about seeing where you fit into the world.

Life is about finding something new to challenge you to grow and expand your mind, things that blow you out of your little world that often becomes narrow and overly claustrophobic.

Life is about what is next.

You will live with more intensity, more passion,
and more depth if you worry about "next,"
and give up thinking you have to know what you want to do forever.

FITNESS MADE SIMPLE

If you are wearing it, you ate it.

If you want to lose it, you have to move it.

If you can't pronounce it, don't eat it.

If nature grew it, chew it.

If man made it and it comes in box, don't feed it to your dog.

Your goal should always be "one butt, one chair."

Too many men suffer from terminal Dickie Do, where their bellies stick out farther than their dickie do. Hard to use it if they can't find it.

If your butt is still wiggling three minutes after you stopped walking, keep walking.

If sex is hard work, you should either be in a porn movie or join a gym.

Fat is a choice. If you're fat, you made a bad choice, but if you are fighting the great fight, then may the universe bless the sweat.

No skinny, healthy person ever got that way from drinking "diet" anything.

Sweating is sexy.

No out-of-shape person should ever have the power to challenge that.

If you are any type of fitness professional, you have to be in decent shape.

Finally, there will come a time when you consciously make an effort to put in the work and live healthy, or you simply quit. Choose life, and remember, as long as you are still moving, they can't bury you.

FAILING DOES NOT MAKE YOU A FAILURE

A failure is a person who quits and heads home, whining all the way.
Do you really believe you are the only person who has had tough times?
Do you believe you are the only person who might have lost a business?
Do you really believe you're the only person to get divorced and worry about your kids?
What ex-spouse has never tried to make you feel guilty
because you refused to live life another way?

We are all messed up.

It is how we deal with the mess that determines if we will be known as a success
or a complete and total wreck.

You will fail.

So what? In the course of your life, a failure doesn't matter.

You have the strength to rise again.
You have the talent to start again.
You have the love to always do the right thing with those kids.

I wish you had the ability to stop the damn whining and get out there and kick some ass.

Right now, today, as you read this, you have permission to live your own life and get over others trying to ruin it. You are not a failure; you are just a regular person working on becoming the real you.

When that happens, it is going to be worth the wait.

IT'S SATURDAY.
I AM AT THE AIRPORT, AND I AM BAFFLED

Airlines are shrinking the average seat to 17 inches,
but the average butt circumference for women is 40 inches and men, 39.

It's not like they are trying to get a big watermelon in that seat.
The watermelon would either fit or not fit.

With people, it is more like you are trying to shove 40 wriggling ferrets into a trash bag.
You push the bag down into the seat, and after you get enough ferrets on the cushion,
the rest of them scramble up the sides and spill over into my seat.

Imagine if that big butt was set free from those overstuffed jeans. The vision would look
like you just landed the plane in water and were letting a life raft out of its storage bag.
One pull of the string and that small condensed raft becomes as big as a delivery truck.

People make their own choices about their weight,
but when part of your butt is in my seat, I am not happy.

I paid a lot for my little 17-inch slice of paradise, and I do not want to share it with a herd
of squirming ferrets shoved into yoga pants or cheap cargo shorts.

Yes, I am baffled today.

Maybe the universe is telling me it is time to go home—too many days on the road and
the only message it could send was a big butt partially parked in my lap.

Let's not forget the seatbelt extenders.
They are the airlines' answer to putting a leash on those ferrets.

IF YOU WANT TO SURVIVE LIFE

If you want to survive life, you have to find your own definition of wealth.

Wealth used to be defined by the accumulation of stuff, meaning big cars, big houses, and the big payments that go along with them.

There are even "coaches" on the social media—and I use the word "coaches" with a pained expression—who still use the old "live like a millionaire like me" approach to selling their method of success.

Nothing says success from the 1980s like a guy in a tight white tee shirt washing his own cars lined up in front of his new mini-mansion.

But what if everything we think wet know about success—the lessons passed down by a generation caught up in someone else's madness—are wrong for us today?

What if success is:

> *The ability to spend more time with your family*
>
> *The willingness to live in a smaller house,*
> *so you can spend your life chasing adventures and experiences*
>
> *The ability to create wealth with the only thought*
> *that money is nothing more than the freedom to live life on your own terms*
>
> *Having enough money in the bank so you are never held hostage by a job you hate,*
> *or have to live in a town where you are miserable*
>
> *Maybe success is being able to help a friend or family member*
> *who needs a hand and you have the money to do it*

What if success is simply being able to work a job you love,
where the most important thing is the lives you change?

What if success is waking up with a spouse you love, a kid draped over you,
and a dog in the blanket?

What if success is what you already have plenty of, but you ruin your life chasing more?

Money is important.
Money allows freedom and choice.

You have to make and save money
to build a future where you and your family are safe.

But money doesn't have to be the collection of stuff.

Money doesn't have to be big debt and the illusion of wealth.

Wealth isn't defined by what you drive, but by what kind of person you are and the friends who surround you.

Maybe wealth is the experiences of life and not the collection of stuff your kids sell cheap at a yard sale after you die.

Maybe you are already wildly wealthy and don't realize it.

Maybe everything you need is what you already have,
and you are the wealthiest person you know in what really counts in life.

YOUR PURPOSE IN LIFE IS TO MAKE A DIFFERENCE

You change a client who has failed everywhere else, with every other coach,
and you made a difference in the world.

You spend a few hours totally focused on your kids,
and you can change their world by loving them for a few hours.

You help someone in trouble or in need
with no expectation of glory or any personal return,
and you just made the world better place.

You show up at the local grade school as a volunteer doing your own version of physical
education and expose kids to something that might last a lifetime...you made a difference
that day.

You support a local charity through your gym and the entire community benefits
because you cared and did something most others just talk about.

You became that older coach who has seen it all, and now you can look back
and say, "I changed a lot of lives. The people who have worked for me and my clients
benefited from this gym and from being with me."

If you can say that, you understand your purpose in life...to leave the world around you a
better place than when you arrived.

You give a few bucks to a homeless guy, donate to the local food bank, hand some money to
the guy ringing the bell at Christmas, patiently answer questions about leading a healthier
life, train someone who needs it but can't pay, and all of this makes a difference that ripples
through people for more years than you can imagine.

People ask, "Why am I here?"

Many spend a life searching for something right in front of their faces.

You are here to change the world.
You are here to make a difference.

When you leave, you made the world better because you were in it.

Simple really...just change the world a little each day
and you have a life worth living.

YOU CAN BECOME SO PASSIONATE ABOUT FITNESS

You can become so technical, you become boring.

You can charge so little, you have no value.

You can become so pure, no one can follow you.

You can become so self-absorbed with your own looks, you can't help others reach their goals.

You can seek so much analysis, you reach a point of paralysis and don't know what to do.

You over-think so much in training and in life, you can't function.

You can live for moderation, and are passed in life by those obsessed.

You can devote your entire life to training, but then realize you can't make a living doing it and can't change jobs because you never learned how to do anything else.

You can work the client hard and get results,
but still lose him because you never changed his mind by teaching him "why."

All the talk about seeking change in your life prevents you from actually changing.

You work so hard for your family, you lose them because you were never there.

You try so hard to prove what you know, you lose clients who just want to know you care.

Life in the training world is nothing but a series of contradictions.

Your life will be better, your family will be better, and your clients will be better
when you learn when to attack and when to back off and just listen.

Just listening to the needs of others
may be the ultimate level of sophistication any coach needs.

The training life isn't about what you know or how you live;
our world is about how you can help others reach their dreams.

THE GYM BUSINESS SIMPLY EXPLAINED

You cannot out-train a stupid lifestyle. Little sleep, bad food,
and too much drinking cancels the best workouts.

The phrase "no pain, no gain" was created by a stupid trainer.
He is dead now. And he deserved to die.

If you are wearing it, you ate it. Denying that won't make it easier for either of us.

What you hate the most is what you need the most, so yes, you are doing squats today.

No one has ever gotten fat from eating apples. That does not apply to apple cider beer.

You know the difference; you understand food, you just choose to make bad decisions.

You have someone do your taxes. You have an attorney; you have a doctor, but you think you
are smart enough to figure out your own workout because you played football in high school.
You are not that smart—get a coach.

Over half the wasted calories in your diet are liquid.
Put down the fruit juice box and eat like an adult.

How many fat people do you see drinking light beer?

Lifting big doesn't mean lifting stupid.
If you can't handle the form, lower the weight.
Your personal ego will hurt you more than any trainer will.

And trainers, stop worrying about people thinking you are right.
Instead, worry about getting your clients the results they paid for.

What works for you may not work for someone else.
There is no perfect workout, only figuring out how to help the struggling person in front of you.

It doesn't matter how many credentials you have; it only matters that you can get results without hurting someone. No, a trainer with three months of experience and a one-day certification cannot supervise 20 tired people doing power cleans to failure. Not now, not ever, no way.

Yes, I love women in yoga pants. I have issues, but I am sticking to my story.

THE FUTURE OF THE FITNESS BUSINESS

The future of the fitness business belongs to the people who hate us most.

About 19% of the people in the United States, and fewer in most other countries, belong to any type of fitness facility. This means 81% do not belong to gyms, have had bad experiences and have quit gyms, or are so afraid of going to a gym, they don't even try.

What this really means is that 81% of the people in this country
see no value in what we offer,
or have tried our services and hate us.

Why?

It's because we can't speak "beginner," and are so far removed from being beginners, we can't understand them.

We over-train the first few visits, leave them sore and humbled, talk about nutrition as if it is black magic voodoo, put them into groups too soon and with people who are far ahead of them, and then set unreasonable attendance goals that only the purest 25-year-old trainer could achieve.

We staff our gyms with people who have never been out of shape and have no true empathy with someone who struggles with weight and personal image issues. We say the right words, but our actions never match those words.

Young and perfect coaches dressed in workout bras and tight shirts aren't role models; they represent everything the potential new client hates about us.

We are an egotistical group, full of selfie-taking fools who would rather talk about themselves than help anyone new. This viewpoint of the client isn't wrong.

Most importantly, our potential clients and the public in general hate us because we assume the reason they are fat is they are lazy. Maybe a few are, but the vast majority need leadership, gentle guidance, early success, and reframing through a long-term understanding of fitness and how to live a healthy life in motion.

So many want help, but we blame their inaction on them
instead of considering maybe,
just maybe, they simply need a plan and some support.

The fitness industry won't grow until we grow up.

This field will not expand until we understand that gyms have to cater to those who need us most, but who don't fit into the model we currently offer.

If you want a more successful business, start with the idea that the things you believe are best about yourself are what is keeping the world away.

CREATING MAGIC IN YOUR LIFE

Just heard the old song *Somewhere over the Rainbow/What a Wonderful World,* by Israel Kamakawiwo'ole, the one with the ukulele and slow, steady beat. The song was recorded in 1988 and the singer died in 1997.

I wonder what was in his head when he recorded that song?

Did he know at that moment he created something magical that would last 20 years past his death? Does any great writer or artist realize at that moment he has mastered his craft and the work is perfect?

Most people never live up to their potential because they don't chase the magic in what they chose to do with their lives. Everyone can be an artist in life. Somewhere there is the perfect workout, the perfect class in school, the perfect presentation, and the perfect day in your life when you achieve mastery in your work through your passion. When mastery occurs, there is always magic.

Mastery simply means that for a few minutes on a given day, all your insanely hard work paid off, and for a brief time, you were the best that has ever been. Seek the passion, and see if you can create some magic that will be remembered forever.

YOU OWN A BEAUTIFUL CAR

You let it sit out in the rain and snow year after year.

It slowly rusts, the paint fades, tires go flat and that new-car glow is replaced by something that once looked like a perfect car, but is now nothing more than a shadow of its best days.

Someday you are going to restore that car, because you love it and this car is the only vehicle you will ever own. But each year you wait to start the restoration, the job seems more and more impossible.

Wait.

Are we talking about your car, or are we secretly talking about you and your level of fitness starting in your late 30s, 40s, and beyond?

You and that old car have a lot more in common than you realize.

Every year you wait to start getting your health back, it becomes a harder, seemingly impossible task. If you are out of shape and feel bad about how you look at 38, how do you think it will be when you are 48, after all those years of more rust, decay, and those flat tires of yours that just keep drooping lower and lower. You might even need magic pills to get that special tire of yours firm and hard for the road.

Part of fitness is about "now."

Fitness for today is about how you feel in the morning, how you look in clothes, how confident you are in the world, and the level of energy you find in yourself every day.

But the secret of fitness
is that getting in shape is really about how you will live in the future.

The workouts you do now will determine the quality of life you will have 10 years from today.

Fitness isn't about getting in shape in 21 days and then done for the summer.

True fitness is about laying a foundation now for a quality life in the years to come.

Get that old car back in shape, find a real mechanic to tune you up, and remember that every day you wait will make your chance of finding your way back to health less likely.

LONG BEACH, CALIFORNIA
Quaint, tacky, and everything California

YOU CAN'T HIDE UNDER YOUR BLANKET LIKE A FOUR-YEAR-OLD

IF YOU ARE WALKING THROUGH HELL

If you are currently walking through hell, do not sit in a corner covered with your favorite blankie, drinking a bottle of cheap wine, and whimpering like a four-year-old.

If your life is tough, take serious action.
Do something now, even if that action might later turn out to be the wrong move.

When you do nothing, you did something by doing nothing.

Doing nothing is a move. Most of what we suffer from in life and business is the failure to take action. We know we are miserable, but we sit, we wait, and we wait, and we suffer. Few problems in life get better by ignoring them.

When you have a major issue in life or business, but decide to do nothing—just keeping the course even if you see other shipwrecks on the rocks coming your way—you have given up the only thing that matters, your ability to take control of your life through personal choice delivered by action.

We often refuse to change because we don't know what to do next. Instead of admitting we have no idea how to move forward, it is easier to posture, block, and stop new ideas from being put into place. We are so afraid of doing the wrong thing that we do nothing...just sitting and waiting to get crushed by life.

Do something, even if it is wrong. Exert control in your life through action.

If you are miserable, doing almost anything is better than suffering from inaction.

Bad job? How long are you willing to be miserable at someone else's expense?

Bad business partners?
Are you willing to ride the business down instead of confronting the problem?

Bad choice in marriage? How many years of your life are you willing to waste instead of doing anything that improves your marriage, or at least ends it so you can move on?

Doing the wrong thing is usually better than doing nothing.

Doing the wrong thing at least moves you ahead
and gives you a chance to see the problem from a new perspective.

You can fix wrong, but no one can do anything about you doing nothing at all.

When you are trapped taking that slow stroll through hell, often the best advice is to start running as fast as you can to give yourself the chance to get to the other side.

The positive course of your life is determined by the actions you take,
the negative often by the choices you refused to make.

DO WHAT YOU PROMISE IN LIFE, BUT NEVER PROMISE TOO MUCH

Sometimes the best answer in life is, "No."

Thank you for asking, but no, I do not want to do that for you.
I simply don't have the time to do as you ask.

There are too many of you asking for my time, and it's just me trying to do too much, for too many, so the answer is no, I am sorry, but I just can't promise something I may not be able to do.

We get caught up in promising everyone everything because we cannot say no to anyone. But then we get to the point where we can't get it all done, and the yes we promised turns out to be, "Sorry, I have to let you down."

Or worse, the promise takes away from your own life, your own time, and your own family. You say yes to so many people, you find yourself on your only day off carrying boxes up a long flight of stairs for a person you hardly know.

The yes drained your life and you did not have to do it.

Maybe the only yes you should have given that day was to your family,
who were again robbed of their time with you because you can't ever learn to say no.

Start saying no.
Say it often.
Say it like you mean it.
Protect your time.

Protect your personal integrity by promising very little
and then doing exactly as you promised.

Saying yes to everyone leaves you over-committed, mad at the world,
and it frustrates the people you may have to disappoint.

Promise little and then live up to those commitments,
but never, ever promise anything you aren't willing to do.

FIVE THINGS
YOU SHOULD LEARN BEFORE YOU ARE 30

Number One—That most beautiful person you are madly and secretly in love with and whom you fantasize about every second of your waking being is someone else's pain in the ass.

Number Two—You can never be old and wise unless you were a young dumbass first. You will screw up many things in a life well lived and it just doesn't matter.

Wisdom comes from this life experience, and the more you have of the experience of crashing and burning, the more wisdom that follows.

Number Three—The workouts you do now and the food you eat today determine the person you will be 10 years from now.

Fitness for life is a linear projection, with each layer based on the previous one.

In other words, when you are young and stupid and can eat and drink everything and stay somewhat in shape, you never think about who you will be in 10 years...but you should.

Number Four—If you disagree with me, it doesn't mean you are wrong or I am wrong. This disagreement just means we don't agree on this one subject.

Hating someone over opposing positions is a children's game.

Number Five—Your parents are usually wrong about your life. Look at how the world has changed in just the last five years; very few parents have the experience to deal with how your life is today.

Seek those who have lived the life you want, and rely less on those who guide but have never done.

Finally, the years between 30 and 60 pass in about 23 seconds.

Plan for tomorrow, live hard today, and don't give a damn about a past you cannot change.

WATCHING PEOPLE DOING CARDIO
IN A MAINSTREAM GYM

The club rule must be to hang on to the side rails so you don't fall off.
One guy is walking about two miles an hour and is badly out of shape.
One healthy-looking woman is walking fast,
and one woman is at a full-out run and is lean and vibrant.

Asked the slow-going guy how long he had been a member.
He said three years.
Asked him if he was getting what he wanted out of his membership.
He said no.
Asked him why he walked so slowly.
He said he just wasn't into the workout thing and walking slow was enough.
But what you are doing isn't working?
He just shrugged.

There seems to be a relationship with intensity.
The worst shape you are in, the slower you go,
but maybe going slow is why you are in that shape.

Maybe intensity describes everything in life.
Go fast, go hard, and get it done, or go slow and just meander through life,
achieving nothing, and getting nothing done.

Intensity is the feeling of being all in to whatever you do.
If it is worth doing, it is worth doing it intently.
Intensity is a commitment to seek a higher level of play,
where you know what you are doing at the moment is the best you can possibly do.

Why be married if you aren't committed?
Why go to work if you don't care enough to do it well?
Why have kids if you aren't willing to be the parent of the year?
Why own a gym that barely gets by and all you did was buy yourself a job?

Intensity may be the definer of a life well lived.

If you are going to be a friend, be the best friend ever or don't play.

If you are going to get into shape,
commit and get into the best shape your body will allow.
Go big dog and bark and chase life down the street,
or sit on the porch, little poodle girl, and snap at those who choose to live your life.

Commit to fewer things in life.
Say no to being distracted from your plan.

But if you decide to commit to something, apply the rule of intensity and go all in,
with the intent of doing whatever you choose as well as you can possibly do it.

Or you can just be a guy walking slowly on a treadmill who wanders through life,
frustrated his life isn't different but who is not willing to do the work that would
give him a life worth living.

IT IS YOUR LIFE, TAKE CONTROL

Take control and stop wasting such a precious gift by trying to make everyone else happy.

Here are five things to start doing today to get your life back and make it your own:

Number One—Say "no" a lot more often.

The more you say yes just to make someone else happy, the more of your life you give up. You cannot make everyone happy, so stop trying. Pick and choose your "yes" commitments carefully, because every time you say yes to someone else, you have to say no to doing what you need to get done for yourself.

Number Two—Say "no" to guilt.

People attempt to control your life by using guilt to manipulate you. Sadly, for those in our profession who dedicate their lives trying to help others change, we fall quickly into the guilt trap. Ignore any sentence starting with, "If you really loved me," or "If you really cared about my feelings." Turn slowly, walk away, and refuse to do guilt.

Number Three—Get rid of the energy-sucking vampires in your life.

The negative, the perpetually pissed off, the "mad at the world" people, and the "life is so unfair" whiners need to be exiled from your life. Life is hard enough without a life-hater in your ear all day.

Number Four—I don't care how much you can snatch, you are not strong enough to carry everyone. There will be one person in your life who expects you to give up everything you have to do nothing but what they want you to do. You live to make this person happy, and since nothing you do will be enough, stop wasting your life trying. Their unhappiness is what makes them happy. You can never win.

Number Five—You have to find an hour a day that belongs to you, focused on moving your life ahead. Get up earlier, stay up later, hide for an hour mid-day, but find an hour when you can just work on being you. You get so busy being busy, you are now too busy to do the right things. Pick the few things that are important and will change your life, and create an hour when you can get life done.

Twenty years from now, what will you say?

My life, what a gift it was? Or my life, I can't believe it went so quickly and I wasted so much time trying to make everyone in the world happy but me.

IT IS SO HARD TO GET PEOPLE TO LIVE NOW

You go on vacation, but obsess about what you left undone at home so you waste the entire trip.

You open a business and dream about what it can be someday
and fail to do the work that has to be done today to keep it alive.

You have a partner suffering from neglect because you are always dreaming about somebody more perfect, someone who is a fantasy in your dreams, and that is killing your relationship.

You walk in the woods with your kids and lose the magic because you are texting someone somewhere else and can't see the beauty that surrounds you in nature and in your kids.

Now is all you have and all you will ever have.
Wait for the future and it never comes,
because the future is always something waiting to happen.

Live in the past and you lose today.
Where you are today, who you are today, and what you are doing today,
now, at this minute, is your only reality.

Live in the moment and understand that right now may be all you will ever have.

If you can master living in the now, life can be a beautiful thing designed just for you.

NOTHING CHANGED IN YOUR LIFE TODAY

You still hate your weight, hate your job, and hate your quickly failing relationship because being miserable is easier than admitting the problem is you...and then changing.

Change requires the will to work. Work is something no one wants to do, other than those willing to let go and change, which isn't you.

Change never happens, and the work never gets started, until the misery of being you surpasses your willingness to make excuses for who you are.

It's easier to be unhappy with your career, body, or family than to admit what you are doing isn't working. It's also easier to live being miserable than dealing with the brutal realization no one can change you but you.

Change requires personal responsibility, which is a subject discussed in whispers at bars, but is easily ignored in a culture where blaming the world for your failure gets you followers by the thousands on social media.

Today, you are a day older and still unhappy, but didn't change a damn thing that might have given you a brief glimpse of a happy life.

Change isn't one huge thing; change is simply deciding you have had enough and today, right now, right at this moment, you accept it all as on you. You can change if you do the work.

Change is the first small step where you declare you have had enough.
Only you can get it done.
This admission is 90% of all change in life.

Change is hard, but you are worth every second of the work.

Being happy is a good thing; you should try it someday.
But this happy thing may require change and only you can get it done.

NEVER LET THE BIG KARMA BIRD OF LIFE POOP ON YOUR HEAD

You are either a giver or a taker in life and the universe will accommodate you accordingly.

Takers are those who drain the life and assets out of everyone they know, never giving anything in return. They need your help, time, and money, but when you are no longer willing to give, they move on to the next victim.

These people often operate as friends or relatives, making it harder to walk away. These are also the people who hurt others with their schemes and madness, justifying any pain as, "I deserve this and you need to give it to me."

Givers are the people who create beauty in the world.
Givers help, guide, and support others, expecting nothing in return.

Ethics and moral code are important to the givers,
while the takers couldn't spell either one.

You will see few takers who end up with anything in life.
The universe will always correct those who prey on others,
and the takers always end up with nothing in life.

Believe in the big karma bird and understand that givers may have tough times in life, but in the end, you will win.

Just don't stand next to a taker for long.

Karma bird poop will not come out of your workout clothes.

NEVER LEAVE ANYTHING UNDONE

One moment you are there, and the next you are gone. One day you are a vibrant, fully functioning person, full of life, big plans, and thinking there will always be time to correct the negatives of life, and then it becomes your turn to say goodbye. No one is guaranteed a long, glorious life. Your day could be today.

One day you will leave for work, and it will be the last time.
One day you will say goodbye to the kids, and that will be your last goodbye.
One day you will simply be no more.

Leave nothing undone, every day, starting today.

Never leave home without telling everyone you love them.
Never go to bed angry at anyone, ever, because you may not have a chance to make it right.
Never drop a kid off at school without words of love.

Never fail to live your life today as it might be your last day, because one day it will be. Do you really want to leave with so much of the business of life unfinished?

Ask yourself what you have left undone.
What if this hour was your last hour on earth?

Are there calls you wish you would have made, reaching out to someone you haven't spoken to over something so trivial it is embarrassing to even think about?

Did you leave the house fighting with a spouse over petty things that prevented you from a serious hug, kiss, and a special word?

Are you living today, believing your life starts tomorrow when there might be no tomorrow?

Your arrogance is that you believe you have all the time in the world to fix and do anything. But your reality is, today can always be the day when it ends, when there are no more chances, no more hugs, touches, or forgiveness.

Today might not be your day to say goodbye, but it should be the day you understand that all life is fleeting—including yours—and nothing important in life should ever be left undone.

WE DIE SLOWLY IN TODAY'S WORLD

We die slowly in today's world—die,
because we can't breathe and this cause of death is self-induced.

We sleep until the last minute, then spring to work. On the way out, we yell goodbye to anyone awake, people we won't see again for 10 hours.

We stand doing the scrolling thing until we get to the front of the coffee line.

We bust into work with five minutes to spare, and our workday jumps on our chest with full force, knocking the wind out of us for eight to ten hours.

We eat lunch standing up or at a desk, still scrolling, still stressed,
and minutes away from round two.

Finish another five or seven hours, sleep walk through an undernourished,
lack-of-water, barely there workout, and then stagger home.

Grab a beer, sit on the couch, and pretend to be a father for a few minutes while still scrolling because who knows, we might miss that next wildly important social media post written by someone we don't know doing a workout we find stupid.

The spouse sits down to talk and we can barely listen. We eat dinner, still scrolling along, fall into bed with the phone in hand, or where we can at least reach it. We sleep too little, leaving us more stressed the next morning, less prepared for family and work and a stuttering nightmare.

Or maybe you realize you are human
and not the super hero you want your clients to believe you are.

You get up early, sit quietly in a private room sipping a cup of something good,
read or study, or think and write, and it is all about you for one hour.

You plan 30 minutes of kid time before leaving for work.

Hug the spouse for an extra 15 minutes before even getting out of bed
(don't worry, you will think of something to do)
and leave for work at a reasonable time.

You check the phone once in the morning and again in the afternoon
and then leave the damn thing in the drawer.

You understand working smarter is better than harder, and you learn that 50 hours a week is enough if you use your head. You come home, eat with the kids, maybe read to them, and then maybe, for about five minutes, you scroll before bed.

You sleep for eight hours, get up refreshed, and repeat. You always save one day a week for family, because that is the only reason you do all this other crazy crap.

Your choice: live like a stressed-out animal in a small cage at the zoo, or join the human race and have a life.

Pick carefully; you only get one chance to get it right.

YOU CANNOT CHANGE ANYONE
WHO DOESN'T WANT TO CHANGE

You can coach a person, lead, educate, support, scream at, call bullshit on, walk away from, or do a dozen other sometimes-questionable behaviors, but no one changes until reaching the point of, "This behavior isn't working for me. There has to be a better way."

People seeking change need all the support and coaching you can give them.

The people who refuse to change but thrive on the attention they get from their behavior— you have to have the strength to run away from professional victims at top speed.

We all know the person in our life or that one particular client who finds it more important to repeatedly tell everyone who will listen, "Poor me, I want to change, but I can't; you just don't understand how hard it is in my life," usually explained with tears, a big sigh, and the endless woe-is-me story.

You fight; we fight alongside of you as your personal reserve of strength.
You don't want to change; we don't want to hear your story again.

You only have so much energy to spare.

Do you really want to waste your life chasing people who exist to drain your kindness? Or do you want to spend your life lifting those who want to rise up and beat their demons?

Lifting those who listen and respond to your offer
of support and strength will give you a lifelong career.

Drowning in someone's nonsense will leave you sitting up late at night wondering how you failed, when the truth is you didn't fail at all. You just became a victim of your own kindness.

THE FIVE STAGES
OF THE CLIENT AND COACH RELATIONSHIP

*Stage One...*The client discovers you and can't believe someone like you exists to answer questions and help and guide in life.

*Stage Two...*The client wants everything now and does whatever you say, and it starts to work. She can't believe she has missed this in the past, and now anything is possible and she wants it all, right this minute, and will do anything to enjoy the new success.

*Stage Three...*The client achieves a major success. He can't believe he wasted all these years without you doing something that never worked for him. You are the man (woman) and you are the source of all knowledge.

*Stage Four...*She brings everyone she knows to you. You are her coach, and she has to share this with the world. She writes about you, posts about you, attends every workshop or mentoring group, and gives you credit for changing her life.

*Stage Five...*She never fucking heard of you. Now, in her head, it was all her; she made the changes, and in fact, she probably taught you a few things, and you really should be grateful to her that she was your client at all.

This client is now so important, she feels she can't acknowledge she had help. She believes admitting any lesser life in the past will kill her credibility with her clients.

If you are lucky, you help a lot of your people to Stage Four, whether they are training or mentoring clients. But if you are good, you get some to Stage Five, and have to learn to not get mad or take it personally.

Remember, you created the Frankenstein; you can't get pissed when he eats the village.

This is also a lesson in remembering where you came from in life and in business.

No one ever made it big without a hand up, whether willing to admit it or not.
Stay humble.
We all needed help to become us.

TIME IS THE ENEMY OF FITNESS

You never want to give a fitness client the "I don't have enough time" excuse.

Keep most of your sessions, classes, or other offerings to 50 minutes. This allows the client to park the car, walk in the door, do the workout thing, and get back to the car in less than an hour.

Most fitness professionals can devastate a client in six minutes doing nothing but body-weight exercises, but there is also a threshold where money spent equals value. That magic number in fitness is 45 minutes. Your clients have to be sweating for at least 45 minutes, or they think they aren't getting what they paid for, no matter how badly they are getting burned at the time.

You can occasionally offer special sessions that go longer, but it is important to keep the bulk of what you do to less than hour. This means not one hour exactly, but 50 minutes.

The 50-minute session is a powerful approach to retention and even makes the initial sale easier since you completely take away the time objection.

Finally, if you do 30-minute mid-day offerings, do not discount them. You are offering a convenience, not selling training by the minute. This is a more intense offering, not a discounted session sold by the minute.

TRAFALGAR SQUARE, LONDON
Never time in London without an afternoon watching the world go by at Trafalgar.

A PRAYER FOR THE MENTALLY UNAWARE

A PRAYER FOR THE MENTALLY UNAWARE

I give you a prayer for the mentally unaware, the terminally childish, the socially inept, and those who simply live to create pure hell in your life.

May you stretch your short little T-Rex arms down
to that never-opened billfold and buy a drink now and then, you cheap ass.

May you at some point in your life learn to say thank you to all those who have carried your lame ass for so many years.

Just one "Thank you" would ease a lot of pain when coming from people who expect it all, but who give nothing back in life, not even a recognition of the help they have been given.

May you remember that working for someone is a privilege, and if you take my money, be grateful you have a job and do some work now and then. I don't pay you to scroll all day; you are paid to create some revenue. Me telling you to put your phone away is fair and is not punishment. Please, do something besides cashing that check every week.

May you remember dressing like a homeless guy who just popped out of a dumpster is not a cool fashion statement. It is a reflection of what you think of yourself, and your inability to adult wears out your friends' patience.

There is style, and then there is you—too stupid to at least put on a shirt with a collar and sleeves at dinner.

May you remember that takers drain the universe and always end up broke and dead last in the race of life. Givers get better with age and end up with all of your toys, and maybe your spouse and probably with your old job you did so poorly.

May you understand that pounding a client with a multi-level marketing scam is poor taste, a loss of ethics, unprofessional, and simply bad business. It's also embarrassing when you are trying to pressure me into this month's latest and greatest scam.

May you also understand that there is nothing wrong with living pure, but no one wants to hear the lecture that goes with your lifestyle. Yes, the cavemen did drink a Guinness back then. I know, because I was there and partied with them.

May you also always remember where you came from in life. Disavowing the help you had always leads back to the person you might need most in your life refusing to help you again.

May you remember that no one, and I mean no one, cares about your excuses for living a shitty life. This constant whining and denying of responsibility doesn't work past the age of three.

Cheap people who live to take and disrespect their friends and clients are the scourge of the universe, and deserve exactly the same respect they give to others, which is none. If you have these people in your life, move on. They are not worth the cosmic pain of carrying them year after year.

DEAR OUT-OF-SHAPE PERSON

Yes, it was me watching you at the mall.

No, I wasn't making fun of you because you are out of shape.
I was simply looking at you because you frustrate the hell out of me.

You are only in your 30s, but you struggle to pick up your child. You were leaning on the back of the shopping cart because you are so out of shape, your body can't support itself for a simple walk.

And if that is your life now, what will it be in 10 years if you don't change?

Why am I frustrated?

The frustration exists because, as a professional coach,
there are so many things I wish I could help you understand.

Movement and simple exercise would add a quality to your life you may have never known.

I noticed you were wearing layers of oversized clothes because you don't feel good in your body.

Just walking more, eating a little better, and making movement a part of your daily life would give you a confidence you may not have felt in years.

I would like to help you understand that what you do now will determine the quality of your life for the rest of your life, and not just for your children now, but for the days when you have grandchildren too.

I wish I could teach you that there are professional coaches who understand your fears, your needs, and your struggle with your weight, and there are caring people who can help.

I would like you to understand that there is no perfect shape;
there is just you being the best you can be each day.

You do not need to compare your body against a perceived image that can't be achieved.
You just need to seek a healthy version of who you are and who you wish to be.

I especially wish you could understand the feeling that comes from being healthy from the inside, when you achieve a sense of personal satisfaction from knowing fitness is movement and movement is life.

I apologize for watching as you passed through the mall today.

I was only thinking that my job is changing lives and helping people lead a more vibrant life.

I know if you don't change, the quality of your life will deteriorate with each passing birthday.

Most of the diseases of aging are self-inflicted, and as you passed,
I realized there isn't anything I can do to help until you decide to help yourself.

Yes, you might be perfectly happy being you, but that does not change what an unhealthy lifestyle is doing to who you will be in the future.

I wish you wellness and health. If you ever need help, please find a professional coach who cares. We are out here, and when the time is right for you, we will be around.

Please don't wait too long. It won't get any easier in the future.

With respect, your neighborhood fit pro.

IT IS ALL LIES, LIES I TELL YOU

This whole fitness thing is based on lies.

The United States just reached a milestone: We are now the fattest country on earth.

But why?

Many people hate fitness because what they think they know about fitness is wrong.

Here are a few truths to get your butt moving before it is too big to move at all.

Remember, the goal is one butt, one chair,
and keep your shoulders at least an inch wider than your butt.

We do not work out to have a bikini bod, to stand on the beach and flex, or to wear skinny jeans.

We work out to be as healthy as we can, so we can live as long as we can, and enjoy all the cool benefits of this health, such as self-confidence, sex, play time with the kids, sex, a life spent moving, and most importantly, to simply get up every day and scream at the mirror, "I may get old, and I may slow down, but not today universe, not today."

Fitness doesn't take immense amounts of time. Fitness is just moving a little more every day. Fitness is walking up the stairs a few extra times. Fitness is understanding how your body moves, what it needs to be its best, and then working with a professional coach to get some direction.

There really is no DeLorean time machine despite what the movies lead us to believe. No coach in the world can take you back to the day you were the most beautiful, most handsome, best-day-of-your-life-at-that-wedding self.

Fitness is simply about being the best you can be today. If you are 45, be the best version of 45 you can be, and be happy with that feat of mind over butt.

You do not have to eat every meal out of a plastic box.
You do not have to make your meals for the entire week on Sunday.
You can have a beer.
You can drink wine.
You can have a life.

Diets do not work and never will.

Fitness is learning to eat better food and less crap food.
You already know how to eat healthy, so that is no excuse.

Potato chips—bad. Apples—good.
Sugar-coated kid crap in a box—bad.
Green veggie things in a salad with a big chunk of chicken—good.

See? Food isn't hard. We just think it is because we have been taught that starvation and special diets are the only ways to lose weight, and that is a lie. Healthy people eat...and eat a lot.

Working out every day isn't about who you are today. Working out, eating right, and moving more is about how you want to live 10 years from now.

Look at people who are 10 years older than you are now.

How are they aging?
Is that how you want to be?
If yes, they are probably moving every day.

If they scare the hell out of you and are becoming your, "on the couch drooling" big beer-belly older brother, or your over-the-big-top-aunt hanging on the back of the buggy at The Walmart, remember, 10 years ago they made a choice. That choice was to not care about the quality of their lives.

Where do you want to be in 10 years?

How about really healthy, active, feeling good about your body,
and irritating everyone in your life with your ceaseless energy and willingness to go?

Or you can do nothing, reap the benefits of poor health, and simply wait until the doctor says, "Move or die, your choice." Moving today is such a better choice for the life you dream about in the future.

Choose life and choose to live every day at your best.

IT IS HARD TO UNDERSTAND
WHY YOU ARE SO PISSED AT THE WORLD

It is hard to understand why you are pissed at the world when who you are is your fault.

You are, and always will be, a product of your own creation. Who you are today is nothing more than a combination of all the decisions you made through last night.

If you are in a job you hate, look within and figure out who accepted the job. If you actually accepted responsibility for the job, could you do it better, be happier, get paid more, and turn a mediocre job into the start of a possible career?

Horrible relationship and you blame the other person?
You, and only you, made the choices that set you on that path.

Struggling in life and blaming the world?
You are who you are by choice, and the choice was yours.

Once you accept that the responsibility for your life is yours and yours alone, everything will change. It is at that minute you will understand that along with the responsibility for your own creation, you also have the power to change what you don't like.

The day you realize you own this power is the day you become the strongest force in the universe—a person who accepts that the responsibility for your life is no one else's but yours.

You have the power to do whatever you want with it.

WE ARE WHO WE ARE

We are who we are because of the decisions we make every single day.

We wake up, we decide to either just survive the day,
or we decide to be a force of nature changing the world around us.

You still had to get up.
You still had to go to work.

All you really had to decide was how you want to live that day.

We decide every single day to be healthy, fit, and seek a quality life, or we decide to quit trying and have our life shrink away from us as we seek to ruin ourselves one bad decision at a time.

Fitness isn't a big shift in life; fitness is 100 small choices adding up to a life well lived.

You could go for a long walk, yet there you sit on the couch staring at a fake reality, watching people have pretend lives while you give up yours. Sit on the porch and bark like a scruffy poodle, or run big dog, run and live a life unique to you.

You make a decision every day to touch people, smile, be patient, be generous, or you decide to be the lame prick the world would quietly celebrate if you left it early.

You decide to read to your child or you decide to park the kid in front of a video while you scroll for an hour. You can decide to put the phone down and for 30 minutes try to be the best parent ever, or you can check messages one more time while yet another chance to love your child is lost.

Every day, you decide to be in love with your special person, or you decide to let it all go and slowly fade away because you won't do the work. Get in, or get out, but don't waste your life and your spouse's too.

Every day, you decide to be the best employee ever, or you accept another wasted day being average, taking someone's money for doing work so much less than your potential. You withhold your talent; you waste your talent and, do it long enough, you lose your talent.

You decide to accept aging 20 years before you should. You decide to be a lesser version of your potential. You decide to be a great friend or a lost friend. You decide to be successful or to live a life of quiet frustration; you, and only you, decide how you want to live your life.

Tired of being broke, tired, old, petty, pissed, average, fat, angry, distant, and just a lousy human being? Then make better decisions, because you control all of this, and only you can decide to change it...one decision at a time.

YOU CAN NEVER BE GREAT

You can never be great at any endeavor in life until you are willing to suck at it for a long time.

Look at 100 people in any skill-based business, such as being a fitness professional or a professional manager of people, and you will find those who are considered the best were willing to spend years being mediocre, slowly developing their skills.

Practice is the tool that enables talent to slowly emerge.

There are a lot of young fit pros who think of themselves as master coaches, yet they are at best average, and often worse. They are not willing to spend the years it takes trying, failing, and trying again that leads to becoming a master in their craft.

In life, you are only as good as your patience to pay your dues and learn, coupled with your willingness to fail along the path.

There is talent in almost everyone, but the willingness to do the work over the years that lets talent mature is the rarest of gems.

CHICAGO, ILLINOIS
Two of Chicago's finest watching the late-night city

THE BASIC FORMULA
FOR FAILURE

HERE IS THE FORMULA FOR FAILURE

Success + Ego = Stagnation (in business and life)

This formula states that the higher the success rate, the higher the ego associated with that success.

This increased ego then leads to the increasing speed a business will fail.

What made this guy successful in the past is the very thing that will keep him from staying successful in the future. You can't teach an egotistical idiot anything new since he knows it all, based on earlier success he assumes will last forever.

This is why chains fail.

What made them great at some point is the very thing keeping them from being great today.

What made them successful in the past kills their leadership in the end. They are no longer willing to learn or listen, because, "We know how to do it; just look at how good we were back in the day."

The trouble is, most of what you knew before doesn't translate to today.

Look at the major fitness chains from the last 20 years—most are but a shadow of what they used to be.

The ability to let go of your ego and what got you to that level of success, and then focus on what will keep you successful by continuing to learn may be the greatest and least-appreciated skill in business and personal development.

You seek success in life and business, and then your ego causes you to self-destruct and lose it all. At some point, the ego shuts down your ability to listen, learn, admit you don't know it all, and most importantly, understand that success is a fleeting thing based on a time and place, and as time changes, you have to grow or die.

The old adage in business is still true: Evolve or die. There is no evolution without the recognition that nothing lasts forever in business, especially those ego-driven machines that never realize there is no way to sustain a business without change.

There is no change without the ability to learn and grow.

DON'T WASTE TIME TRYING TO
WIN OVER THE HATERS IN THE WORLD

You are not the dumb-ass whisperer,
and you have no chance against their wall of hatred.

Eternal haters who usually condemn the rest of the world to some form of hell because we won't accept their version of reality don't want your help. They want your attention, and no matter how much you give, it will never be enough.

Many haters hide behind a cloak of self-righteousness. To them, their vision of training, religion, food, or even their opinion of the work you do is the only right belief. If you don't share that opinion, you now are the beneficiary of their hate.

Many haters simply hate everything and have no real core values or internal beliefs. They hate anything good or different, or because you like something and believe in it yourself.

Being a living hater of everything works for them because it gets you to respond. It becomes about the attention you feed them in response to their hatred that keeps them going.

You cannot change a hater.
You cannot live with a hater.

You cannot become who you were meant to be if there is a hater dominating your life.

Run away; run and let the hater die of loneliness, the ultimate death for a seeker of your pain and who lives for the attention of others.

A PRAYER FOR THOSE WHO COACH

The year-end holidays should be a time of reflection, but we are often too busy with family, friends, and work still undone to sit and think about the year and what we accomplished. This is also a time to be grateful for who you are and what you do for a living.

What you do as a fitness professional looks so easy from the outside and yet is so hard from within. You are responsible not only for your own wellbeing, but you also have to take care of other people who look to you as a guide. What you do matters.

If you are making a living in fitness, you were given special talents to accomplish the difficult tasks you face every day.

People who live in the fitness world often gain a sense of spirituality they don't always think about or discuss with friends over the occasional glass, but the perfect workout with friends could easily be viewed as a spiritual event that brings you closer to a universal truth. Fitness is motion and motion is life as life was intended to be. It doesn't matter who or how you worship, but it does matter that you are on a path that constantly leads you to seek a higher power in the universe.

The touch of spirituality that people living in fitness often feel comes from the ability to use what we know to change someone's life. Because of you, other people are better, and by any definition of any religion, when you leave the world a better place due to your presence, you have gained an understanding of the spiritual side of the universe.

What you choose to do for work should matter to other people and what you do should make a difference in the universe. The following is a prayer written for all of you who get up every day at the first light of dawn, kiss the family goodbye, and set out to help people who struggle in their lives to reach goals and find happiness through feeling better about themselves.

An open prayer to the universe

Allow me the knowledge and the power to change lives and help those who trust me with their lives to find the happiness that comes from the simple pleasure of being a healthier person.

Guide me to always do the right thing with the people who seek my help and to keep my ego and personal agendas out of my teaching.

Help me always remember that small steps are important and any change in someone's life is valuable if that change is a positive step forward.

Please help me remain patient with and nurturing of the people who fail on the journey.

Grant me the means to keep doing the right things and to support and protect my family through the dedication to my dream.

Please help me be a friend and guide to those around me who are also on the same path and are seeking the same goals in life.

At the end of each day, please grant me the knowledge that what I did made a difference and everyone I touched became a better person because of my efforts.

And at the end of my days, please grant me the privilege of looking back and knowing that my life made a difference and I did not waste the talents given to me by the universe.

Take a few days off; you earned it. Sit quietly and think about the good you did this year, the people you helped, and the lives you changed.

There is a new year coming that will bring many more people into your world.

Your job is very simple: You exist to change lives and no one does it better than you.

A PERFECT LIFE MADE SIMPLE

Stop whining; no one wants to hear it.

Do what you say you are going to do with no change of mind or heart.

Honor the one you love.

Make sure you make time for yourself every day.

Failure is part of life; learn to accept the fact you will get your ass kicked someday.

Making money is simple if you learn the rules.
The first rule is that you do not create wealth by spending everything you make.

Never wait for someone else; be the friend you want everyone else to be.

Life is better if you are in shape.
Life sucks when you can't keep up.

Taking risks and running full speed naked down the beach is far better than sitting in a hot tub sipping cheap wine with a dozen wrinkled old people you met at The Walmart.

Never take advice from anyone who hasn't already done what you are trying to do.

A sunset, a bottle of wine, and holding the hand of the one you love
is God's way of telling you there really is a heaven.

Don't let a band of idiots hold you back.
If you move ahead in life and your friends don't, get new friends.

You get the life you create.

Accept nothing less than perfect because secretly, deep down in those moments before you fall asleep, you know you deserve it.

"I'VE NEVER WORKED WITH A COACH BEFORE— JUST WHAT CAN ONE DO FOR ME?"

When you have been a coach for a long time, it is easy to forget what an inexperienced client thinks about when considering a gym.

Most newbies have no idea what a coach does, thinks, expects, or how the relationship is supposed to work. Here are a few thoughts every coach should patiently explain to a new client before the relationship begins.

Good coaches teach. We will tell you what to do and why we are doing this.

Good coaches bring out your potential by patiently encouraging.
In-your-face, screaming coaches are fake TV trainers and not professionals.

Good coaches individualize the support process, such as nutrition or chasing dysfunction, according to who you are, your goals, your life, and never give you a "one size fits all" approach. You may work out as part of a team, but how you eat and how your body reacts to the workouts is unique.

Good coaches motivate, but they aren't your mama. If you expect the coach to call you at home to make sure you show up, you have a problem the coach can't fix.

Good coaches set goals and project your fitness into the future. If you work with a coach, where will you be 90 days from now...six months or a year? Every workout should be part of a long-term plan with an expected outcome. If the coach can't or won't do this, get a different coach.

The coach should have a lot of experience solving the type of problems you bring to the relationship. A middle-aged woman needs a bodybuilding coach like a ferret needs a trampoline. The coach has to fit you, not the other way around.

A good coach should help you get out of your own way by pointing out the behaviors that aren't working for you. It is good for clients to be challenged, and it is good to get an outside dose of reality.

Good coaches always know you had more than one glass of wine,
no matter what you wrote in your food journal.

A good coach should challenge you to your limits, but never destroy you.
Training to failure is last century and not productive.

A good coach should have the depth to keep you challenged as you progress.
As you get better, the coach should have more choices to help you progress.

Any good coach or mentor should have enough knowledge to keep you moving over time.
This is rare in coaching, mentorships, and life.

Good coaches understand that your goals are your goals; coaches should ever impose their personal standards on you. Once a week at the gym is better than sitting on the couch; twice is perfect for most people.

Anything beyond that is a gift of time you should enjoy.

Good coaches are worth every penny you might pay...
and more if they can get you to change your life.

No matter who you are and what kind of shape you are in, there is a coach who can inspire and lead you to a better you. This client is what motivates a good coach to get up every day and get it done.

WE ARE SO BUSY IN LIFE,
WE FORGET HOW TO DO NOTHING

We forget how to sit quietly and just think.

We forget how to read without music blaring or our phones in our laps. When was the last time you just sat in silence, enjoying your own company for an hour or two without a single distraction?

The pleasure isn't in having nothing to do; the pleasure is in having a lot to do and choosing to do nothing…nothing at all—total inactivity for a few hours, with no purpose and no expected outcome.

We go to the beach loaded with books, music, and phones, and never notice how beautiful the beach is. Just sitting, staring at the water, watching people walk by, noticing the birds, and laughing at the kids—all are things we have forgotten how to do.

We fill time because we can't stand just doing nothing,
but doing nothing is one of the great healers of the human soul.

We are so busy being busy, we are too busy to stop being busy and do nothing.

When is the last time you and your favorite person just got into the car and took off? No destination, no direction, no time frame, and no reason to be in the car except that want to spend the afternoon doing absolutely nothing with someone you care about.

When was the last time you poured a glass of wine and sat by yourself, without your music, without your phone, without a blaring television, and without a care in the world because you were doing nothing except what you wanted and needed to do, which was doing nothing?

Doing nothing but living may be one of the hardest things to master in life, but the rewards of an afternoon without a care in the world and with nothing, and I mean nothing, to do might be the best thing that ever happened to you.

HOW YOU KNOW YOU ARE A TRAINER

You have no idea it's Monday because you've trained the last 30 days straight.

It's been so long since you've been home in the evening, you notice you now have three kids instead of two and are afraid to ask when you got the new one.

Your husband has a pool girl and you don't have a pool.

You signed up for a certification, sat down, got comfortable, and slept through the whole thing because it was the first time you stopped moving in three months.

You are going to a wedding and realize you just laid out
a dress tee shirt to wear with matching socks.

You saw a dead rabbit on the side of the road and wondered about the calories and fat content.

You wear your Fit Band thingy during sex because you hate to not include the burn and then are disappointed because your mate only racked up 100 calories.

Other people get drunk and do shots. You get drunk and do pushups on the bar.

Finally, you know you are a trainer when you go to a restaurant
and are surprised the meal is served on a plate instead of a plastic bowl.

Now get off your weekend ass and go to work. Train hard this week and change lives.

NEVER A DAY

Never a day when I will let something petty ruin my day.

Never a day when I won't get up and try to change the world,
even if the best I can do is put a smile on some miserable person's face for just 30 seconds.

Never a day when I will lose my temper with the weak, the young,
and those who never earned or deserved petty anger.

Never a day when I will forget where I came from and who helped me along the way.

Never a day when I won't open my eyes in the morning
and be truly grateful for another chance to do it right one more time.

Never a day I won't tell those who mean the most to me that I love them.

Never a day I will disrespect the one I love.
Better to leave quietly than spend a life with someone I can't and don't respect.

Never a day I will let a client make me crazy.
Better to say goodbye to the client than to lose my self-respect.

Never a day I won't try to do some crazy act of random kindness.

My life is perfect, and there is someone every single day who can use my help and kindness.

Never a day wasted being mad at things I cannot change. Life is hard enough worrying about the things I can affect without worrying about someone else's nonsense I have no control over.

Never a day worrying about money.
If I need more, I need to go to work more...and perhaps work a little smarter.

Never a day wasted getting drained by the takers of life.
Help when I can, but if I linger, they want it all.

Never a day I won't move. Movement is life, and there is no pleasure on the planet more satisfying than the ability to flow through life.

Never a day without a thank you.
My life is good through the graciousness of others and I will say thank you.

Never a day scared in the dark.
If I am scared of anything, I will ask,
because there is an answer to what makes me afraid of life.

Finally, never a day without a smile on my face.
The world is a miserable enough place at times
and I can be part of the problem or the solution I was meant to be.

Never a day without changing the world.

I accept nothing less of myself.

MY PRAYER TO THE UNIVERSE
THIS HOLIDAY SEASON

Please give me coffee for the strength to change the things I can change, and wine for the things I just plain don't understand.

Please help the young coaches who understand business be successful, and please make those who don't have any clue about business real cute so the clients will date them and give them lots of money.

Please, just once in the coming year, help Mrs. Johnson realize gluten-free pancakes, gluten-free muffins, gluten-free snack bars, and gluten-free cookies don't really do her much good if that is all she eats, and please help her understand a bottle of wine a day cannot be canceled out by three mediocre workouts a week.

And please help her understand I am a professional coach, not a magician who can make her butt disappear with a magic wand.

Please help all people who join a gym for $10 understand that expecting to get in shape in those places for the price of one visit to Starbucks is a very stupid concept. Joining those gyms are what you want to do when you don't want to get into shape. May the universe take away their vision of free pizzas in the gym, and fill these misguided fools with the need to sweat for their own health.

Please, if you can, make pints and wine and friends all part of my life this year.

Please have Santa run over any young coach who has a one-day certification and three months' experience, and then calls himself a master coach on his business card. And please have the reindeer dump on him as they stomp him in the dirt.

And please, next year in the women's division of all Spartan races, make clothing optional.

And please allow the universe to give a special gift to whoever invented yoga pants. I tear up just thinking about the good that person has done for men around the world.

Yes, if the universe is a fair place, anyone who drives a car while shooting an "I am live now" spot on Facebook would have the phone and car taken away. And does anyone really want to hear the lessons of life from a 23-year-old coach who has tried nothing and failed at everything, and who has a thousand dollars in the bank?

Finally, when you are sitting with your children or are out with the love of your life and you spend more time on your phone than touching their hearts, may the universe take them away from you and give them to someone smart enough to put the phone down and love the people they are with.

Karma is a good thing, but sometimes karma can take too long.
Perhaps the best way to get change is to get in someone's face and scream.

YOU HAVE TO HELP
100 CLIENTS CROSS A DANGEROUS FIELD

Twenty of them are out front, 60 are in the middle, and 20 are way behind, bitching about their training, complaining about you and your staff, their diets and why they failed, their spouses, their endlessly bad jobs and lousy kids, and as a group are draining your very soul just keeping them moving.

Which group are you going to put your energy into day after day?

The rear 20 are where you get trapped.

The rear 20 are the black holes of your universe, sucking the air, light, and energy out of everything around them and returning nothing but cold darkness.

The rear demands attention, and the more they bitch, the more attention they get until they eventually squeeze everyone else out of their world. The more you give, the more they want, and there will never, ever be enough.

Run up front and thank that group, your best but underappreciated clients, for not bitching, not complaining, and for supporting your business and you for so long.

Then encourage the rear group to try another coach.

Neither you nor any other good coach has the energy needed year after year to save them all. Put everything you have into those who want to be with you, and who understand bitching does nothing but irritate the universe. You simply don't have the time for their eternal nonsense.

THE BIGGEST REASONS
YOUR CLIENTS CAN RUIN YOUR DAY

The biggest reasons some of your not-so-dedicated fitness clients can ruin your day or make you laugh until you snort coffee through your nose:

Number One—They confuse curvy with big muffin belly.

Number Two—They confuse walking the dog to the wine store with 10,000 steps.

Number Three—They believe protein that equals the palm of your hand was in Andre the Giant's hand.

Number Four—They believe $100 yoga pants are better for their butts than actually doing yoga.

Number Five—Although they would never dream of taking abuse from their own clients in their businesses, they feel fine beating you up for a $5 increase in their hourly rate.

Number Six—They believe canceling 12 minutes prior to their session is fine, but if their doctor charges them full price for the same stupidity, they pay the rate and don't complain.

Number Seven—They believe a new, freshly certified coach with three months' experience charging $40 delivers the same results as a master trainer with 10,000 sessions under her belt over 10 years charging $100.

Number Eight—They believe two bacon sandwiches equal eight ounces of organic free-range chicken.

Number Nine—He believes two minutes of sex, shower included, equals a 30-minute HIIT session with a weighted vest. He also can't believe the fitness device on his wrist only read the two minutes as 12 calories and he will trade the thing in on Monday.

Number Ten—She believes all women with muscle are born that way, and the only workout she can do is Zumba with a one-pound weight that magically tones. She has been doing group exercise for 12 years and can't understand why her butt is bigger and everything sort of sags.

We love them and are grateful for each one, but some days you just have to laugh.

STOP TALKING ABOUT EVERYTHING YOU ARE GOING TO DO AND JUST DO SOMETHING

Stop putting everything in your life off until the right time.
There will never be a right time, so get moving and do it now.

Your personal life is a mess because you won't make decisions in a timely fashion. There is no perfect time to get your life right. There is only today, so why not get started now?

Stop bragging about all you are going to do and just do something now.

Stop living in the past and telling everyone you used to be somebody. We all used to be somebody, and no one really cares about who we were; they only care about who we are going to be tomorrow.

Stop comparing yourself to others.
It does not matter what they do in life; it only matters what you do.

Stop living in the past. You cannot change a damn thing, so why obsess? I would be a lot more concerned about what I am going to do today than what I screwed up years ago. We all pee on the monkey at one time or another, so laugh, shake your head, wonder how you could have been so dumb, and then get on with your life.

There will be a point in life where you won't able to get it all done. You will have more to do than time left to do it. Start now, while you can, and get it all done.

You do not want to be sitting on a bar stool 20 years from now telling people who do not care that you could have been someone, you had the talent, you had it all...and never tried. Be someone now; all it takes is getting off your "glued to the couch" butt and to make something happen.

Do something, even if it is wrong.
I would rather fail at a level higher than you were even brave enough to play at.

Enjoy the process.

There is no perfect; there is only you, taking on the world
and that should be enough to get anything you want in life.

If all else fails, go home, have a beer, hold the hand of someone you love, and then start all over again tomorrow. Every day you are out there trying is an absolutely wonderful day.

SUCCESS OFTEN LEADS TO ISOLATION

The more successful you become or the more successful you are perceived to be by others, such as your clients, the more difficult it becomes to ask for help or gather new information from others.

These leaders or supposed experts then often fail because their egos prevent them from moving beyond what they already think they know.

Open a gym, make a little money, and now this person is an expert and others ask how he did it. Ego prevents this guy from ever attending another workshop, because what if others see that he doesn't know it all and still needs to learn?

Start your first mentorship and you are now the leader...the expert, the guru. Ego dictates you will never grow past this point, because if a 100 people look up to you, how can you ever ask for help, especially when you might really need it?

Success over the long term can only come from a willingness to admit that what you are doing isn't working, and perhaps you really don't know everything there is to know about your business. Even gurus need an outside opinion now and then, a different perspective that allows the mind to grow and solve problems.

Good leaders stay willing to learn, while poor leaders reach a point where their self-importance outweighs their ability to grow as leaders or as people.

The day you think you know it all is the day your business started to fail,
your personal development stopped, and your friends started deserting you.

And most likely, this day is also the day your dog started to hate you, your spouse decided to move on, your friends are too busy to hang out with you, and your mother stopped returning your calls.

No one likes a know-it-all, not even your mother.

YOU JUST MIGHT HAVE A PHONE PROBLEM

Do you sit on the toilet answering calls, checking email, and hoping the person in the next stall doesn't flush?

You might just have a phone problem.

If your spouse says, "Hey, want to mess around?" and your answer is, "Yeah, sure, but let me see what is going on with Facebook first. And hey, would you make me a sandwich?"

You might just have a phone problem.

Do you sit on vacation, face down, ignoring the beauty around you, ignoring the kids, ignoring your friends, ignoring your soon-to-be-ex spouse, texting people who could be ignored until Monday?

If you have to answer email on vacation, you didn't train your staff right. You should not be held hostage by your own business.

And you might have a phone problem.

Do you leave the house going out for dinner, drive five miles, and then turn around to get the phone you left at home? Can't go to dinner without your little buddy?

You definitely have a phone problem.

Do you sleep closer to your phone than your spouse?

You might have a phone problem.

Ever walk into a wall because you were face down in your phone?

You have a phone problem.

Ever sit on your couch, look up, and realize you have been scrolling for 30 minutes, completely ignoring your family, who are all sitting there with the look of realization that there is nothing they can do to compete with whoever is on the other end of that text?

You need help...and you have a phone problem.

We use phones to become more effective, but immediate email, immediate text response, and the immediate need to scroll social media all make you less effective.

Answering a text in 20 seconds doesn't make you efficient; it makes you an idiot who didn't even think about the problem at hand for over a few heartbeats.

You want to improve your business and personal life?

The answer is in your hand.

Put down the damn phone and concentrate on your business without interruption, lock yourself in your office without the phone for an hour or two at a time, and work on your business while not being held hostage by a piece of plastic.

Focus on being present with your family and learn to block out an hour or two a day to return calls and catch up, but never let your phone dictate your day. Or dictate the attention you give the kids.

Or ever be so involved with your phone you are missing life altogether.

AT SOME POINT, BEING ABSOLUTELY CORRECT MEANS YOU ARE ABSOLUTELY WRONG

Evolving professionally means at some point much of what you have spent so much time and money learning over the last decade no longer works.

Look at the trainers who grew up in the bodybuilding era who snickered at the fools using kettlebells. One day they were experts, and then they couldn't understand why Monday was no longer National Chest Day in every gym in the world.

This is especially true once you collect a lot of initials after your name.

It is hard to admit the information you learned at a $2,000 weekend certification three years ago—the one that fired your ass up for months—might now be proven out of date, maybe even dangerous.

If you want to be a master trainer, you have to know when to let go.

If you find yourself laughing at a new method of training, you might be the problem and no longer the solution.

LONG FORGOTTEN ELEVATOR
IN ANOTHER NAMELESS HOTEL

WE SELL HOPE! WE SELL WHAT IS POSSIBLE IN LIFE

REMEMBER THIS!

We sell hope.
We sell what is possible in life.

We don't sell TVs or tires; we sell the possibility of making that quiet dream the client has in her head for five minutes before she falls asleep at night come true. It's a dream where she is feeling good about her body, feeling sexy, or able to live a normal life not trapped by another failing diet.

We sell the idea that with our help that dream can be a reality, but only we can see that dream along with her. Only we have the vision to help ease her deepest fears and encourage her dream to become the best version of who she can be.

We do not sell workouts, program design, sessions, packages, or nutritional advice. Any time spent explaining these to a client is worthless chatter time by a trainer who feels this is about what he knows, and not what he can do.

No one cares about what you know; they only care that you can change their lives.

We sell a solution to a problem the client may not even share with herself, let alone you, but we know the dream is there, and this dream is what drove her to the door.

All our techniques are just tools in the box to make that dream come true.

The client does not care about your methodology or what is in your tool box.
The client only cares about your ability to help visualize the dream and make it come true.

We sell the future. Your job is to help the client understand that dreams can be real.
Dreams do not have to remain a fantasy used to keep the tears at bay.

EVERYONE HAS THE RIGHT TO FAIL

Everyone has the right to fail, even the person in your life who keeps making the same stupid, arrogant, mind-numbing, crotch shrinking "I have my own style" mistakes, and who gets the same worthless, clueless, inefficient, losing results every single time, every single day, year after maddening year.

Even this person has the right to fail on his own.

Even the person in your life who gets a little older but no smarter and refuses to ask for help even though doing nothing but repeat the same arrogant, self-righteous, isolated, uneducated behavior that has led to a life of constant turmoil, weekly drama, the need to endlessly borrow money, and yet another sitting on the sofa crying episode asking, "Why? Why does this always happen to me?"

Yes, even those people have the right to live their own lives and have the universe endlessly chew their butts like an old dog munching a slobbery tennis ball.

Then there is the person who is getting a world-class beating by being trapped in a bad marriage, by constantly making horrible, senseless money mistakes, who lives on too much alcohol, does too many drugs, and who answers every attempt at help with, "No, I am cool dude, I have it all together."

Hard to accept, but even that person has the right to fail.

Sometimes the best way to help someone is to close your eyes and walk away, silently cussing to yourself.

Sometimes all the good intent in the world
is best used somewhere else where you can make a difference.

Sometimes the best help you can give someone is none at all. Everyone has earned the right to fail in life on their own terms and sometimes there isn't a damn thing you can do about it.

ONE OF THE HARDEST THINGS TO TEACH A PERSON WHO IS 30 IS THAT HIS FUTURE MAY BE HIS FATHER

Our population in America and in most of the world is becoming top-heavy with aged people, but little of what we do in the name of fitness was designed for a herd of people over 50—with many now extending into their 90s.

We can keep the young beautiful. We can repair the moderately overweight, and we can rebuild most injuries, but we cannot offer much to the person caught up in the process of aging, which is currently the biggest percentage of people in most developed countries. This is where the money will be in coaching during the next decade.

Aging is frustrating. You sit in an older body, still the person you have always been, but now with bad packaging, a bit scuffed up, sort of like your favorite pair of weekend shoes—still serviceable, but not something you want to wear out in public.

And then you notice the most basic movements become noticeably more of a struggle, even though you are doing "the workout thing."

We can train anyone to hit a golf ball farther,
but we spend little time helping him bend over to get the ball out of the hole.

We talk about diet and can keep a guy over 50 somewhat leaner if he pays attention, but this same guy struggles to get his foot across his knee to tie his shoe, even though he is at the gym three days a week.

We can create beauty, but we ignore functionality.

The future of fitness is the restoration of natural movement patterns—beyond functional fitness, beyond the kettlebell mentality, and beyond the creation of bodies that look perfect but are held together with a pretty color of duct tape.

Does the woman over 50 want to enter a contest based on a manufactured sport concept, or does she want to keep her weight down and not be embarrassed in front of her friends, still have interesting sex, and just be able to move better when playing with her grandkids?

Does a guy in his 60s need to power clean until he pukes in the name of some insane definition of fitness, or does he want to be able to get out of a chair gracefully, still be the other half of meaningful sex, and keep his weight under control?

What both of these people want is not what we sell in most modern training gyms, and the first gym pro who figures this out will make a lot of money.

The next big thing is specialization in fitness for age 50 and beyond. The tools you need to capitalize with this group are what most of our current training models exclude, which is advanced nutrition and the restoration of movement.

This specialization isn't as sexy as sports performance, not as much fun as team training with 20 people in their 20s, and not something coaches aspire to when in their 30s. But a focus on those who are feeling their age is where the money will be in the future, and where the mature coach will find a home.

We tend to make fitness too difficult, when it really can be explained simply:

Fitness is movement; movement is life.

When did we forget that?

RUN AWAY, AS QUICK AS YOU CAN

There is always that one person in your life who wraps himself in a blanket of unhappiness and misery and then makes it his life's work to pull as many people as possible under the blanket with him.

We make the mistake of thinking we can change that person.

If we just do a little more for him, cry a little longer at night, ruin a little more of our own lives, maybe we can find a way to bring the happiness so desperately needed.

Maybe you can change the person.
Maybe you can't.

Maybe you should run away as fast as your little legs will carry you.

Some people love that blanket of misery.
Their unhappiness is their identity.
These people love being professional victims.
Their unhappiness is all they have.
Their unhappiness is all they ever want from life.

Their happiness is living a life of misery to be shared with everyone they know
or even meet for a few minutes.

They bask in the attention of "woe is me." No matter what is happening in your life, their illness, loss, pain, or struggles are greater than yours could ever be and there is nothing you can share that can't be topped.

These people live to make you miserable. There is no sunshine in their lives, just pulled shades and drawn blinds that keep them forever in the dark. They love the darkness and wouldn't change a thing.

You can lose much of your life living to make that person happy.

What you failed to understand is that your pain and sacrifice in their name is what makes them happy. Their continued misery is the only thing keeping you there.

Run. Run fast. Do not look back.

The perpetually unhappy will find someone else to take your place in about an hour. Crawl out from under the blanket, throw open the shades, raise the blinds, and seek the light.

Sometimes, the only way you can win is to give up and quit trying to help someone who is perfectly happy being forever unhappy.

WE ALL LOSE OUR WAY IN LIFE

We all, at some point, reach a day
when we do not know what to do next.
We all will find ourselves living in
a quiet fear where going forward terrifies us.

Our fear is often nothing more than fear of change.
We are miserable in our current life,
but the fear of going forward scares us more.

Living this way takes your life away.
The wasted days turn into months, then years.

Finally, you reach the end of your life as a lesser version of what you could have been.

Living in fear means your talent, beauty, and strength is diminished.

Living in fear means you never rise to your gifts
or come anywhere near your potential as a fully functioning human.

There is hope.
Embrace your fear.
What you fear most is usually what
you need the most to complete your life.
Moving forward often cancels your fear.
Fear is amplified by inaction, but subsides with movement.

Embracing change is shedding
the darkness and chasing the light.

The most powerful way to overcome fear is to take one step toward change,
and when you realize the change won't kill you, run as hard as you can to the light.

THE FIVE RULES OF LIFE

You will never find happiness through others.
If you cannot find happiness within yourself, you will never be happy.

If you are waiting for someone else to make you happy, you will waste your life waiting.

If you are dependent upon someone else for your happiness, you will always be held hostage by that person. You need to live within yourself before you can be truly happy with anyone else.

Some people need to have the universe drag their butts through the cosmic mud before they will learn how to live on their own. There are people in your life who prey on the strength of others. They want to live off the kindness of an intrinsic-driven person, such as a professional coach, but when you struggle, this person simply jumps off your back onto someone else's.

Carrying someone does nothing but enable that person, and the universe needs to have its way with that guy before he will ever change. A hand up is one thing; enabling a person to stay worthless in life is something else. It lessens your life and will not change the other person for a single second.

Money isn't everything...but it is. Live as a minimalist or live as a hedonist; it doesn't really matter as long as you have enough money to live independently of others.

Money is freedom and nothing more.
How you determine what your freedom costs is your decision.

It is all your fault. Your life is how it is because of the decisions you made or didn't make; good or bad, it is all yours.

You cannot blame anyone for your inability to take care of yourself in life. Nothing bad ever changes until you take personal responsibility for the situation. You are who you are because of the decisions you made, and if you screwed it up, so what? Get over it, get on with it, and get your butt moving.

We all fail, and it doesn't mean a damn thing,
except that you are human and just as messed up as the rest of us.

Because you are you and have it all, you have to give back every day,
or everything good in your life will be taken away from you someday.

You must to do a hundred small acts of genuine kindness a day to improve lives around you.

You, who have it all, must share it all, or lose it all.

Your personal problems may be tough, but the rest of the world sucks worse than you do.

Even on your worst day, you are still capable of changing someone's life.

YOUR PERSONAL PHYSICAL PERFECTION

Your personal physical perfection lasts for about an hour and a half on the best day of your life, and then is gone like a fart in a strong wind.

You peak physically for a short time in life and then, if you reached the middle rung of being a mature adult, you understand from here on you become a work in progress that can only reflect the best you can be today. Being the best you can be today has little to do with that single day of perfect years in the past.

How can you be a trainer if you aren't perfect, ask the trainers who believe they are perfect, who believe physical perfection is more important than any credential. They can't understand how anyone could turn 30 and realize maybe it takes too much time and that a body doesn't always want to be "perfect."

Coaching isn't about perfection. Coaching is about being the best you can be today, and is never about trying to be who you were on that one perfect day. We get hurt, burn out, fade away, and become so frustrated we quit because we spend so much of our lives chasing the person we were.

We also hurt our clients because we let them believe that with just the right pills, coaching, and drugs, we can get them back to the glory days when they were 21 and in the shape of their lives. Now, though, they are 35, beaten up by years of sports and life, have three kids, a stressful job, and absolutely no time to chase those fading dreams.

We let them go too hard and too fast. They break, and this destruction is our fault for never saying, "How about we don't chase perfect; how about we just see how we can make you the best version of who you are today?"

Savor your perfection when you find it that day. Take great naked pictures on that single day of being absolutely flawless and share them with your friends at the bar someday in the future screaming, "See, I had it all back in the day." Enjoy the short time you are the best you will ever be, because that short window into your physical perfection gets quickly slammed shut by the reality of life.

All you imperfect coaches out there, thank you. You inspire and motivate. All you works-in-progress, you are often the best coaches in the world, because you have to work at it so much harder than the perfect human beings.

To all you self-proclaimed perfect, self-righteous idiots, just look at your older relatives with the baggy pants, belt buckle pointing straight down, and who creak when they stand up. Your day of no-longer perfect is around the next jagged corner in life, just past "had a few kids" street, and maybe a mile from the "damn, I turned 40" intersection.

THE LEVEL OF SUCCESS YOU ACHIEVE

The level of success you personally achieve in your life
will always be determined by how good you are at elevating the people around you.

You can rise and be considered good at something on your own, but you will never be
great at anything until you understand your limits are controlled by the levels of success
the people around you achieve through your efforts, your caring, and your leadership.

Great people make other people great.

Small people spend all their time trying to rise at someone else's expense.

You have people around you who can benefit
from your experience and personal interest in them.

Spend some time with those people and help them grow. You will be surprised how
great your life can be through the simple act of helping others rise to their own talent
and ability.

WHAT IS THIS "BEING HAPPY" THEY TALK ABOUT?

Does "happy" come from the sense of well-being you get from moving every day?

Or is "happy" what it means to get up every day knowing today is the day
you will change the world...and you start every day that way?

Maybe "happy" is finding your own internal strength after being in a relationship that
has drained you for years. Today, for the first time in years, is your day without "crazy"
in your life.

Defining your own life instead of having it defined by others
might be one of the happiest days you will ever experience.

But "happy" could be lying on the floor after your last chemo treatment, realizing you
are alive and will continue to be that way; the darkness in life didn't win, and never will.

You smile at the ceiling and promise yourself when you get off this floor, you are going
to kick the universe's butt. That thought makes you happy when other people suffering
the same process might have quit the fight.

And don't forget, "happy" might be as simple as an hour holding hands with the one you
love, watching the sun set and not saying a word because you don't have to say anything.

And the day you die, you will remember that hour until your last breath, because you
were loved and happy, something some people never let themselves experience. Maybe
you had it all along and just didn't appreciate it.

But happy is also spending an hour with your kids, walking along a back road talking.
No phones, no urgent need to get anywhere—just you and the kids for an hour, laughing, walking, and talking. Maybe that is more than happy...that might be perfect.

And maybe "happy" is knowing what you want from your life.
Is having a purpose in life the foundation of happiness?

Maybe happiness is all of these things.

Maybe "happy" is nothing more than the simple experiences we neglect because we are
always so busy trying to chase happiness that we never take the time to just let go and
be happy and enjoy what we already have.

You might be the happiest person on the planet if you let it happen.

WHAT INTEGRITY SHOULD MEAN TO ANY COACH

You do what you say, as promised, with never an excuse.

Everything you do is for the benefit of the clients. Never talk clients into training or into buying a product that does not directly enhance their health or workout.

It is better to lose a client than to lose your integrity.

You always do the right thing no matter the consequences.
The right thing is always the right thing to do.

Never badmouth another professional trying to enhance your own position. If you think you are better than others, prove it. Keep the lies and rumors to yourself.

If you are an employee for anyone, honor that person. If you are unhappy, leave, but leave with class and dignity, never trying to harm a business where someone gave you a chance.

Never spread rumors or stories about any client. Most of those are lies anyway. Stay out of the gossip world and honor every client in the gym, even if a client may not deserve it.

Stand up for others.
Defend your friends and clients against negativity.

Never hide your talent to please someone else.
You were given talent, and talent is a huge burden.

Living down to someone to make them happy is a waste of your life
and goes against your integrity.

It is better to lose your job than lose your integrity. If someone asks you to do something that goes against your beliefs, walk away. There is always another job for a person of strong integrity.

Integrity is all the small things too.

Return the $1 extra change to the coffee shop, correct your check if you were overpaid, accept no money you did not earn, be true to what you want in life, and honor those who help you get through life every day.

Integrity is being thankful and grateful.

The world is a crazy place and there are millions of people who would give their lives to have what you take for granted every day.

Integrity is living within yourself and being grateful for your talent and all the other things of value in life.

Integrity is about you, how you want to live your life, and who you want to be to others. You make 100 choices every day; choose to live with integrity.

WHAT IF YOU RISK EVERYTHING

What if you risk everything you have to open your own business or take that dream job, and then you fail?

What if you don't take the risk and never discover if you could have been somebody?

Which is worse: the fear of failing or the regret you never lived a full and complete life because you weren't strong enough to let go of what you had to chase your dreams?

Someday you will look back and laugh at the mistakes you made in life. Screwing up is part of the journey, and there is no chance you will get through life without making some legendary mistakes.

These mistakes define who you become in life.
There isn't anyone who is interesting who hasn't made a mess of something.

True regret comes from never trying.

We fear risk so much, we often do not try at all,
but we should fear not being brave enough to try even more.

Having regret that you didn't take the risk will destroy your soul far more than making a few mistakes.

You have a dream.
You have a vision of what you want in life.
You have a hidden fantasy of what you want from your life.
And you are afraid to risk what you have to get what you want.

But how long will this dream wait for you? How long before you are too old to try? How many more excuses are you going to hold tight that are slowly draining away everything you wanted in life?

If not now, when?
If not you, who will take the risk?

There is no tomorrow for dreams, only the precious minutes of today.
If you don't get your butt moving now, you might lose it all before you ever had it.

A GOOD PLAN NOW
IS WORTH MORE THAN A PERFECT PLAN NEVER

Classic over-thinkers can kill a good idea by trying to make it perfect, but there is no perfect plan, only your ability to get started and then adapt the plan to the reality at hand.

I have seen people trying to open a business spend years thinking about and building the perfect gym on paper, yet the gym is never built.

I have also seen someone with a good idea, a decent plan, and a willingness to commit make a million a year chasing the dream.

Many of you over-think your careers, your businesses, and even your relationships, and this over-thinking leads to inaction and failure by freezing in time.

Movement in life is everything.
Waiting for the perfect time to do anything
means most of what you want will never get done.

If it is your passion, chase it until you earn it.
If it makes you happy, you probably should be doing it.
If it makes you unhappy, run away.
Life is too short to waste a day being miserable.

Life in many ways isn't complicated. It's avoiding the meaningful decisions in life that makes life seem so much harder than it really is.

OUTSIDE LONDON
History is in every village in England if you are willing to look

THE HIGHEST RISK IN LIFE IS FROM DOING ABSOLUTELY NOTHING

THE HIGHEST AMOUNT OF RISK YOU WILL EVER FACE IS FROM DOING ABSOLUTELY NOTHING

We avoid going forward in life because we perceive the risk to be greater going forward than to just keep doing what we are doing.

We compare the risk of change, which is really the fear of the unknown, and compare it to the relative safety of staying in our comfort zone.

Ten years from now someone asks you, "What have you done with the last 10 years of your life?"

You answer, "Nothing! I stayed in a job I didn't like. I live in a place I hate and I am with someone I don't want to be with. I was mediocre at all of them because none of it was what I wanted to do with my life."

You avoided the risk of the unknown. You were afraid to take a new job or walk away from a relationship that was killing you, but you sacrificed your life in the process.

The greatest risk in life is not in seeking an unknown future; the greatest risk is getting trapped by a known past.

You risked nothing, but lost it all by doing nothing.

We seek safety in the comfort and routine of life, but all that could be taken away quickly.

That comforting job you don't like but won't leave will be taken away because no one is ever good at something they don't like, and you will eventually fail.

That relationship you won't leave will never be special, because while you stayed and are there to avoid risk and dealing with pain, you spend more mental energy wishing you had the courage to be somewhere else. You waste the years, time you can never regain in life.

There is no true safety where you will be forever risk free, but there is talent. Your talent is never developed until you find the courage to move forward and challenge yourself again and again.

The only thing you have in life no one can take away from you, the only thing in life that overpowers risk, is the talent you develop in yourself.

Someone can take everything you own, including the clothes on your back, but no one can take your talent without your permission.

You risk more by sitting still than you ever will by giving yourself a chance to be the best you can be.

Seek risk in life.

DEATH HAPPENS

The door opens, your person passes through,
and those left behind try to find meaning in the loss.

We can mourn this loss.

Or we can celebrate the passing of someone we loved.

Mourning is an act of selfishness that fulfills our own needs.
Celebrating a life is an act of respect.

Celebrating a person who has left us is a tribute to that person's journey.
Celebrating gives meaning to the life.

Death is inevitable, but we how we choose to live our own lives is a choice.

Many of us waste this precious gift by failing to understand
that a life of meaning is a life lived to its fullest each and every day.

Live life as hard as you can.
Make every moment of every day important.

Make the small things, such as the touch of your child,
something you will carry through to your last day.

Do this, and when you are gone,
you will have left a life worth celebrating by those who will miss you.

When you get up tomorrow,
make the day the most special day of your life.

And pass that passion for living to everyone you meet.

HOW MENTALLY DERANGED

How mentally deranged would an adult have to be to willingly spend a day at Disney?

Disney is not the happiest place on earth.

How could anyone be happy surrounded by millions of little kid monsters in messed-up hats?

Kids at Disney are like fleas at the beach. You brush one off and there is another one staring up at you with melted crap on his face, giant mouse ears, and a grumpy "I hate all adults" sneer that could penetrate a concrete wall.

And then there is the mob of princesses, dressed up by parents in their little tiaras, strangely colored dresses, and magic wands. Hey, kid, if that magic wand really worked, you would turn yourself into a giant beer and make me really happy.

Flying into Orlando, Florida, is one of the more miserable experiences you can have in flying.   You are surrounded by a hundred overly sugared kids screaming to see the Big Rat, the artist formerly known as Mickey Mouse, who lives to capture the souls of small children and financially bankrupt all parents.

Flying out of Orlando is also painfully miserable. You now have a hundred kids stuffed full of candy, hot dogs, 26 sugared sodas per day, who are tired, crabby, sunburned, and crying because they have to leave the Big Rat. You know this to be true when the parents order double vodka Bloody Mary drinks at 7:30 in the morning.

Then there are the families with matching Goofy hats, with the long brims and floppy ears. Come on, Louisiana people, are you really going to wear those on the plane all the way home?

Dad, you are wearing a, "Go LSU!" tee shirt, worn so many times it is faded into oblivion, and hey, Dad, you have gained maybe 50 pounds since you bought that sucker. There is a whole lot of Louisiana belly hanging over those cargo shorts, all topped off by the world's biggest Mickey ears.

By the way, the matching purple and gold striped tube socks really do make that outfit.

Why don't they arrest people like that? Do you realize how much wine I will have to drink to purge that vision from my eyes?

Thank the universe for high-end water bottles filled with vodka and if one more mother shrieks, "There is Princess Ariel, run everyone, we can get a picture," and smashes into my leg with that damn baby stroller again, there is going to be a small princess floating in the Disney Lake.

My new business plan is to open a vasectomy store there.

"Hey, buddy, how is your day going with those five kids? Stand in line again for two hours to ride a three-minute rip off? Just paid $86 for lunch for that little mob? Step right in here, my friend, no waiting. I guarantee there won't be a number six."

Happiest place my ass.
Disney is a taste of hell on earth.
Save your money.
Take the kids to a nice beach.
They will be happy with the other fleas.

HEY, HAVE YOU NOTICED

The smile on your kid's face when you spend a few unplanned hours together?

The smile on a client's face when you say thank you for the business?

The smile on your spouse's face when you come home early and head out to dinner?

The smile in a friend's voice when you call just to say hello?

The smile on the homeless guy's face after you give him a few dollars?

The laughter in your parent's voice when you call for no reason?

The look of shock on someone's face when you commit a random act of kindness?

The smile on your own face when you live a healthy, happy life?

You just might be the most powerful person on earth simply because you have the power to change lives every day...and you never even knew it.

Superheroes aren't just in comic books.
Sometimes they live in your own mirror.
Live up to those powers.

Do something nice this weekend.

Change the world around you because you have the power.

HARD TO HURT A GUY
RUNNING FULL SPEED TOWARD BETTER DAYS

It's easy to hurt someone who sits in the dark,
obsessed about yesterday and afraid to live today.

We give up control of our lives one day at a time.

It is like the proverbial frog in the slowly heating water that ends up boiling instead of leaping.
You go through life day after day, letting control slip away one decision at a time, until you end
up bitter, frustrated, and feeling like a failure because your life is no longer yours.

It's difficult to hold people down when they believe they control their own lives.

You will find power you never even knew you had the day you declare it is your life.
If you don't start making decisions to move your life ahead, someone else will,
and that will always end badly for you.

Time passes quickly when you are out of control.

Days become weeks, weeks become years. Then you wake up and realize you have wasted
everything you had and everything you could have been, because you were never strong
enough to shout, "My life, my decision, and I am in control of who I am and how I will live."

And if not today, then when?

How long are you willing to be miserable because you refuse to live your own life?

How long are you willing to let someone take control of the only thing in life worth owning—
your own life, lived on your own terms?

It's hard to hurt a guy running fast into his own future, one he created for himself through his
ability to make his own decisions and control his own life.

GET OVER IT; THE WORLD OWES YOU NOTHING

Just because you are a trainer doesn't mean you are a good one.

You still have to do the work, put in the years, and learn from the best before you can make it, or ever be considered a master coach by your peers or the clients you serve.

Other coaches make more money than you do because they dress better, speak better, do the work, build the relationships, and master their craft. If you do the work, you will get the money. You don't make the money you believe you deserve because you aren't as good as you think you are...yet.

Just because you open a gym doesn't guarantee the business will work or will be financially successful. You are not entitled to succeed just because you try. You succeed because you are willing to learn about business, run it as a business, and work your ass off until you make it.

Having kids does not make you a good parent. Your kids can grow up as good people, or they can become stupid people doing stupid things in stupid Facebook videos. It's your choice, and it depends on whether you are willing to be there and do the work.

Any idiot can get married.
Staying married takes more work than most people are willing to do.

You chose every day to be healthy, or you chose to slowly lose the greatest gift ever. Being healthy takes more work than being fat. You have to learn about food; you have to move and think to stay fit and healthy—work few people will do.

You can give of yourself every day to help people around you, or you can spend every day using people to get what you want. How do you think that turns out over time?

Takers always fail because eventually there is nothing left for them to take.
Givers are the people you respect and who change the world.

It isn't that hard.
Give more than you take.

The world owes you nothing.

THERE IS ONLY ONE RESOLUTION
YOU NEED TO MAKE THIS YEAR

"I will not, under any circumstances, give up control of my life."

Your life is like a huge canvas yet unpainted.
You paint, every day a few strokes at a time, the story of your life.

At the end of your days, the painting will be a masterpiece reflecting your life,
your individual journey, and will be unique to you alone.

The mistake we make is letting others paint on our canvas.

Your life is your life.

We often let others dictate how we live our lives. We let others dictate the type of work we
do, where we live, what we believe, and we become secondary players in our own lives.

Listening to others is wise. Reading and studying is mandatory in life, appealing to a
higher power works for many who find direction and peace there.

But all of this comes down to the absolute fact that if you, and you alone, don't make
decisions that set the path of your life, you can never find true happiness.

There will be countless resolutions made this year, but there is only one that matters.

Never give up control of your life.

Your life is your gift and your canvas to paint, and only you should make the decisions
that govern who you will become, how you will live, and the work you will do.

THERE IS NO SUCH THING AS PERFECT...
AND THAT MEANS YOU

We all struggle.
We all work out and then stop.

We all fall off whatever wagon we're riding that week to stay good,
and often just don't fall off, but the horse backs up and poops on us too.

Seeking perfect is seeking failure.

We have too many adults, and now too many kids, expecting perfect from themselves.
Nothing messes a life up more than trying to be perfect.

You will have days when the pants are too tight.
You will have bad hair, bad breath, funny clothes days, and food stuck in your teeth.
And it doesn't matter a damn bit.

You will even have days when it seems the entire universe hates you,
but that is usually just you trying to be something you were never meant to be.

Stop thinking of life as an absolute, either A or B,
and that you are either perfect or not perfect.

Start thinking of life as a long continuum between A and Z, where A is not perfect.
There are all kinds of stops along the way toward perfect, which can't ever be reached.

Your goal is to understand life as a sliding scale. One day you might make it to Q and
feel pretty damn good, and then you wake up the next day a G and have to start working
toward the right yet again.

You didn't fail that day.
You just realized for a brief moment that you might be human after all...
nowhere near perfect.

Be kind to yourself.
Understanding you are not perfect is the day you set yourself free to find the perfect life.

THERE WILL BE THE DAY WHEN I CAN'T

It will be my last day at the gym, my last kiss, my last hug from someone I love.

The day will come when I can't do any of the things I most cherish in life.

But not today.

Today, what drives me isn't because I can; it is the fear that someday I can't.

I can accept being a lesser version of myself through the years, but there will be a point when I just can't at all. That day is coming for all of us.

Today, I want to linger a little longer with friends. I want to savor a kiss a few more seconds. I want to sit quietly and watch the sunset and listen to kids laugh and play.

Today, I want it all, because today might be all I have.

Today I will, because I can, motivated by the shadow that the someday I can't.

But not today.

Today is mine, and all the good things in life are possible because I can.

THINGS THAT SET YOU APART IN LIFE

Staying later after everyone else left the gym and making one more client call. Winners do the work others ignore.

Getting up an hour early to read quietly without your phone in hand. You work to build a more muscular butt, why not try to improve your head too?

Learning to become a competent speaker, able to talk for an hour and not bore people into doing drugs. "Well-spoken" is just another way of saying, "I want to give that guy money."

Mastering decent table manners. The older you get, the sadder it is when you cut that steak holding your knife like you are trying to stab a chicken to death—and no one, on any continent, ever leaves the napkin on top of their finished plate when they are done. Heathen!

Developing a style in clothes that is professional, but still all you. The best-dressed person in the room, even if you are a sweat dog coach, is perceived as more professional. Coaching pants beat baggy shorts every single time for professional image, although a man just has to love yoga pants, but I have issues, so ignore that comment.

Learning to ask questions. You will meet people you respect. What do you want to learn from each one of them? Learning to ask real questions that will help your life is an art form. Ask anything except another exercise question.

The ability to get things done is a lost art. There are a lot of talented people, but the ability to get things done, on time and done correctly, makes you a rare gem worth much money running or working in any business.

Being gracious. Being grateful, thankful, respectful, and courteous all combine to set you apart from the rude, the arrogant, and the pretenders. How you treat the kid at the coffee shop when no one is looking defines who you are as a person, and what is in your soul. Respect everyone, but be intimidated by no one.

Building a career is the accumulation of a hundred little things done correctly that defines your professionalism. Setting yourself apart from the thousands of people fighting to succeed is the goal of being a professional. Every detail counts.

"Better" is how we work, but "different" is how we are remembered, and how we differentiate ourselves from the pretenders.

TWENTY REASONS YOU ARE A BROKE TRAINER

You were 10 minutes late again for a session, using the traffic excuse one more time.

You do an entire session holding your phone and checking messages.

You lowered your price, thinking you would steal everyone else's clients. Wrong again, and proving one more time that you can't be the cheapest and the best at the same time.

You have every client, every time, doing the same workout.

"I didn't get my personal workout today, how about you just doing my workout with me?"

Nice outfit. Try something a little less wrinkled, and maybe show some respect for the clients who pay you money.

"Yeah, I did hear about her (your other client) and she is a bitch."
Lack of class and poverty usually go together.

"Me? Give my clients a 'thank you' and a present?"
I would never even consider saying thank you to the people who make my life possible.

"You really need to buy this vitamin line from me. It is exactly what you need."

You have signed up for another MLM scam and are sharing it with the clients yet again.

"Can I talk to you about my personal life?"
Every client likes to listen to your latest breakup.

"Yes, I am an employee, but why should I respect this gym?
I train these clients and they are mine."

Oh mighty cup of coffee, my personal savior of mornings,
I will hold you with both hands and worship you for the first three client hours.

"I am a little short of cash this month. Would you mind paying early?"

"What don't you understand? If you buy one session, it is $75 per hour, but if you buy five sessions, it's $40 per hour." What you are saying to the client is you are a $40 an hour, low-end trainer. Hey, if you buy 20 sessions you are even cheaper.

When was the last time you learned anything new? You think you know everything there is to know about training. You learned it at your first job and haven't learned a damn thing since.

Master trainer here. One-year experience and a one-day certification, and the ego to back it up.

"Well, Guru (insert any real guru or master coach here), I know it took you 20 years to learn that, and I realize you have five books in publication, but if I would have done it, I would have done it this way. No, I haven't tried it your way yet."

"Money? I don't believe in money. I am pure as daylight and only coach for the goodness of the universe. By the way, my kid is sick, can I borrow a lot of money to get by?"

"Fired? How can you fire your best trainer? All the members will quit if I am gone. Why yes, I did Facebook everyone to tell them I am working out at that other gym. You got a problem with me working out at another gym and inviting your members?"

You can't make this stuff up.

Being a poor trainer is a state of mind, an attitude, and self-destruction all rolled into one. You are paid exactly what the market thinks you are worth, and if you are under-paid, maybe it isn't them.

Maybe it is you.

BEING GRATEFUL FOR WHAT YOU HAVE

Being grateful for what you have and being aware of how you achieved it is often lost at the end of the year when we should be most grateful for being allowed to do what we love.

No one, no matter how big the ego, got to be anyone without a hand that reached out and helped at some point. Here are a few people you need to remember with something a little more touching than a text or Facebook post.

If you have clients who pay you and that pay allows you to do what you love, buy a bottle of wine, hand out Starbucks cards, or do something besides mumble as they leave the gym. You exist because they pay, and it is time to be grateful.

If you can't afford to give them all a gift, understand that all clients are not created equal. Give thanks to the top 20 clients who made your business a success, who show and pay without complaint, and who keep you alive each year.

If you work for someone and the job doesn't suck, say thank you for the opportunity with a small gift. You work because they pay you, and it is time to be grateful.

If you have a mentor who patiently opened a door for you and you are a better person because of that person, say thank you. You achieve because someone else believed in you, and now is the time to be grateful.

Don't forget the family. If someone sacrificed something in life to make yours better, you owe a debt that can never be repaid. You had a start because someone in your family gave time and energy to you, and it is time to be grateful.

The universe is a funny place; the more you give, the more you get back. There are a lot of people who owe a big debt because of the talent and gifts they have been given.

Acknowledge that debt this year,
and surprise the hell out of everyone by remembering who you are and where you came from.

SYDNEY HARBOR, AUSTRALIA
Sunset through a wondrous city

IF I ONLY HAD ONE DAY LEFT,
I WOULD BE A DIFFERENT MAN

IF I ONLY HAD ONE DAY LEFT,
I WOULD BE A DIFFERENT MAN

With just one day left, I could be the man I always dreamed of being, the one who lived life at a higher level and who lived, loved, and learned as hard as he could every single minute of that day.

Just one day gives me the time to be the perfect father, with no thought other than to spend those precious minutes with the perfect children...at least perfect that day.

Only one day left gives me plenty of time to call everyone and tell them the things I should have told them every day these very long years.

With just one day left, I can finally admit I was wrong and things don't always have to be my way.

Just one day, I can be the person my dog believes I am when she scampers around me at the park.

Just one day focuses me now. Slowing down life to one day makes me realize the person of my dreams is the one right next to me, and there isn't a better person on the planet to spend the day with.

I would have to move during my last of all days. Spending a life in motion means you go out in motion. Fitness is life and life is motion, and with only one day left, there might be nothing better than a walk in the woods, hills, or beach with the one you love.

All the crap I have gathered in the name of chasing someone else's idea of success doesn't seem too important now, but it is fun to sit and talk about the adventures and experiences I have had just living one perfect day after another.

Just one day made me the man I always wanted to be.

Just one day can make you the person you always dreamed of being.
Just one day.
Today can be that day.

Today is your perfect day, if only you are smart enough to realize that every day is your last day...or at least should be lived that way.

Just one day, and that day is perfect, because I know just how I am going to live it.

EVERYTHING EVERY WOMAN OVER 50 KNOWS

If you are a woman over 50, you grew up in the dark ages of fitness.
What you learned back in the day was wrong.
The books you read were wrong.

The cultural norms about women and fitness were wrong then and are still mostly wrong today.

Here are a few things that might be right for you...and remember, the workouts you do today determine the woman you will be in your later years.

The curves and definition you see in other women you respect are muscle, yet you believe lifting weights makes you too big, which is a lie. Your mama told you women do not lift weights and going to a gym is for men. How did that work out for that generation who mostly died young, were in nursing homes too early, and who hung on the back of shopping carts when they were only 40?

Muscle gives you the curves, the sexy look, keeps you upright and proud, and enables you to live life on your own terms way beyond those silly people using tiny pink weights.

Real women understand that strong women are beautiful women,
and every woman needs strength to be the best version of herself.

Diets do not work.
Diets never have worked.

If you have failed on a diet by losing weight and then gaining it all back,
you have personal proof diets do not work and never will.

The biggest lie in fitness from your era is the "eat less, move more" syndrome. Cutting calories doesn't work. That only leads to temporary weight loss that always comes back.

What works is healthy eating, strength training, and learning to move every day.

That you can walk it all away on a treadmill is also a lie. Women from back in the day believed walking on a treadmill every day will help lose weight. It does for about six weeks, and then you hit a plateau and the endlessly mindless rat stuck on a treadmill routine stops working.

This is the same problem for most class-style aerobics programs. You end up a skinny fat person because you forced off the weight, but did nothing to change your structure.

If you have one workout a week, lift weights.
If you have two workouts a week, lift weights twice.
Beyond those two sessions, find a way to move every day with a little intensity.

Slow cardio does not work for weight loss over time. Walking an hour a day makes you feel better, and the entire human race would benefit from that life choice, but strength training tops endless cardio any day of the week.

You also believe you can master fitness through a book or a video on social media, and that too is another lie from the Jane Fonda era.

You need a professional coach.
You get sick, you call a doctor.
You have tax issues, you find an accountant.
You have legal issues, you call an attorney.

But you are fat, feel bad, have no energy, and are miserable,
so you buy a book and try to figure it out on your own?

That is crazy talk. You need a professional coach, because this isn't just fitness.
This is you for the rest of your life, living a better life through movement and health.

If you are a woman of a certain age, question everything you know about getting in shape, because everything you believe might be preventing you from becoming the best version of who you can be.

THERE ARE SOME CLIENTS
YOU JUST CAN'T WORK WITH

Years ago, when visiting a client was part of the normal routine for our company, I spent some time with a client who lived in a small town. He had a lot going for him in life and with his business.

During an early morning run along some beautiful backcountry roads, he began to bitch about the town, the people in the town, how he hated small town life, and how badly he wanted out.

And he bitched.
And he bitched.
And he bitched...until I stopped him on the side of the road,
started poking him in the chest, screaming at him.

He was making a lot of money, the town supported him in so many ways, he had an attractive spouse who loved him, three healthy and happy kids, money in the bank, and a cute house on the edge of town.

He had it all, except nothing in his life made him happy.
And that was the day I swore to never work with that type of client again.

Many of you have everything, yet don't understand that being happy today
and enjoying what you have now doesn't mean you still can't strive to be better tomorrow.

Many of you are truly blessed but miserable
because you don't understand who you are and what you have in life.

Many of you have more than you will ever need,
yet still find the need to ruin your life looking somewhere else.

You can be rich in so many ways, yet so poor morally, ethically, and professionally.

Being successful is a state of mind, not a bank account. If you are unwilling to celebrate what you have, understand that what you have now is more than most will ever have.

Be grateful for what the world has given you.

CHARLOTTE, NORTH CAROLINA
Art, race cars, southern food, and workshops

THE HOURS IN THE GYM HAVE BEEN SOME OF THE BEST IN YOUR LIFE

THE EVOLUTION OF A TRAINER

Year One

A one-day wonder certification is like a learner's permit for driving, but you don't know that if you are first-year guy. You already think you are better than all those old coaches. You have been working out for years (about three in reality), know everything there is to know about coaching because you have spent 20 hours watching YouTube, and now you are a Trainer...Gym Trainer...with a license to kill.

Year Three

You are married to specific methodology. Your way is the only way. You are pure; the rest of us are flawed, and while you crap outside in a peasant squat, eat only food you prepare, go to bed at exactly 9:00 every night and have no sex because it might drain your "vital energy," yes, you might actually live longer than the rest of us, but who cares, because you won't have a single friend. You have irritated everyone in your life for so long that everyone avoids your craziness and you haven't been laid since your prom night 10 years ago.

Year 10

You now become the master trainer the first-year guy thought he was after three months. You have thousands of sessions done and recorded, have trained and mentored other coaches, and have mastered a variety of methodologies. Finally, you are able to say, "I don't know; I might have to refer you out."

Congratulations, you are now one of the best in the world.

Year 15

You are standing on a stage in front of 300 coaches, wondering if you were as ever as young and dumb as some of the faces staring at you. Then you remember you were, take a deep breath, sigh a little, and proceed to try to change a whole bunch of lives who secretly think they are better than you at everything.

Year 20

"Hey kid, just pick up those kettlebells and walk down to the end of the street and back for 30 minutes. When you get back, we will sit and have a scotch and talk about the rest of your life."

It seems the older we get, the more "simple" seems to work.

Finally, you become that old guy working out quietly in the corner of a real gym.

Your workout is your meditation.
The hours in the gym have been some of the best in your life.
Your gym friends are your only friends.

And still, sometimes sitting alone, you smile at the young clueless bastard you were back in the beginning and wonder how you survived such a long and perfect career.

DEAR THOM

You are ruining the coaching business because all you talk about is the money.
My clients will pay me just because I am the best trainer in town.
Training isn't about the money, it is about helping people.
I am un-liking your page.
You suck.

Dear New Trainer,

First of all, you still live with your mama, so your perception of money may not be all that good.

In the real world, people work very hard to gather skills and experience to build careers that matter. Once you become a master at what you do, you should not only charge a lot for what you do, but actually be proud you charge more than other coaches who aren't as good as you are.

Money is never important until you need it, and then it becomes the most important thing in your life. Turn 40 and a kid gets sick or you lose your job, then maybe your house and family too, and you will wish you had been smarter about money earlier in your life.

Money is a way we validate our careers and life's work, but not the only one.

New Trainer, you have my permission to charge what you are worth, take pride in your skills, and say no to clients who don't appreciate and aren't willing to pay for your time.

By the way, thank you for un-liking my page and you suck too.

DAYS LIKE THESE ARE SO VERY RARE

The days when you are strong enough to accept you, as you are.

No guilt today because you are not perfect.

No stress today, because today you aren't carrying the burdens of people who take all you have and give nothing back.

No uneasiness in your soul, because today you said "no" to a 100 people who drain your life, expecting you to take care of them every day.

Days like these are so very rare.

Days when you got up early, before the kids to just sit, think, read, and write a little, but ended up just staring out the window sipping tea and enjoying who you are and how you got here.

Days when you made time to work out and accepted the fact every workout doesn't always have to test your limits. Maybe today you discovered that the real joy of working out is just the process of enjoying being healthy and alive.

Days like these are so very rare.

When your "not quite perfect" kids are perfect. You realized today you love them for not being perfect.

When the person of your dreams called for no other reason than to say hello and that you are loved.

And when you realize you are a beautiful, unique creation, and even with your flaws, weirdness, imperfections, and the 100 failures every human encounters in a life of growth, who you are is enough to change the world and leave it a little bit better because you were here.

These days shouldn't be so rare.

There will never be peace in your life until you accept who you are and accept that there is no perfect in life, but there is wonderfully messed up and that is enough for a life well lived.

FIVE THINGS
THAT DRIVE PROFESSIONAL COACHES OUT OF THEIR OVER-CAFFEINATED MINDS

Oh, the things we want to say on bad days living the coaching life.

Number One—You are not a vegetarian. You are a crazy person who eats nothing but bread and pasta. Eat the damn eggs and put down the fat-free, gluten-free, taste-free special muffin sold by calorie fairies at the mall.

And no, you aren't big boned; you are carb-loaded almost beyond repair.

Number Two—You complain about the cost of training at this gym, but you will spend thousands and thousands of dollars when you are sick to feel better, and you will spend $40 to get your toenails done, and you spend $50 on golf balls to hit into the lake.

You need a coach—you need help. I am a professional coach and I charge to save your life, even if you would rather have red toes than live 10 years longer and be able to pick up your grandchild. And the grandkid is fat too; take the damn grandkid for a walk.

Number Three—Pills do not cure everything. You are better off not taking those cheap supplements from The Walmart. In fact, you would be better off dumping all those brightly colored little bites of sugar on the floor once a day and then getting down on the floor and picking them up one at a time. That is more exercise than you have had in 10 years.

Eat real food and move, and only take supplements if your professional coach tells you it is a good idea. The Walmart is not a professional coaching organization. It sells cheap supplements for a big profit. Oh, my aching head.

Number Four—I know you drink too much wine. Your spouse knows you drink too much wine. Your friends know you drink too much wine. You were declared Customer of the Month at the neighborhood wine store.

When you claim one glass a night in your food log, I, and the entire world, know you are lying. Just write down, "One Big Ass Bottle per Day," and get over it.

Number Five—You have time to go to the gym. You had time to sit and watch TV and get fat. You had time to sit on your butt, scrolling through videos of funny pets all afternoon. You have time to stay up watching late-night television. You have time to watch the Kardashians prove there is no reason for them to exist.

Please stop telling me you don't have time.
And even your little dog is fat.
At least walk the damn dog.

This list could go on and on.

Some days, the pain just needs to be expressed.

Enjoy your quiet day this Sunday, because Monday it is back to Crazy City, home of the greatest coaches on earth. There's no need to write and tell me this isn't politically correct; I really don't care.

IF THE SITUATION DOESN'T DIRECTLY AFFECT ME

If the situation doesn't directly affect me, why do I care and why am I so upset?

If a guy doesn't agree with me, is he a bad person, or does he just have a different position?

If I changed how I looked at a situation, would the situation change?

Are my kids okay?
Is my significant other okay?
If yes, why in the world would I ever let anything make me mad?

If I asked for help, why am I so mad at the answer I was given?
Was I looking for validation, or really asking for help and guidance?

Am I really going to let something that happened years ago, something I can't touch or change, affect me today and control my future?

Am I really going to be mad at a kid for being a kid?

I made every decision in my life myself; how can I blame someone else for my failure?

I took the job; if I don't like it, I should leave and stopping complaining about it.

I had the chance to step up and improve my life, but didn't.
Should I really be jealous and hate the guy who did?

Am I so petty that I let insignificant things in life make me mad?

When did I make working so hard a bigger priority than my family?

Read this list often if you are having a bad day. There really isn't a reason to have a bad day except you probably made a choice to do so on your own.

THE MOST PEACEFUL DAY YOU WILL EVER HAVE

The most peaceful day you will ever have is the day you stop giving a damn what other people think of you, and start focusing on what you think of yourself.

People who spend every waking moment worrying about what others think of their work, their clothes, their lifestyle, or whom they sleep with are the "pleasers" in life, those who try to make everyone love them at the expense of their own happiness.

There are several big questions in life that any on-the-road-to-maturity wanna-be adult has to ask at some point or you will never arrive at that adult destination:

"Are you making yourself happy?"
"What do you think about yourself?"
"Do you respect yourself?"
"Have you created the values allowing you to live ethically and morally?"

In other words, are you happy being you?

We often get caught up trying to please others
because we never have the courage to look within and ponder if we like ourselves.

We fail at this vital introspection, because our standards for ourselves are often so high and so unrealistic that no one, including ourselves, can live up to them.

Accept you aren't perfect.
Accept you are a work in progress.
Accept you will have bad days and screw things up.

You can't help others until you come to peace with who you are and will be in the future.

I DON'T KNOW

I don't know who you were meant to be.
I only know you should be who you really are.

Over time, we build shields against the world, made up of bits and pieces of what everyone else expects of us.

We hide our talent, our dreams, and the potential of our lives because we carry this heavy shield, built by all those who believe they know better what we want and need than we do.

The best day of your life will be when you get up and be the naked you who is underneath that shield.

For once, be the person who doesn't give a damn if other people care whether you are a fitness nut in funny clothes, gay as a football cookie, want to move a 1,000 miles to take a job only you could love, are obsessed with coloring books, eat Paleo and butter and are happy about it, are 10 pounds overweight and don't give a damn what anyone thinks of your butt, would rather drink wine with a few friends than go to all the parties in the world, and literally for the first time, become the person who doesn't care if the world accepts your personal weirdness.

Just one day, it's all about you, without a thought of trying to make everyone else happy.

Hey, why not today?

I WANT IT ALL

I want to be the person my parents hoped I would be.

I want to be the person my kids think I am when I look into their eyes.

I want to be the person my dog thinks I am when she wants her head rubbed.

I want to be the friend everyone brags about because I am in their lives.

I want to be the person my spouse thought I was when we got married.

I want to be the person who does the right thing every day,
because doing the right thing is always the right thing.

I want to go to sleep at night knowing I did something today
that made the world around me a little better.

I want to be the person who inspires others to be better versions of themselves.

I don't want to be perfect, but I am totally happy being wonderful.

I want it all, and will settle for nothing less in my life.

IT ONLY TAKES ONE

Just one caring person can change someone's life.

Just one motivated coach can make an entire community a better place to live.

Just one hug can last a kid a lifetime.

One "thank you for the great service" can turn someone's miserable job into a good day.

A single phone call can let an old friend know you still remember.

A smile can change an unhappy day into a work of art for you and for those around you.

One kind "patience, my friend" can save a struggling client who can't find his way forward.

One small "thank you, good work today" can change a good employee into a great one.

One "I love you, honey," unexpected and for no reason, can heal a relationship.

It is just me, you say, what can I do by myself?
You have the strength of hundreds in your words.
You are enough, alone, to make the world a better place.

It just takes one.
It just takes you.

YEARS AGO

Years ago, I attended a trade show in San Francisco and was walking in the city's chilly, misty rain from the hotel to the venue and I was late.

Along the way, there was a 20-something woman sitting on the sidewalk, back against a building, gently crying with that vacant, drug-induced stare.

I hesitated, thought about helping her to a chair under an umbrella and buying her a sandwich and coffee, but I checked my watch, muttered to myself and walked on. I can now say that leaving her sitting in the rain has haunted me every single day of my life.

Most of us are blessed beyond comprehension, yet few of us take the time to notice the world around us. That day, five minutes and a few dollars might have made all the difference for one woman.

Take a step back now and then, look around, and realize you—who have everything good in life—can take five minutes and change the world.

It doesn't take a lot of money and it doesn't take a lot of time, but it does take thinking about who you are and the talent, abundance, and health we often take for granted but don't always share enough.

You don't have to take on the burden of changing the entire world; the small part where you live is more than enough.

THE 10 WORST IDEAS TO HIT THE FITNESS WORLD

Number One—The guy who invented Lycra, modeled it on a super model, and then sold it to a generation of Walmart women.

Number Two—The guy who first turned his ball cap backward and asked, "Man, how cool do I look?"

Number Three—Arnold, who changed how the world works out. We still can't get people to stop doing chest and biceps every Monday.

Number Four—$300 yoga outfits on women who can't spell it, let alone do it.

Number Five—The guy who first said, "No pain, no gain." I hope he is a bathroom attendant in hell for all eternity.

Number Six—Man, I hate Zumba.

Number Seven—Hot nude yoga. Strange visuals and worse smells.

Number Eight—The idea of six small meals a day. Eat too many carbs, starve, eat every hour because the carbs became instant sugar, and repeat the cycle until severely overweight.

Number Nine—The guy who first invented moderation. Moderation sucks. Drink good wine and just do more pushups.

Number Ten—Any trainer who forgets that fitness should be fun and part of everyone's life, and not a goal to be on television, held together by tape competing in an event only a small handful of human beings can or should ever attempt.

I probably should add ephedra workout drinks too, but I kind of liked those to get the day going. Smile often and change a few lives while you're living the dream.

THE WORLD IS A SIMPLE PLACE

Help others the best you can each day. Your job is to change lives. Plan to do this daily, forever until you die or are too old to wobble to the gym. If you are already wobbly, just keep going; they can't bury you if you are still moving. It is the law.

Give someone who deserves it help, without expecting anything in return. No one saw you slip that fiver in the homeless guy's pocket, or did they? Don't mess with Karma—he will burn down your house if you aren't careful.

Hug your family a lot longer than you think they need because they need a little love a lot longer than you usually hug. It is okay to hold hands with the one you love in public. Get over your silly selves, macho people.

Call a person you love and make someone's day. Call, not text, you moron.

Make a little money and save most of it, so you can have a life now and a lot of life later too.

You should be a fully functioning adult at this stage of your life. Does anyone need to tell you to spend less than you make and put the credit cards away?

Sit quietly, and read.
Sit quietly, and think about who you are, and want to be in life.
Sit quietly, and just be grateful for all you have, even if you don't have a lot yet.
Sit quietly daily; you will figure out what to do.

Respect every human the same.

Respect them all, but be intimidated by no one because there is no one better than you, no matter how much money or fame they might have today. You are as good as anyone, but no better.

These are wise words to remember when you pull your superior human being trick with someone trying to help you in a business.

Change the world around you for the better today.

Do not be the petty mean ass the world can live without. Is your life so pathetic that someone cutting you off in traffic or making you wait an extra five minutes for coffee can really ruin your day?

Are you okay and safe? Is your family okay and safe?

Then laugh through the rest of it.
If you and the family are safe, nothing else really matters.

Life really is simple. We only make it hard because we believe complicated is better.

The longer we live, we come back full circle and understand a simple life is a perfect life.

THE UNWRITTEN RULES OF FITNESS

No one ever gets in shape believing they can eat all they want, drink all they want, sleep four hours and then go to the gym for an hour to save their souls.

A 25-year-old man left to his own devices without a coach will bench press and do sort of a squat thing followed by curls three days a week until something breaks.

If you are wearing it, you ate it.

Purists die alone in a dark room without friends because they irritated everyone in their lives and drove them away, and then lived to be a 100.
Maybe better to die a little earlier with a few friends and a last beer.

There is an inverse relationship to the number of selfies you post on your business site and the health of the business. The more of you, the fewer clients you will have.

You squatting with your butt to the camera doesn't inspire people to join your gym, but it might make a lot of stalkers happy.

Every coach who wants to be considered a master trainer should have advanced education in nutrition and behavioral modification. You can't fix the client if you can't fix the food, and only the worst of the worst of all coaches believe there is one diet for every client.

The best coaches in the world will say, "I don't know. I need to think about this. Can I get back to you tomorrow?" Young coaches quote their favorite line from their favorite guru and destroy the client.

Any coach who thinks your personal behavior, personal image, and the way you speak doesn't matter to a client, that the client just cares what you know, is an educated but financially poor coach.

Any young coach who arrogantly says, "Money doesn't matter to me. I think it is wrong to do this for the money," never had a sick child or tried to buy that first house. Money doesn't matter until you really need it, and then it is the most important thing.

Any coach who sells a client some MLM product trying to make a few quick bucks will find there is a special room waiting in Trainer Hell.

If you sell someone a mentorship, you better be damn good, because if you take someone's money, you better never, ever hurt the person by not being prepared to truly change that life.

Karma is a special thing.

It is amazing how many of these "I have the secret to success" guys disappear quickly and deservedly. Did the guy make money doing what he says, or does he make money teaching you things that never worked in his own business and he is now sharing his secret?

Finally, ethics and professionalism matter.

If you always do the right thing with your clients, do your best to get results, and concentrate on charging a fair price for what you know, you will win.

No one goes broke doing the right thing.

THE RULES OF CRAP

There are always those few in your business who insist on giving you crap every single day. Throw them out, fire them as clients or employees, and replace them with crap-free people who actually appreciate who you are and how you do things.

There are friends who always seem to have too much crap in their lives and want to give you some to carry. Carry for a while; help, but remember, many of them are only happy when you are burdened down by their crap. Carry briefly, help when you can, but always remember, taking care of your own crap is more important.

Accumulating too much crap can kill you. If you are drowning in payments for crap, realize you don't own the crap—the crap owns you. You can live with less crap; and owning expensive crap doesn't define you as a person.

Eat crap, you look like crap. Crap hanging over the top of your pants, flopping on your arms or swelling up some stressed-out pants...well, looks like crap.

Being in a crappy mood ruins your karma. The universe says, "This person likes to give everyone crap. He must like it, so we will pile up all the crap we can find on his doorstep."

Sharing your good crap is not the same as giving someone endless crap.

Finally, not giving a crap about anything is not a badge of honor; not caring is a statement of you as a worthless human being.

Pick the crap in your life carefully,
but when you pick, make it the best crap in the universe.

No, I have no idea where this crap came from.
It just popped into my head while I was staring at the computer.

GENERALISTS EAT LAST

Generalists are people who try to do everything well,
but in reality end up doing everything average at best.

Specialists are those who niche themselves in the market,
and who focus their education and training on working with groups that fascinate them.

If you are a women-only specialist, sports performance in golf, or maybe fitness after 50,
you know that people will drive past the average "I do everybody" trainer to work with one
who understands their needs and problems.

Find an area you are passionate about and then kill it by being the master of that niche.
When you focus your energy on mastering a specific segment, it doesn't take long to be
the expert.

Experts eat while generalists fade away.

Three years from today, you could be the best in the world in your chosen niche. If you
want to be the leader, the writer, the front-of-the-room presenter and expert, declare your
niche and go crazy mastering everything it takes to be that person.

THE FITNESS INDUSTRY HAS CHANGED

The fitness industry has changed for the positive more in the last few years than it has since the 1970s. We now know how to get results, train effectively, and gyms are no longer just nasty man caves for the badly dressed and overly muscular.

One of the biggest drivers of change not talked enough about online or in old-school magazines is the new generation of fitness women. In the past, women were all but banned from most weight rooms in commercial gyms, especially in the golden era of the bodybuilder.

Women then were told to go down the hall and dance, doing that aerobic thing, or if they lifted weights, the dumbbells were pink or chrome and two pounds. Most often these gyms had a women-only area tucked back in the corner where women could do their thing, but never really be part of the gym.

If a woman worked in a gym in those days, she was at the front counter, in childcare, was a sales woman in a short skirt, or was an aerobic queen. Female trainers, while they did exist and were as good as most of the guys back in the day, were rare and usually focused on their own clients and not often part of the bigger trainer evolution.

Today's fitness women are highly educated, in better shape than most '80s bodybuilders dreamed of, and are training equals in every sense of the word. The industry has changed during the last decade, with more women clients entering training gyms than ever before, and as usual, it has taken a bunch of dedicated, kick-ass women to get it done.

Welcome to the dance. I wish you had shown up earlier; we really need the help since guys left to doing things their way usually ends in ruin. Thank you for pushing for change. Hanging out with a bunch of sweaty guy trainers and sweaty guy clients has really been boring.

BREAKING THE HOURLY ADDICTION

Getting paid by the hour sounds so logical when you are a fitness professional. You show up to work, do your training, get paid for the time, and go home. If you work for someone else, this method of compensation makes sense because how you get paid is out of your control. If you work for yourself, however, getting paid by the hour is the least effective thing you can do to generate revenue for yourself and for your team.

The problem with hourly pay is that there are a bunch of negatives that kill this method. Here are just a few to think about:

- There will always be a monetary perceived per-house ceiling you can charge—either in your mind or in the client's.

- The client immediately finds an equivalent rate, comparing you to what he pays others in his life who provide an even-vaguely similar service.

- You can only work so many hours per week; therefore, you can only earn so much before you top out your income.

- Selling yourself by the hour always brings the discussion down to money instead of how you can help the client. Why is help in our world limited to one hour at a time? Why is fitness sold per hour and not per solution to a problem? For example, a client asks for weight loss and we turn around and sell an hour. The person asked for a solution to a long-term problem and we come back with an hourly fee.

Let's say a trainer can charge $100 per hour in her market. In the trainer's world, this amount is often a lot of money, especially since we currently believe the idea is to charge as much as you can per hour worked. This proves to be an ineffective way to charge anyone, which we will discuss. The trainer says, "I am going to push my rate up to $100 and go for it—the most I have ever charged anyone."

Since this is a lot of money to the trainer, her ability to ask for this money is weak. It takes a mature money person to stand in someone's face and ask for the most money you have ever earned. Most trainers, especially the younger ones, stumble here.

Trainers usually get into the field because they are internally driven people who love helping others. It is a strange comparison, but trainers are like the social workers of the fitness industry. Social workers are usually good people who dedicate their lives to helping others in need, often for extremely low pay. Many trainers love helping and training so much that they will help others for free if necessary. This intrinsic drive is admirable in a trainer, but it doesn't feed the kids or pay the rent.

The client, on the other hand, often has either direct or indirect knowledge of what trainers in your market get paid, and compares your rate to others. You should be the highest priced trainer in your area, but there are limits to how far you can push this concept. Money people who are your training clients understand better than you that the higher the rate someone charges, the higher perception of service and quality that goes with it. This thought is a direct contradiction for trainers, who often feel they have to continually make deals or charge the least in their market to get work. This is often the hardest lesson for any trainer in the business.

Where we fail, and where there is a serious disconnect, is that what we ask for doesn't usually match the circumstances of the sale. For example, your client wants to hire an attorney. The $50 per hour attorney usually matches the rate charged. Bad suit, small office, no assistant, poor location, and little experience are all signs of a $50 an hour attorney. On the other hand, the $250 hour attorney completely matches the rate, working in a big office, with assistants, is often part of a bigger firm with offices in the best part of town, and all the trappings, experience, and poise it takes to charge the highest rate in town.

Our trainer, however, is trying to charge the highest rate possible or the highest rate the market will bear, but is trying to sell it in the same context where all the other cheap guys live and work. Our hero wants the most money, but is dressed the same as and works alongside the low-priced guys who sell their services at the lowest price in the market, doesn't understand added value or building value for the client, and simply tries to charge a little more, but does nothing to support the context of being worth more. It isn't always what you know; it is how you deliver that knowledge that makes the money.

In the world of attorneys, the range between the lowest and the highest hourly can exist because the differentiation is so apparent. In our world, the gap between the high and low a client will accept is often much smaller, because there is often no perceived differences between the players. Your price is based on learning that perception of quality is the real separator in the client's head in most business transactions.

Another problem with charging by the hour is that the client compares your rate to other professionals, and we often fare badly in that comparison. If you charge $100 per hour, and the client's chiropractor only charges $65 per visit, you are now being compared to a medical professional. In the client's head, you are charging more than a medical professional on his team. We can survive this comparison, but our delivery system, which includes the support materials for the client, how we dress and act, where we train the client, the support services we offer along with our training—such as nutrition and all the other small details that make up our product along with the actual training—has to be more distinctive and offered at a much higher level than the other trainers we are competing against.

The need for having a life also works against you charging hourly for your services. Yes, you can work six days a week. Yes, you can work splits so you can be there in the morning and come back in the evening for those later clients. And yes, you can train clients for 40 or more hours per week. The question is, how long can you do this, and most importantly, how long can you do this well?

Your ability to maintain this level of training over a long period of time is limited. The average trainer lasts fewer than six years before burning out. Trying to maintain this type of schedule is the prime reason trainers fade away early.

There are several issues involved here. First, your ability to work past this hour limit will put a max on the money you can make. If you can only work 32 sessions per week, your money ceiling is 32 times your hourly rate, minus your cost of servicing that client. Trainers who want to make more money keep trying to gain more clients and work more hours, but realistically, at some point you will have to take a nap, eat, see your kids, visit your soon-to-be-ex spouse, or simply sit somewhere for a few hours with friends to decompress. Whether or not you admit it, there is a limit to the hours you can work, and therefore, the money you can make.

The second issue is that the more hours you train clients, the more ineffective you become. There will be those of you who read this who adamantly deny this and swear, probably at me, that every session you ever offer is the best you can do, and every client gets your best every time you're on the floor. The passion is appreciated, but sit quietly and ask yourself if that is indeed true. Are you really giving your best every session, every week, every month, year after year? Or are you giving it about 80 percent of what little energy and passion you have left after five years of split shifts, 2,000 meals out of plastic bowls, clients in foul moods, late nights with friends, and the fact that you haven't had five consecutive days off since summer vacation in grade school?

Training for a living, despite what your relatives and friends think, is extremely difficult with a full load of clients. Every client is there to take a little of your energy home with them that day; no trainer, no matter how good, is capable of sustaining that level of commitment year after year without rest, decent food, and a chance to stay fresh and excited.

The answer to all of this is to move from hourly to solution-based client sales. There are several ways to get this done.

First, you can switch from one-on-one training as your primary tool and start with small group training with up to four in a group. Your return per hour goes up, the clients get better results over time due to the group dynamic. Most importantly, you can work fewer hours each week and make more money. You also gain the advantage of shifting the focus away from you and to the group, making your job easier and more sustainable over time.

The key to getting started is to switch from per-session charges to charging by the month with a 12-month commitment—or at least three months if you are nervous to try this.

For example, instead of charging $60 per session or 10 sessions for $500, which would be a typical charging system for a trainer in the one-on-one world, you could switch to $259 a month for 12 months for five visits per month. Or perhaps $359 a month for 12 months with unlimited access, defined as 12 sessions per month, including guided workouts for the off days, where you write the workouts, but the clients do them on their own on the off days.

You set times on a schedule and the client books the times. The client does not have to bring a friend or fill the slots; she simply goes to your scheduler and books as needed. The average client will train about 9.6 times per month, so you win by accumulating a large receivable base of client money owed to you. The client wins by being able to train as desired, in a group setting with motivated people alongside.

If you don't want to do it this way, you can sell a solution to a problem. For example, a client wants to lose weight and get healthier. It doesn't make sense for this client to buy a five-pack of sessions, and it is worse if you discount your services to sell more sessions at a lower rate.

Using the $50 rate from above based upon the session package, you could sell this client a three-month complete rebuilding program for only $549 per month for three months, which includes 8–12 sessions per month done in a group setting, full nutrition support and supplements, a workout journal, and a tee shirt. This is just a model—what you charge and what you add is up to you—but the key is that you make more money selling the client a solution to a problem rather than trying to sell sessions and packages.

The goal is to net 40% on everything you do, but the long-term move is to build a system where you get paid for what you know, not just the hours you are willing to work each week.

You're already doing the work; you just aren't getting paid enough for it.

LONDON
The London Eye along the Thames

STOP
THE DAMN ENDLESS
WHINING

STOP
THE ENDLESS WHINING AND COMPLAINING

Step back.
Be aware of what you have in life, and just say "thank you."

Your life is amazing. If you only took a few minutes to realize it each day.

You opened your eyes this morning, stretched, and realized you were still alive...your life is good. A lot of people who would have loved to have one more day didn't get it today, but you did.

And still we aren't grateful.

You had a chance to get your pathetic butt to a workout today, your life is good,
and yes, a few more of those workouts and life might be even better.

Your health is your greatest gift. What you often take for granted should be a one-day-at-a-time celebration of how perfect you have it in your life, because who you are now is not always who you will be, no matter what you believe about your own immortality.

You had food to eat today, and money to buy it if you didn't...that is a wonderful life half the world would trade a kid to have for just a day, but we complain about the food, the cost, or the inconvenience.

You eat regular meals; welcome to the gifted side of the universe.

You called a friend and someone answered ...someone even loves a person like you—how much better can it get?

You have friends, people who care, yet you often take your friends for granted and do not give back. Celebrate your friends by valuing them.

Your kids beg you to hang out for an hour...how cool is that in anyone's world?

Your kids still want you in their lives, but you sometimes do everything you can to not be there.

You went to work, changed a few lives, made a few bucks, and stopped for a beer with friends. This alone should make you the happiest person in the world, and one of the most grateful.

Your kids love you, the dog loves you, your significant other loves you...and yet many people in the world will still find a reason to be miserable.

You return home to a roof over your head and a place filled with your stuff and life...and yet you find a reason to be petty and mean instead of grateful and happy.

You walked by a homeless person today, one you can tell is hitting bottom. You look in your wallet, realize you have a little extra money that might make a huge difference to this person, and you share what wealth you have.

You changed someone's life...how unbelievably cool is that?

We often go through life unaware of how good we have it.
We assume our health will last forever, but it won't.

We assume we will always have everything we want and need, but someday we might not.
We take our friends, our family, and our work for granted, but these are all things denied to so many. These people will not always be there no matter how much we care.

You truly do have a wonderful life.

It is a shame you never stop to say thanks, be grateful,
or share the endless abundance you take for granted.

Life is good, and yours is better than most.

FORGIVE, FORGET, SMILE AND MOVE ON

Nothing wastes your life more than carrying anger.

Still pissed at your ex?
Hey, that old fantasy is now someone else's pain in the ass.
Rejoice in the quiet thought
that your formerly crazy person is now ruining another person's life.
Forgive, forget, and move on.

Mad at your parents?
What, you really believe you were the perfect child?
You really aren't going to call them ever again over money, over family, over politics?
Forgive, forget, and get moving.

Mad at friends who let you down?
Disappointed at friends you perhaps outgrew and they resented the new you?
Get new friends and forgive and forget.

There is no reason to lose your soul and waste your best days being bitter at the world
and everyone in it.

Forgive, forget, and move away from the toxic people.
You are too valuable to lose your life being angry.

Get up tomorrow, sit quietly, and forgive everyone, forget the nonsense that makes
you angry, smile to yourself—you have to let go and move on.

START THE NEW YEAR RIGHT FOR A CHANGE

Maybe the resolution thing isn't what you really need in life.
Maybe all you need is to forgive yourself.

You will make mistakes.
You will hurt someone.

You will go through a time where you can't mentally get past the damage you have
done to yourself, and maybe to someone else.

Forgive yourself.

You will make serious mistakes in your business and career.
You might get fired over a bad decision.
You might even fail in a business.
You might mess up a good relationship by making a bad choice.
That brief encounter could destroy a relationship meant for a lifetime.
You might pick the wrong career and have to start over.

Forgive yourself.

You might trust someone who fails you and get angry.
You might have offended someone years ago
and carry that pain like a ton of weight on your back.
You might commit, and find that it wasn't for you, and you need to run.

Forgive yourself.

There is no growth without experience,
and the only experience in life that can shape you is failure.

You will make mistakes...and those mistakes are what you did in the past,
but have no bearing on who you can be tomorrow.

Forgive yourself and get on with your life.

FIVE WEIRD RULES OF BUSINESS

Five weird rules of business you haven't learned yet, but should never forget:

Number One—Never provide anyone's first job. Let people learn to work on someone else's money. Do you really want to have to teach someone how to show up, how to dress, how to talk, or more importantly, how to put down the damn phone and do the job?

Let someone else take this beating.

Number Two—If you are hiring a manager, do a credit check. If he can't manage his money, why do you think he can handle yours? The worst employee you will ever have is the one who is always broke. You can never pay him enough to cover his out-of-control life, and he will always be mad you because you won't subsidize his quest to spend all his money and more.

Number Three—Hire diversity. The world doesn't need another training gym with seven white guys all 26 years old, who drink together, work out together, and chase the same women. Small business is about problem solving; different viewpoints add up to a lot more solutions than if everyone who works for you looks like a relative.

Number Four—Dream bigger. You usually build the business to fit the money you want to make in your head, and if your dreams are too small, your paycheck will stay too small. The single biggest mistake we make early in business is the failure to realize the true potential of what we own.

Number Five—If a potential employee says making money isn't that important or corrects you on a new idea because the business shouldn't be about the money, don't hire him or fire him now because you won't ever be able to change his mind.

In small business, it is about the money. That is how rents are paid, children are raised, and people eat. And that is where that young dumbass got his paycheck too.

Don't forget the classic rule: The more partners involved in your business, the more the lawyers will charge you to break it apart. You may need investors, but you seldom need partners in a training gym.

Remember, if you think you are above the rule,
the rule is probably exactly what you need to have hammered into your head.

CERTAIN PEOPLE BECOME DARK AND BITTER

These people appear to have it all, but still live every day angry, petulant, and often just plain mean to everyone around them.

You become that person the day you realize your dreams are over, but your life still has to go on.

You see this in older people who become a certain age and have by then given up on whatever dreams once nourished their souls. This behavior is almost expected from that crotchety old dude down the street, but losing your dreams and becoming bitter isn't restricted to age.

You can be 30 and a miserable human being when you stop believing you can reach new levels, achieve a better life, or create the magic you so badly need to motivate your mind to new levels.

Without dreams, you have no reason to get up.

Without dreaming, there is no reason to go to a job you can't stand because that job is endless without the belief there is more out there. Without dreams, you might still be alive, but you will remain angry at a world that gives no hope and a world you believe offers no chance to rise above who you are today.

Dream about what can be.

Take the chances in life, be willing to risk, to chase your dreams. And once you reach whatever you seek, dream again, and again, until the day you die and those dreams are replaced with a peace that rules your soul.

Without dreams to fill your mind, darkness and anger creeps in and you become the person the world most hates: someone bitter without a chance to ever become what they once dreamed of becoming.

Never ever let regret and anger at the world replace the dreams of a better you.

IF I AM EVER ARRESTED

If I am ever arrested, it will be for dropping a rant on some overweight, miserable person who just told me he doesn't have the time to work out because he is too busy.

Hey, listen to me:
You can move for an hour a day or you can be dead 20 years early...forever.

Being too busy didn't force that donut into your mouth.

Saying you are too busy is stating to the world your kids aren't worth the effort it would take to be able to do something besides sitting on your big butt watching TV. Take them to the park, take them hiking, take them skiing, but never take for granted the days you would have had with them if you had only been able to move.

Too busy means you can't bitch and complain because your spouse left you, since you are the one who gained 40 pounds in the five years you were married.

Movement is not an optional choice in life. It is life, and you are ending your life decades early because you are too busy or too lazy to save yourself.

And yes, too busy means you might not be able to watch four hours of worthless television every day, but hey, watching someone on television pretend to have a life is more important than actually having a vibrant life of your own.

Call the police.
Call cable news.

I just can't listen to the lame excuses people give me for dying early.
I am heading into Rant City.
Check your texts; I might need bail money.

YOU ARE A ROLE MODEL,
WHETHER YOU WANT TO BE OR NOT

When you choose leadership in the form of being a coach, a business owner, or a parent, you became the role model you never wanted to be.

As a role model, everything counts.

Coaches who are overweight or have bad health habits are always suspect.
Is it fair? Yes, because you chose to be the one out in front leading.

For every leader, there are thousands of people looking for guidance and structure. People want someone to emulate, follow, and believe in.

If you choose to be in front, you have to make better choices because that young staff member is imitating you, the client believes what you say, and the kids just want parents who never let them down.

If this is the truth in leadership, every detail counts, from how you dress, the words you choose, the habits you live by, and the values you embrace.

Leadership isn't for the weak.

Leadership is only for those willing to understand the world is watching and the world badly wants you to lead.

SAVANNAH, GEORGIA
One of the most historic and beautiful cities in America

IF YOU ARE STRONG IN SPIRIT,
YOU CAN TAKE ALMOST ANY
BEATING LIFE HANDS YOU

IF YOU ARE STRONG IN SPIRIT

If you are strong in spirit, you can take almost any beating life hands you. But if your core belief system is weak, you will struggle because you do not have a system to show you the way out when life gets tough.

Everyone, at some point in life, will feel like they are drowning and there is no way out.

This sense of being trapped happens to the peaceful people, the unusually happy, the successful, the failures, and all the rest of us.

In life, it is not *if* you become trapped, it is when.

There comes a day where you feel like life has wrapped you up, and you have no choice but to believe the situation will never end and there is nothing you can do to save yourself.

But you have a choice and you can find the strength to run.

We are usually trapped by another person, not by a situation.

We end up with a significant other who insists we have to live a different life.

We end up with spouses who use guilt to make us believe that leaving will end their lives.

We end up with business partners who refuse to do their share,
but who expect us to work alone to carry the business.

We are not trapped by the situation; we are held hostage by other people who deny us a life of our own in exchange for being trapped in their nightmares.

Ask yourself this: When is it my turn? When does it get to be about me?

When do I get to live my own life, make my own mistakes, and, fail or succeed, get up in the morning and make my own decisions?

Strong core belief is another way of saying you have to value your own life before you can consider carrying someone else.

There is nothing anyone should be able to hold over you that is worth your life.

No guilt, no loss of money, no walking away from a bad relationship, and no sense of entitlement should convince you someone else's nonsense is more valuable than living your own life on your own terms.

The strength to run comes from a core belief you are worth it, that your life is valuable, that you were put on earth to live the life you were given.

Yes, you may choose a life of serving others.

Yes, you may dedicate your life to helping others change their lives, but only if that is your choice, your decision, and your core belief.

And if not now, when?

FEELING SLIGHTLY OLD TODAY AND VERY JADED

There are some things in life that still amaze me.

That getting after it and getting sweaty still feels good.

That some people who have everything complain about life, and others with little celebrate being alive as if the world has given them everything.

That although the stories are tried (and maybe true),
a dinner with old friends is still perfect.

That there are some people you don't talk to for a long time and then there they are,
back in your life, and you pick up mid-sentence...
proving there are perfect friendships.

That being at home for an hour can make up for a week of bad traveling.

That there are fitness professionals so dedicated,
they forget it is okay to make money doing what they love.

That too many people do not understand that who they are
and who they will become is their fault.

I am also amazed that in a world flowing with millions of people,
it is sometimes so hard for someone to find a trusted person to talk to.

When you lose your ability to be amazed at the world, or worse, when you take your life for granted, you lose the appreciation of all the small things and experiences that define your life.

The small things are who you are, such as the smile of a child or a pint with a friend.

I guarantee that when you are old and tired, the small amazements of life will be your shelter against the storm.

IF ONLY

If only we could at least once in our lives tell a new client on his first day what we really think about his approach to fitness.

Yes, I realize you just got divorced.
No, you will not be in "get naked with a stranger" shape by Friday.
I am a coach, my friend, not a Norse God with super powers.

You were a member of that cheap gym for three years.
You gained 20 pounds during that time.
You paid $10 a month to gain weight.

We charge more here, but our goal is to go the other direction with that weight thing.

Yes sir, I am sure you were a high school athlete and a star.
You are now 45 years old.
How about we just work on you being able to glance down
and see what sex you are without a mirror?
Small goals, sir, let's start with small goals.

So you are 30 pounds overweight and only eat salads?
I was standing two people behind you at the donut shop getting my coffee this morning.
I didn't realize they made cream-filled salads with jelly on the top.

If I had five pennies for every person who kept an honest food journal,
I would have...well, nothing.

If one more woman says, "I don't want to lift weights; I don't want to get bulky,"
she is going to get a little pink weight stuck in her ear.

Ma'am, how about we lift those weights, and I will watch carefully and stop you one day before you transform from an overweight housewife who needs some muscle into a professional football player.

I will watch and promise to stop you in that sweet spot between the best shape of your life and a truck driver gone to hell. Please, just pick up the stinking kettlebell and swing, woman, swing.

You don't have time to work out?
What could possibly be more important than your life?

You know every contestant on *The Bachelor*, but can't find time to move every day?

Yes sir, I know the guy at that other gym gave you and your buddy a two-for-one deal with no membership fee and a tee shirt, but I don't do that here. Threatening to leave if I don't give you the deal just makes me want to watch you leave even more.

You see, we have these little things called professionalism and integrity.

And may I ask sir, when you went with the lowest bidder, how did that work out for you?

No deals, sir, not now, not ever.
Deals are for today, but integrity is for all the years I have to do business in this town.

And, sir, those running shorts from the 1980s are scaring my other clients every time you bench press. Might I suggest something a little more private?

IF MAKING A CHANGE IS HARD NOW

If making a change is hard now, how much harder will it be in 10 years?

Every single day you put off changing, the negative becomes more ingrained, and the possibility of success slips further away.

I see people in their 20s or 30s who are overweight, yet are not doing anything about it. Ten years from now, will change be easier or almost impossible in their minds? If you are in your 40s or 50s, how much harder will it be to change in your 60s or 70s?

Every day, you have the choice to make the decisions to move your life ahead, or you make the decision to put it off.

Yes, avoiding something is a decision…it is a decision to do nothing and change nothing.

If you are not happy, change now, because somewhere in the future, the "older" you will be more entrenched, more out of shape, less likely to take a chance, and carrying the baggage of years of avoiding the very things that would have made a difference.

Find the courage to change today. The older you will look back and thank you.

IF YOU ARE CONFUSED ABOUT YOUR FUTURE

If you are confused about your future, stop obsessing about what you want to do and start focusing intently on how you want to live your life.

If you want to live a life of meaning, start with lifestyle.

Are you the type of person who can work for others?

Are you the type of person who prefers to work alone, or do you need a team around you?

Is having a family early in life important,
or would you rather be the person who travels the world first, and settles down later?

We get trapped in life by letting our choice of work dictate how we live,
but it should be the other way around.

If you want a life of meaning, you have to discover how you want to live and then create or choose work that lets you live the life of your dreams.

How do you want to live your days?
Where do you want to live?
How much money does it take to be you?

Can you live simply yet happily,
or do you need more money and a bigger life to satisfy you?

All these questions have to be answered before you choose a career or work path. How you want to live your life is so much more important than the work you choose, and any work you pick has to enable you to live on your own terms.

Money has no purpose but to create freedom.

Living life on your own terms is the goal—find a way to finance that life.

That work has to provide meaning and fulfillment,
but only within the scope of allowing you to live free.

If you are currently stuck in work that provides income but little other satisfaction or fulfillment, start again by asking, "How do I want to live my life?"

Only you can answer this, and only you can choose the work to let it happen.

IF WE ACCEPT RESPONSIBILITY
FOR THE SITUATION

If we accept responsibility for the situation, the situation almost always gets better.
Denying responsibility or blaming others doesn't ever change anything.

No marriage was ever made whole by blaming the other person.
No child ever improved self-destructive behavior as a result of being blamed.
No bad business deal was ever healed in court by former partners blaming everyone
but themselves.

Accepting personal responsibility doesn't mean you let someone else win.
It means you are tired of a bad situation and are accepting the burden of making it better.

Too many people suffocate in bad situations that could immediately be improved by standing up and saying, "Enough—it doesn't matter who is wrong; it only matters that we fix it."

Want a better life with less drama and stress?

Start today by knowing that the mess in your life usually stops
when you stand up and own the responsibility for it.

Ask yourself this: Do I want this to go away, or do I want to waste my life blaming others for
situations that will kill us all unless one of us is strong enough to say "enough" and fix it?

In the end, it doesn't matter who is wrong or right; it only matters that your life is better.
Only you can make the pain go away.

YOU ARE BEING FORCED

You have no choice.
You have to give up one of these two choices today, forever.
Would you give up your stuff, or would you give up your memories?

The most outrageous new phone is old in a year, but the pictures of your baby playing on the bed are all that makes it worth keeping.

You have the latest, greatest new TV the size of a full wall, but there was that perfect dinner with friends where you laughed for three hours, spent too much on drinks, and still talk about three years later.

You took the love of your life on a trip, which cost you more than you wanted to pay, but you still pull up the pictures when you are alone just to put a smile on your face.

Stuff is stuff.

New stuff is flashy and you can't live without it and then, as all stuff does, it fades, breaks, and becomes so last year.

But the experiences of life—those moments that define your very soul—are what you should be chasing.

You have enough stuff.

You can never have enough adventures, good times with a loved one, enough time with your kids, or never, ever have enough pints with that special circle of friends who make you shake your head wondering how you ever found them.

Learn to live simply, do with less crap, and spend your hard-earned money chasing the stories that will remain with you until you die.

Come on, would you really give up every good memory for a bigger house or nicer car, or are those memories the essence of who you are and how you lived?

MELBOURNE, FLORIDA
Home is a wonderful place when you are home to enjoy it

SOMETIMES
THE WORST THING
THAT CAN HAPPEN TO YOU IS
THE VERY THING YOU NEED

SOMETIMES

Sometimes the worst thing that happens to you in life ends up being the very thing you need.

You go through a devastating breakup, ending a stressful relationship,
and a year later you are with someone new and are the happiest you have ever been.

You cling to a job but finally lose it, which gives you the courage to chase your passion and do what you always wanted to do.

You are sick and feel you will never survive, yet you come out the other side with a new perspective on all that life can be, and realize how much of your previous life you wasted.

Bad things happen to good people.
That is life.

Sometimes, when you feel what you are going through is the worst thing that could ever happen, just let go and embrace the fear.

Change will happen in your life, whether you want it to or not, and sometimes the very change you need only comes from the ultimate struggle to remain the same.

FIVE RULES FOR LIFE AFTER 50

Number One—Every single workout matters. Six days a week for life. Your body isn't forgiving at this age, and food and working out are what will save you.

Number Two—You will have fewer friends, but they will be better friends. You will most likely be less tolerant of bullshit at this age, and you will slowly find a tight group of people you love is better than a posse of idiots.

Number Three—When you are 50, you are who you are, not who you will be. The goal at this age is to become the best of who you are now. Stop worrying about trying to be someone you will never be but always pretended you would become.

Number Four—Spend less on stuff and more on experiences. That $5,000 watch or giant screen isn't the same as a weekend with someone you love. You will leave your kids enough crap they won't appreciate and will most likely throw into a dumpster 30 seconds after you are dead. Spend their inheritance living a beautiful life instead of accumulating stuff that collects dust along with your under-stimulated mind.

Number Five—There are a lot of things you thought you would get to in the future—things you will never achieve—and now that you are running out of time, you need to pick and choose what you do a lot more wisely.

Aging is a process.

The goal is not to try to regain a long-ago youth, but to realize who you are at this moment is who you will always be. Accept your current self, flaws and all, instead of wasting your life trying to be 30 again.

YOU ARE HERE WITH ME, BUT GONE

You are here with me, but your phone beeps and you are gone.
Who is more important than time for us together?

You lose sleep agonizing over decisions from the past no one can change.

Your willingness to live in the past is destroying our present. The continually looping video in your head is the ghost of a past we cannot touch, and that cannot touch us.

Maybe the things in the past are why we are together, and why we are strong.
Maybe the past is what makes us better today.

You stress about a future that never comes.

The more you worry, the worse the future appears, but why does the future never end up as badly as you anticipate? Is it because we make good decisions in the now, choices that keeps our future from being the disaster of your fears?

The kids want nothing from you but time. Not your phone, not your messaging, not your obsessive checking social media...just some attention and your hand for a few hours. What is more important on that phone than your kids, with you now and who need you now?

Out to dinner and you check the phone in the middle of hand holding and talking...Why did you even bring that phone to dinner? Isn't a relationship between two people nothing more than holding hands and talking about life?

Why would you ever let anyone in during the small time you have with the one you love?

You cannot touch the past, and the past cannot touch you. You should not stress about a future that will never happen; you can only work today to give it a direction. You cannot get back time with the ones you love; a day lost now can never be regained.

There is today.
It is all around you.
It is all you really have in life.

Show up today and live now, with the ones you love, and be present in your own life.

SOONER OR LATER,
ONE OF THE BIG FOUR WILL KICK YOUR ASS

Life is tough, especially in the fitness business,
and no one can hold it together for too long without blinking.

The Big Four are death, divorce, distress, and drugs.

You can't live for long without one of them affecting your life,
someone you care about, or your career.

It is how you handle these issues that defines your life and who you are. The people
with strong core values, such as personal strength, integrity, and the willingness to fight
back, always come through the other side.

You can't hide from any of these, and it is inevitable one will find you at some point.
These issues may set you back or damage you for a while, but none of them can change
who you are and what you believe, or take away your belief in yourself and what you
want from life.

THERE IS NO PERSON ON THE PLANET

There is no person on the planet who has not experienced fear in life...
but are we afraid of the wrong things?

You should be more afraid of not taking risks than terrified of the fear of failing. You never want to look back and tell yourself, "I could have been somebody, if I would have only tried."

You should not be afraid of death.
You should be afraid of death by mediocrity in the middle of your life.

You should never be afraid of mistakes. You should be afraid if you are not making a mistake every day, which proves you are simply human and not held hostage by such a need to be perfect that you do nothing.

You should never be intimidated by anyone who has money or power, but you should be terrified of jerks, cheap people, and the petty traits that are contagious. Those people should be avoided like a plague of fat, badly dressed, shorts-wearing, baseball-capped American tourists in central London.

You should never be afraid of your own dreams,
but you should be fearful of anyone who tries to take those dreams away from you.

You should never be afraid of children, but you should be terrified of a birthday party of four-year-olds. Vodka in adult sippy cups is the only way to overcome that fear.

You should never be fearful of your own talent. Talent is not a gift; talent is a burden that has to be faced and overcome. It is a harsh reality for many people to face living up to how good they can be in life.

You should never be afraid of love, but if love fails, you should be afraid of not trying again. People change and grow apart, but your ability to love does not diminish.

You should not be afraid of getting older...
but you should live in absolute terror of aging without fitness.

Aging is not a choice. How you age is your choice. Tremble in deep fear of the thought of having to hang on the back of a shopping cart at 50 because you are so out of shape you need the support.

You should not fear being different in life,
but you should be afraid of being hopelessly normal and boring.

Life is better out there on the edges, just past the line where craziness defines uniqueness. It is not whether you are crazy...it is whether you are crazy enough for life.

Fear is normal, but never live a day in fear of the wrong things.

Stop fighting what you can't change. Instead, embrace being afraid of life; this fear means you are alive and engaged in something worth struggling for...your own life.

STRATFORD-UPON-AVON, THE UK

What is a visit to England without visiting Shakespeare's home?

THERE IS NOTHING NOBLE
ABOUT BEING BROKE

THERE IS NOTHING NOBLE ABOUT BEING BROKE

No one believes you when you tell everyone you are broke because you are not in it for the money. You only appear jealous when you bad mouth others willing to make money in this business.

Here are some reasons so many coaches end up financially living one week at a time, get out of the business in just a few years, or worse, lose a business they dreamed about for years.

You refuse to charge what you are worth.

You don't understand money, so you charge too little.

Price is perception, and the highest priced trainers usually get the best clients and the most respect. You cannot be the cheapest and the best at the same time. Any money person knows the best always costs more than the worst.

You save nothing.
You have to save at least 20 percent of each check you get.
Blow the rest, but save the first 20 percent.

There will be a day when all you have is what you saved,
and that better be more than a few hundred dollars.

The hardest conversation you can ever have as a consultant is telling a 57-year-old coach who has just a few thousand dollars in the bank that he can't catch up financially no matter what he does, and will have to work until he dies.

You spend every movable hour doing one-on-one training, the least effective way in the industry to make money. Compound your hours by charging more and by mastering multiple-client training.

You don't understand the purpose of money.
Money exists for one reason: It allows you to live life on your own terms.

Money gives you the freedom to work where you want, never be held hostage by a bad job, live where you want, and take care of your family when someone is in trouble. Money is freedom and power against others trying to control you.

You think you can train forever so you will be able to make money forever.
Sometimes you can; often you can't.

For many, there will be a day when you can no longer coach or train the way you do now because physically you will reach a point where your body says "no more." Assuming you can work forever is a false assumption.

How much you save and the skills you have to move on are the only things that will save your future if you reach the point of "it is over."

The next time you hear someone say, "I am not in it for the money," you will know it is only poor people with no understanding of the freedom gained through money who say stupid shit like that.

IF YOU ARE GOING TO GO DOWN

If you are going to go down, at least go down fighting.

We make excuses in life so we don't have to try.

Many of us simply take failure rather than putting up a good fight. When you choose not to try or fight, you choose to live a lesser life, a life where you trade your own self-worth and personal value for the path of least resistance.

We are overweight and tell ourselves, "Why even bother? I just can't do it." We don't even try. We accept being miserable as something out of our control, when it is all in our hands. We will not win every day, but we can win if we don't quit on ourselves.

There is no perfect, but there is you getting up today
and at least be willing to go down hard and never quitting.

We make mistakes in our businesses and quit, not thinking about the thousands of others who have taken a beating and then learn and survive. Opening a business is a license for the universe to find new and unusually cruel ways to humble us, but sometimes we quit just a few yards from turning frustration into a success we chased for years.

We fall in love, fall apart, and walk away without one last try. We quit on our kids because they are having their own version of a tough life. We desert our friends when they need us more than ever, and we quit on ourselves, never understanding that quitting devalues our very souls and who we are in life.

You will fail in life. You will have dark days; you will be challenged to the point the cracks appear in your belief system of who you are and who you can be. That is when the world pushes hard to see who you really are and if you are tough enough to earn all the good things in life worth fighting for.

I may fail, but never without fighting until the last breath.
I may be humbled, but never without the last act of a defiant man.
I may lose, but not without understanding this loss will not define my life.
Knowing how I fight determines how I will live and feel about myself until I die.

At least try.
Get back in the game and fight.

Getting your backside kicked by the universe isn't the worst thing that will ever happen to you, but not trying just might be.

MAYBE IT'S NOT YOU

Maybe it's them, and they have been lying to you since you were a little kid.

Here are the lies in life simply explained:

No, you don't have to be like everyone else.

Being weird, out there on the edge, and a free thinker is what you should have been all along. The big question in life is not if you are weird; the question is, are you weird enough?

No, you're not too old to change. You can be 100 and if for one day you live your dream, you at least had that day.

No, you are not too young. If you are 20-something, and want to change the world and live your own life, get on with it and stop waiting for someone who has never done anything with life to give you permission to do something with yours.

Yes, you are beautiful, but your beauty is not revealed until you let yourself feel that way.

No, you never have to grow up and get a real job. If you love what you are doing, keep doing it; just change the support group who is trying to get you to change.

Yes, your favorite going-out shirt is ugly. They didn't lie to you about that.

No, trying and failing doesn't ruin you for life. Stop listening to people who have never failed because they never had the courage to try anything.

No, that dress doesn't make you look fat. It's the butt in the dress that isn't working for you.

No, the system, or those people, or that ex-wife, or that mean boss isn't why you are a mess.

You are a mess because you blame other people for the choices you make.

Taking responsibility for your own life may be the only truth that matters.

LIFE MADE SIMPLE

Hug someone who needs one today.
If not someone you know, any random person who might need a little of your strength will do.

Get up early and read for an hour. Your mind will appreciate it, your business will do better, and you will have a jump-start on life before the kids even see the light of a new day.

Schedule your workout at the same time every day, and then build your life around that slot. You will be a miserable bastard if you don't work out, so you might as well build a time that stays consistent for life.

Ask yourself four questions before you go to bed each night:

What did I do to change lives today?
What did I do to make money for the family and me?
Who do I need to email or text before I go to bed to say thank you for their help and support?
Did I learn anything from all I screwed up today that will help me in the future?

Keep a journal and write down the answers to these questions each and every day.

Remember who pays the bills and thank your clients every single day until you quit, or they do.

Turn off your fucking phone for at least an hour. Spend time with your family before they all leave you for being the self-centered, all-about-me, electronic geek you are becoming.

Remember that all around you, life will change every single day,
but who you are should never change.

Remember who you are, why you are strong, and what you believe, and then kick some butt when the times get tough. Tough times never last, but tough people are forever.

Admit what you don't know and ask. Doing it your own way until you fail proves nothing except you are an idiot who should have never been in business in the first place.

Hard work beats talent like Chuck Norris cleaning out the room in a bar fight.

Hang out with people who inspire you.
Hanging out with stupid people is only for entertainment purposes.

Never, ever go to The Walmart without your camera.

Some days it is okay to say, "No, not today. I don't want to play life or work out." Sometimes you just need to hide from the world, drink a pint, and let the soul heal. Do this more often than you expect.

Finally, if you didn't make a difference in someone's life today, you failed, and failure is unacceptable with the talent you have been given.

Five dollars to the guy on the street isn't even a good beer to you, and training kids for free is soul-changing for you...and them.

Change a life every day and you will change yours as well.

Smile. You have it all and never even knew it. It is good to be you.
You need to share all that coolness with a world that desperately needs your help.

YOU ARE NOT LIKE EVERYONE ELSE

You were born unique, and you will die unique.

Your uniqueness in life means you have no choice but to find your own path.

Because you are unique means you will never find happiness living someone else's dream. You were born with the spirit and intelligence to seek your own way and to create your own journey, living your dreams, chasing your goals, and living up to your unique talent.

We become trapped and lose our own essence of who we could be when we give up our lives to carry others. If you want to be all you can be in life, start with yourself. If you are not happy, why would you believe for a second you could ever help someone else be happy?

Want to spend your life serving others? Then start with yourself, because if you can't carry your own load, you will be worthless trying to get someone else to carry his.

There has never been anyone like you, and when you are gone, there will never be another like you. You are special in this world. Why not celebrate every day finding out how far in life you can take your unique self?

Sadly, most of the world resents anyone trying to live his own journey. There are people who spend their lives trying to force the rest of the world to be exactly like themselves, mirroring their beliefs, their values, and their lives. Then there is you—the one strong enough to realize there is no one in the world like you—and all that resentment against you finding your unique self just makes you stronger.

Being you is unique.

Celebrate you, quirks, insecurities, strengths, and all,
because the world is a better place when you are happily chasing your own dreams.

WE ALWAYS ENHANCE, WE NEVER DISCOUNT

The temptation for many professionals is to discount their service if the client buys more all at one time. For example, we often see prices like five sessions at $250 or 10 at $400.

Do not do this; it lowers your credibility and return per client.

Learn to enhance instead of dropping the price.
Once you set your price, the price becomes the price.

If someone wants to extend longer with you, add a few bonus sessions,
a training journal or tee shirt, or add supplements, but never come off the stated price.

Treat people as you would like to be treated by rewarding choices that make you money.
That client could have worked with anyone, but chose you; reward her for that gift.

Always add more than you are expected to give.
The old adage of "under-promise and over-deliver" still holds up today.

I signed up for training, but never expected this bag or book.
It doesn't have to be big, but it should be something the person doesn't expect.

Separate yourself from the herd by being the first in your neighborhood
to show appreciation for every session.

Reward the client, but never compromise your integrity by discounting your service.

EAST COAST OF FLORIDA
Let the big storm begin

TIME PASSES—
THE THINGS WE VALUE FADE

TIME PASSES

The things we value fade. Our dreams are now our reality, and we reach a point where there is no more pretending, no more posturing. There is only who we are today; we can no longer find the energy to keep pretending we are someone else.

Eventually in life, we become the truly naked self we are, unable to hide behind our "self-created" image of the perfect "me" we want everyone to see.

We become the people we created slowly through the years, and we reach a point when we can no longer hide our work, whether this personal creation turned out good or bad.

The sad thing is, this vision of ourselves we presented to others as perfect—because we believed this false reality was better than our flawed selves—is less desirable as a friend, spouse, or simply as a human compared to the real but slightly crazy person with flaws and with all the failings we share with every other human.

We spend years trying to get everyone to believe we are perfect, when in reality we are all a mess. If we admitted this to ourselves, we wouldn't waste so much of our lives pretending to be something we were never meant to be.

There are few people comfortable in their own skin. Many of us spend too much time hiding behind a version of the "me" we want the world to see, denying who we really are. This is a loss to your soul, because the real you is often the best you.

The world loves you much better flaws and all,
compared to a vision of perfection no one could ever achieve, or anyone would believe.

LIFE IS TOO SHORT FOR CHEAP BEER

Life is too short to drink cheap beer, or cheap wine…or cheap anything.

Life is too short to be angry.
Anger diminishes your soul.
Walk away, and enjoy the strength it took to do that.

It's way too short to believe you are better than anyone else. And not long enough life to hang out with idiots. Only hang with someone who inspires you.

Never waste a day doing anything you don't want to do, because that day may be your last day on earth. Your life—choose every day as if it was your last on earth because sooner or later it will be.

Life is way too short to not be in good shape.
Who wants to sit on the porch and watch life pass you by
because you were too lazy to chase a higher quality of living?

Life is too short to go to bed early and miss that late-night chat with your friends.
Who knows if you will ever have another chance to be with that group of idiots?

Life is too crazy not to tell everyone in your life you love them when you leave the house.
Some people come home; many don't.
It will be your turn someday, so why not expect it and spread the love?

Life is too short to never forgive.
Is anything really so important that you are so angry you will take that anger to the grave?
Really made your point there, didn't you?

Life is too short to work so hard to gather wealth you never enjoy, and that costs you the family you supposedly worked to take care of in life.

Live hard, love deeply, forgive everyone,
and always be the last guy out of the bar…because life is just too short.

FIVE REASONS YOU ARE STILL NOT IN SHAPE

Five reasons you are still not in shape, despite joining seven gyms and spending thousands on DVDs and sold-on-TV equipment that became a very expensive place to display your underwear in your bedroom:

Number One—You still haven't figured out that fitness is more like taxes or legal issues where you need professional help and guidance, and not something you learn from a magazine article. The hint here is to hire a professional coach like you would for every other situation in your life.

Number Two—You finally hire a coach but still don't listen because you think reading the latest workout book makes you smarter than a trained professional with thousands of hours of experience.

How is that working for you? Still fat? Listen to your coach, you gym dummy.

Number Three—Mentally, you are a mess and don't believe you deserve to be in shape so you self-destruct every chance you get...one miserable cookie at a time. The person you love the most in your life should be yourself.

Give yourself permission to be in shape, even though others in your life aren't. The day you believe you are a unique and valuable human being is the day your body will start changing toward the image you have in your head those last five minutes before you sleep.

Number Four—You eat like a bad-tempered, chubby four-year-old and blame your trainer. Your coach is there as a professional guide and to provide support. He is not David Copperfield, the famous magician who can figure out how to stuff 200 pounds of too much alcohol, too much sugar, and too much everything onto a 150-pound frame.

Number Five—Excuses are easier than sweating. We blame the culture, the fast food companies, the government, the schools, corn, our spouse, and our parents, but nothing changes until you look in the mirror and say loudly: I am who I am because of the choices I have made.

Nothing changes until you admit it is all you, and then everything in life is possible.

MOVEMENT IS THE BASIS FOR EVERYTHING GOOD AND WONDERFUL IN LIFE

Easy to hit a guy standing in front of you.
Hard to hit a guy running away from you.
Movement is essential.

You can't bury a guy who is still squirming; it is the law.
Movement is necessary for life.

Hard to fire a guy who moves faster than everyone else.
Movement is plain good business.

Can't walk on the beach at sunset holding hands with the one you love unless you can move.
Movement is romantic.

Can't run with your four-year-old and chase the ball unless you can move.
Movement is the essence of being a child...and playing like one as an adult.

Technically, you can have sex without movement,
but everyone knows if you aren't sweating, it isn't really sex.
Movement is sexy.

You can't turn 80 and jump out of a plane if you can't move.
Movement is for a long and beautiful life.

You can't walk out of the gym smiling at any age unless you work on movement every day.
Fitness is movement. Movement is life.

Everything in your life that matters is based on the ability to move.

Join a good gym, get a good coach, learn to move again, and walk an hour a day simply because you can. Someday there will be a day when you move no more...but not today.

Move for the simple pleasures of life.

MONDAY, YOU GONE AND DONE ME WRONG

You are the ex-wife of the days of the week.

You are the fat woman at The Walmart who just ran over my foot with her cart.

Monday, you are the cheap bastard at the bar who always manages to be in the bathroom when it is his turn to buy, but who only drinks the best beers.

I hate you, Monday. You are so obnoxious, you block my view of Friday,
the love of my life and the only day I believe I will never see another Monday.

Even children hate you, Monday. Another day, another ride on the school bus from hell. Children scream and hide under the bed just at the mention of, "Don't forget you have school Monday."

Monday, do you even realize the guilt you cause in life? Monday forces me to realize too much wine, too much crap food, and a dozen or so too many beers have a price, something I would never even give a damn about if Saturday was seven days a week.

And the guilt of work yet to be started, projects left from last week, and a four mile–long list of emails to be returned. Monday, if you had a face, I would punch it.

Monday, you are 50 shades of gray without the happy ending; you are the equivalent of four hours at a wedding without an open bar; you are the hangover that will not end.

I hate you, Monday; consider yourself banned from my life.
I hope to never see you again...until next Monday.

MODERATION SUCKS!

Obsessive people rule the world.

Interesting people are passionate about things to the point of being obsessive.

No one ever got into good shape and stayed there through moderation.

You get into shape by committing to a new life because you just couldn't stand to be one of so many who have failed at health and don't give a damn how they look.

Obsessiveness is just another word for "committed."

The best coaches are the ones who don't just understand what they do every day,
the best coaches are consumed by the need to know about everything in life and fitness.

Obsession is seldom about just one thing;
obsession is knowing a lot about everything that affects you.

One-dimensional is moderation; multi-dimensional is what makes a master coach.

We teach children moderation, when we really should be teaching them to follow their insanity no matter where it leads, because children are willing to try and fail. Modern, overly possessive parents can't stand to watch that happen.

Failure is part of obsession, but never part of moderation. Let the kid try and fail.

If anything is worth doing, it is worth overdoing. Do not do anything in life if it doesn't make you excited. Moderation means to try little new; obsessiveness means, "Damn, I just have to see how that feels."

Be interesting, be obsessive about what you feel is important, commit to mastering things that interest you, and remember to save moderation until you are wearing adult diapers, eating plain toast, and are too old to care.

MINDSET ISN'T JUST A BUZZWORD

Mindset isn't just a buzzword used by weak coaches in a gym or by a terrible boss to fake motivation. Mindset defines who you are and whether you will fail or succeed in everything you do in life, from business, to marriage, and kids.

One person looks at a busy day in business and complains to everyone in sight how hard he has to work and how unfair it is he is always slammed at this job. He rants and moans to anyone who will listen about how tired he is, how tough his life is, and that he can't stand the pressure of this job a day longer.

Another guy standing next to him (probably the boss or manager) will look at the same day and get excited and be grateful for all of this business. He realizes he has to pay the bills, take care of his team, and make all these clients happy...and he is downright giggly about business being so good.

One will be a loser in everything; one will be successful in everything he does.

The negative loser will endlessly complain about having to spend time with the kids after work. He will hate having to take his wife to the family dinner. He will be annoyed he has to be an equal in the house and has to participate in taking care of the place he considers his home.

This negative force in the universe will lose every job, lose every relationship, blame the world for his lack of success, and become more bitter over the years. He has a mindset, but it is set to, "I want it all, but I am willing to do nothing to get it, and why should I listen to you or learn, since I already know it all."

The other guy will have everything, including the ex-wife of the negative guy. He will become top dog in every job he has, probably own something that makes money, raise positive, productive kids, and will change the world.

His mindset is simple: "I may need help; I may need guidance, but I have the talent and brains to learn anything and I am willing to outwork anyone you might ever try hiring."

Mindset isn't a stupid saying on a tee shirt.
Mindset is a way of life and a personal choice you make every day.

You can embrace the light or die lonely in the dark, but it is all your choice.

WHEN YOU HAVE NOTHING TO WRITE ABOUT, YOU WRITE ABOUT NOTHING

There is the mental nothingness of sitting in your car after a good workout: wet, tired, and smiling like a four-year-old on Christmas morning.

Or doing nothing except watching a movie with the one you love on a Saturday night, and your favorite person in the world reaches out and holds your hand without even realizing it.

Sitting, touching, smiling, loving—just you two doing nothing,
but realizing there is nothing else you'd rather be doing.

And what better than doing nothing than doing nothing with friends? Nothing is more worthless, and maybe more satisfying, than a round of golf with friends who would rather do nothing together than doing nothing at all.

Or the simple nothingness of watching your child sit at the table coloring in a book, tongue out to the side in total concentration, singing to herself. A small, nothing moment to be lost in a busy life, yet that momentary vision might be the last thing in your mind before you die.

Never forget the power of a simple walk with no phone, no agenda, and not even pretending to call it a workout. Just walking slowly through the woods, or along the beach, thinking about nothing, and enjoying the nothingness of being totally absorbed by the quiet time you spend alone.

Don't forget the nothing repetition of a simple, "I love you," so often taken for granted, yet with the power to change an attitude for the day or a life forever. Those three words mean nothing to so many, yet are so desperately needed to be heard by so many others.

Nothing to write about today but nothing, and yet nothing may be a powerful force in life.

If you are going to do nothing, at least do it well, and with people you care about in life.

We begin with nothing; we end with nothing,
but in between, we have to grasp the wonderfulness of nothing.

Do nothing this week. Seek nothing in your life,
and you might become one of the rare few who realizes that nothing is everything.

THERE IS NO MAGIC

If you have anything in life or have achieved any success,
it is because you chose to do things a little differently than others around you.

There is no magic workshop.

There is no single magic approach to business that makes you wildly successful.

There is no secret motivational technique, no secret to business only revealed if you pay big bucks to get to the next room, no secret combination of words that drive clients your way as if by magic, and no high-priced mentorship that can guarantee that this time your success will be different.

The difference between someone who struggles and someone who makes a success out of most things in life is this: People who are successful are willing to do the things other people cannot or will not do.

Successful people, defined as the ability to live life on their terms without destroying everything around them, are willing to do the work less successful people refuse to do.

Successful people read a little more, work a little longer, ask better questions, make that extra call before going home, and, when it comes down to the core strength, push harder with an intensity others can't muster.

Success can be explained simply: Look at what the unsuccessful people do and do the opposite.

Successful people build teams in their businesses.
Unsuccessful people always think it is about them and no one can do it better.

Successful people study people who are successful and take the best from them for what they do in their own businesses and lives. Unsuccessful people insist their way is the only way and run what they own by ego.

Successful people have families that stay together,
because they work on their families as hard as they work on their businesses.

If what you are doing isn't working, change your behavior.

Repeating failure is not a lifestyle, it is the end of your life. There is no change, until you change

There is no success until you end the behavior working against you.

There is no magic and there is no luck.
There is only a winner willing to do the work a loser refuses to try.

THERE IS NO CHANGE WITHOUT PAIN

Change in your life only comes from self-awareness, and self-awareness never comes without realizing what you are doing isn't working. Change driven by failure is what makes successful people successful.

Change comes when you hit the bottom of life.
When there is no "lower" left, the only way up is change.
Or you can stay face down on the bottom.

Change will often only come when someone you trust points out the need for you to change. That conversation is what many need, yet so many avoid. In your face, "You are a mess, and if you don't change, you will have nothing left," is good advice if you are willing to hear it.

Change comes when there is fear.
The two biggest drivers are fear of loss and fear of death.

Many a weight-loss program has started with a doctor telling a person to change or never see the kids grow up. Even then, many people choose death over change because death is easier.

Ask a smoker.

It is a rare man or woman who can seek change before the world forces it.

Maybe 10 percent of the world is proactive and seeks change because they realize change in life is needed. Ninety percent of the world is reactive and just waits and reacts to the beating.

We refuse to change; we cling to bad behavior, which we know doesn't work, but at least this tried-and-true behavior is in our comfort zone. Even though this clinging to failure doesn't work for us, we persist because we do not know what we want in life.

There is no change without a map that gets us from an A that isn't working to B, our salvation out of the mess. There is no change if there is no goal to move toward.

If you don't like the situation you are in, change how you think about the situation.
Perception is everything.
Being locked into a failing mindset accomplishes nothing and will destroy your life.

Nothing in your life will change until you change it.
Nothing gets better unless you make it happen.

If you are unhappy doing what you are doing,
stop doing it and get on with doing something else.

As people age, their lives shrink,
except for that rare person who expands all horizons until the dying day.

Growth in life is possible until the day you die, and then you begin again.

Embrace change.
Seek change.

There is no life worth living without the constant evolution of you.

WE ALL LIVE BADLY AT TIMES

We all make mistakes we regret.

We will hurt people, and sometimes even by intention we make bad decisions that set us back in life.

But we get up and life goes on.

We have to decide then if we wish to continue living badly. Or we can decide we failed ourselves and those around us, but today, if we want, we can be better people once again and not let the darkness define us.

You will live badly now and then.

There are no perfect people, and those who scream the loudest about their own perfection and judge you the harshest are probably the furthest from being perfect themselves.

Living badly once in a while doesn't mean we are bad people; living badly and making the big mistakes in life just means we are human.

Accept the dark periods in life, understanding that those days when you fail will not matter through a long life well lived. We all have bad days and dark nights where we shatter our own values and challenge our own beliefs, but those lost moments should never prevent you from chasing the light.

YOUR JOB IS A PROMISE

When you work for someone else—when you bring your hard work and talent to someone's business in exchange for pay—you made a promise.

You pay me, and I will do whatever I can to make your business successful. Some employees, however, bring a different mindset to the job. They withhold their talent, always blaming the employer for some perceived slight. These endlessly worthless employees withhold their skills, working far below their talent level.

There are three lessons here.

It doesn't matter what the employer does. If you don't like the job or the person you are working for, walk away, but never, ever withhold your talent, because once you start down that path, you will forget what it takes to live up to your abilities.

If you don't use your talent and grow,
you will permanently lose whatever you had, and fail.

You made a contractual obligation. You took someone's money in exchange for bringing your best effort. Work your ass off every day, and if your current boss doesn't appreciate this effort, someone else will. But withholding your ability as a way to punish a boss is unacceptable.

Stand up, get the job done, or walk away if the pay or the promises fail.

You failed yourself.

You have been given talent, brains, and abilities. Your obligation for those gifts is to use them every day, not to go through life performing at a minimum level and faking life.

Never be anything but the gift you were meant to be.
Working your ass off is a way to define that talent each and every day.

YOUR LIFE

Your life always comes down to just one thing: Did you make a difference?

Did you change someone's life for the better?
When you leave this earth, did you leave the world a better place?

People just starting careers seldom think about this, hoping to get to the important work in life later. Living a life of meaning is not a project; it is a way of living.

There really is no degree of play here. You either live every day with the goal of making the world around you better, or you live every day internally worrying only about you and what you want.

You are in the business of change, but there is a huge difference between seeking physical change and being the person who goes the extra distance and creates better people.

You will not be remembered for the money you have, the house you live in or the car you drive.

You will be remembered for the lives you made better because you cared enough to make a difference.

Come Monday, start the week with only one thought:
The world will be a better place this week, because I will make it that way.

YOUR OBSESSION FOR PERFECT
CAN DESTROY WONDERFUL

Chasing perfect your entire life only leads to total failure,
since perfect is a state of being that can never be achieved.

Chasing something that doesn't exist can destroy a business, career, child, or relationship.
You are holding yourself and others to a false standard that can never be attained.

There simply is no perfect in life, but you can be wonderful.

Who you are—with all your flaws, your imperfect perfect shape, that tendency to drool a little after a few beers, your funny hair, and a bizarre outlook on life—can never be perfect, but the combination of those things can make a wonderful person the world needs.

Letting go of perfect is extremely hard for those who seek it. Admitting you are not perfect means you aren't perfect and never will be, no matter what level of obsession you possess.

Letting go of thinking there is a perfect lowers you down to the rest of us, who manage to get through life happy and fulfilled, knowing that even on our best days we can be a mess, but still be wonderful.

This is also why we have adults held together by brightly colored tape "working through the pain," who can't accept who they were in the past is never who they will be again.

There is no perfect workout or perfect body, but there can be wonderful days in the gym. It's a shame so few understand the difference.

When you believe in and seek perfect in yourself, you always expect it in others.

The date with the perfectly nice person
becomes a checklist nightmare of "If only she was...she would be perfect."

You will never find that person, because that person does not exist.

By the way, you aren't that person either.

There is no perfect on this planet, but there can be wonderful.
And that is more than enough to live a life worth living.

Accept the flaws in others, because those flaws are nothing more than a reflection of your own wonderful imperfection.

YOUR CHOICE TODAY

Miserable person the world hates,
or a person the world is drawn to because you are happy?

Working on being the greatest coach who ever lived,
or just working at a job collecting a check and adding to the miserable human category?

Patient and secure in who you are, or impatient, petty, and a jerk,
because you have to prove to the world you are somebody?

Living a healthy life and getting better every day,
or complaining about being fat and tired,
and blaming everyone else, including your mamma?

Made a difference in the world around you,
or lived the day as a taker who is in it for just you?

Spent an hour today improving your mind, or wasted an hour scrolling to find something useful on Facebook that didn't include a fail video?

Hugged your spouse, kids, and dog, and told them you love them all as you went out the door, or you are arrogant enough to think you will live forever and will get to it later?

Pissed off at stuff that happened years ago, stuff you can't change, stuff that was simply a mistake in life, or laugh at your past and realize you are strong enough to let it go and get on with your life?

Every day, you choose your life and who you want to be.

Want a better life?
Start making better choices, now, today, and get on with it.

You can choose to be a better human being,
or you can choose to live as a shadow of yourself
and waste everything you could have been.

Your choice today.

YOU WILL NEVER HAVE A DAY IN ANY BUSINESS WITHOUT PROBLEMS

The day you walk into your business and every client loves you, the staff is dressed and on time, there is money in the bank, everything is working, your competitor just closed, and your favorite cup of coffee is sitting hot and steaming on your desk is the day you have died.

You are not really in your business.
You are in business heaven, and God hasn't gotten around to breaking the news to you yet.

Problems are part of any business.
How you handle these problems is what separates you from everyone else.

The most naive thing you can ever say is, "Just one day without someone asking me to fix something would be nice." This will never, ever happen in any business, on any day you are open for business.

If you are good, you solve problems better than anyone. If you suck at what you do, you bitch and moan about stuff that happens every single day, and you make everyone around you miserable while you complain about the obvious.

If there were no problems, you wouldn't be needed.
Any drunken monkey in funny shorts can run a business that doesn't have any issues.

But we have issues every day, and that is why a business takes your talent and your effort.

Problems are good.
Problems give you a chance to show how good you really are
at the work you have chosen to do.

Shut up, quit bitching, stop complaining, and fix stuff.
That is why you are here...and not the monkey.

HOW MANY AIRPORT LOUNGES IN 40 YEARS?
How many small hotels?
How many lost days staring at a wine glass waiting, just waiting?

SIT QUIETLY
AND STARE INTO THE PAST

SIT QUIETLY AND STARE

Sit quietly and stare into the past long enough, and the things that haunt you will rise from the shadows and quickly destroy who are you are today.

The past is not who you are; the past is who you were.

The mistakes you made then have no bearing on what you choose to do today.

There is nothing that can change the past, but the past can ruin your today if you let it.

Carrying anger from the past will destroy you even more quickly.
Someone who hurt you in the past did not hurt you today.

If you want any type of future, you have to give up the failures of the past.

What you own, who you are today, and who you will be tomorrow,
are based on making decisions centered on what is in your life now.

The hardest thing for dwellers of the past to do is to take an inventory of what they have in their lives now. Who am I today and who do I want to be is a far more important exercise for the mind than being eternally angry at things no one in the world can change.

Don't waste time telling me how you got here. It might be an interesting story,
but it is bullshit from a past we can't change.

Spend all your time telling me what you are going to do Monday as the person you are today.

Stop destroying your future because you are unwilling to give up a past
that doesn't matter to anyone but the shadows.

DEAR MILLENNIAL PEOPLE

This letter is written by a future friend you will meet soon.

My name is Harsh Reality, and I live just down the street from Monster under the Bed.

I am writing to you now to save you the pain of meeting me in a dark alley someday. This letter will hurt your feelings, something you have yet experienced in your overly protected world. The goal here is to help you adapt to a future that will scare you like a vegan at a Paleo BBQ.

But you have time, you can learn, and you can be the first of your generation to accept the fact that maybe you aren't as special as your mother has been whispering to you since birth. Please, think of the following between energy drinks and trips to the beach paid for by Mama and Daddy.

Do not ever bring a parent to a job interview. You look childish and will be laughed at, especially if you are over 12 years old. And you will be laughed at in that office for years to come.

Do not bring your phone to the job interview.
Checking your messages while being interviewed will not get you that job.

Criticism is not punishment. When you take a job, you will make mistakes, and when you make mistakes, you will be corrected. You are not being picked on and you do not need to cry. This is how new employees learn.

You will not start at the top. You will have to work until you prove you have something your company needs, and then you might get to move up. No, just because you have a great degree and immense student debt does not make you qualified to be the new vice president.

And no, just because you need more money to live
does not mean I will give you more money to work.

Living in your mama's basement is not a sign of hipness; it means you are still a child and your mama has to take care of you. If you want to ever be an adult, go out and adult on your own without Mama washing your pretty little underwear.

Yes, there are great entry-level jobs at the big social media companies, but the people there get promoted just like they do in the real world. They accept responsibility, they work their butts off, they show up and do the work, they don't whine, and their mother doesn't do their laundry.

Amazingly, you have to show up on time to keep this job. You can't leave early just because it is Friday and your buds are at the bar, nor can you stare at your phone all day on my time. No, it isn't unfair if you are asked to put your phone away and do what you are paid to do. No, crying again doesn't work here either.

You are not special. Those 500 medals and ribbons you earned as a child are the signs of parents who refused to let a kid have a chance in the real world. Even though you didn't keep score, your team lost. You finished dead last; you do not deserve a participation ribbon.

If you are bad at something, you are bad.
Now go find something you can be good at and practice like the rest of us.

You are not special; you are merely a human with talent that needs to be developed so you can support yourself, build a career, raise a family, and do all of this somewhere besides Mama's basement.

You are not special; you are simply a new generation of people trying to solve the same old problems we all faced: how to find personal peace and happiness in a world where the only way to survive is to prove you deserve to each day by taking responsibility for your own life.

Happy life,
Harsh Reality and his best friend, Get a Life

MY HOLIDAY WISH FOR YOU

May you be at peace with yourself and your past.

May you never give a damn what other people think of you, for even a minute.

May you never waste a day of your life doing anything you don't love.

May you find quiet time that allows you to heal your soul.

May your body and mind always stay strong.

May you have a pint with your friends and laugh so hard you cry.

May you be blessed with children who won't be as hardheaded as you are.

May your parents look at each other and say, "I think the kid might turn out okay."

May you work until you are too old to care, just because you still love what you do.

May you stop on the street and help a fellow human being, because it is the right thing to do.

May you be dead and in heaven an hour before the devil knows you are gone, just in case.

Be at peace; you need to be strong to change the world in your own special way.

Remember, the world is a better place because you are in it. Helping other people become the best version of themselves they can be is a noble way to live your life.

WHY NOW?

"Why now?" is the single most powerful question
you can ask a potential client sitting in front of you.

You have fought your weight for years; you're miserable,
and yet you have avoided taking action no matter how bad you felt or looked.

So why now?

What is the motivator that finally forced you to take action?

This motivator is called "the trigger effect." It is important to know this trigger if you
want to get the potential client into your business, and to stay there past the first 30 days.

Triggers are things such as divorce, getting turned down for a promotion, class reunions,
and weddings, or a doctor saying, "Move or die."

This one thing—this trigger effect—is the only thing that forced the person to leave years
of inactivity and seek help.

Make sure you ask your next potential client this defining question.

If you don't know the answer to this driving force,
you really don't know anything about the client you are trying to help.

YOU WILL NEVER BE GOOD AT ANYTHING

You will never be good at anything unless you fall in love with it.

Doing work that doesn't inspire you will kill your soul.

Bad choices in work and career often leave people dead on the side of the road in their 40s.

The bad news is, they will still live another 30 years regretting the fear that held them back from chasing the one thing that could have defined life.

People tell me they don't know what it is they should do...but they really do know. Deep down in the dreams you share with no one is the very thing that would let you be happy, if only you gave yourself permission.

If you love what you do, any job is noble and worth your life. If you aren't happy doing what you do, no amount of money will ever make up for the misery you will endure the day you realize you wasted your life.

It doesn't matter what age you are when you realize this and take a chance.
One day lived well is worth a hundred years of just getting through the day.

Shame to waste something so valuable as your life...
and a shame to waste someone so valuable as you.

YOU TIRED OF FIGHTING
A LOSING BATTLE AT THE GYM?

Is this going to be the time to get it right?

Then work with a professional coach who can be your guide past the failures of the past.

The training client's code of responsibility:

I will find a coach I trust and stick to the plan we develop together.
I will not try to outthink a trained professional.

I will accept who I am now, and not try to be the person I was physically 20 years ago.

I understand no matter how many times a week I go to the gym, there is no magic workout that will overcome a lousy lifestyle. If I want big change, I have to make big changes—in not only how I approach fitness, but how I live too.

I will always remember there will be days when I don't feel like training.
The act of just showing up and getting it done is far superior to doing nothing at all.

Good coaches lead, but aren't magicians.
I still have to do the work if I want the change.
My fitness is my responsibility.

I will learn and understand that the ultimate goal of any fitness plan is quality of life. Looking good is nice, but living healthy and feeling great is everything in life and fitness.

I realize 99% of all the fitness crap on Facebook and YouTube may not be true. I will trust my coach and our plan instead of chasing the magic exercise or supplement of the week.

I will not lie to my coach about the amount of food I eat, the wine I drink, or what I ate Sunday watching the game. And no matter what I say, I realize my body can't lie. What I ate is what I wore into the gym today, so I might as well as write it all down.

My goal is to get to the point where I understand fitness is motion, and motion is life. The best day of my life is when I go for a long walk for the simple pleasure of moving.

I understand my coach is a professional, the same as everyone else who supports me in life, such as my doctor, accountant, or chiropractor. I understand the need to get paid decent money for putting up with my nonsense every week.

Finally, as a client, I swear to come in every day in a good mood, not be crabby, or be an arrogant jerk, because I have a nice car or a little money in my pocket.

I will be polite to the other clients, respect the gym and my coach, and most importantly, I swear to stop the whining and just do the work with a smile and a thank you for a good workout.

YOU STAY

You make one or two more calls after everyone else left before you go home from work.

You read one book a week when others are sleeping or staring at the idiot screen.

You get up 30 minutes earlier to get in a quick run through a sleeping neighborhood.

By doing any of this, you are doing what 90% of the world refuses to do.

Winners will always do what the rest of the world refuses to attempt.

Success is not usually one big score;
it is a series of a hundred small things most others refuse to do, done every day.

Your life changes today if you want it to.
Nothing in life will change unless you own the first step.
Life is about doing the work others can't or won't do.

Life is about the choices you make every day to reach up to the upper levels of who you are and the talents you possess.

Do the work others fail to attempt and you will win.

Choose you today.

STONEHENGE
Wiltshire, England

IF I TOLD YOU

IF I TOLD YOU

If I told you that in a few years you would end up in a wheelchair, would you finally admit that sitting on the couch all evening is killing you?

If I told you your looks and sexuality are fading decades earlier than they have to, would you stop telling me you can't afford a coach, and that how you live is aging you faster and harder than you want to admit?

If I told you that you will be dead by the time your daughter graduates from college, and you will never see your three grandkids, would you finally stop bragging about how eating bad food never hurt you?

If someone guesses your age at 15 years older than you are, would you then consider just walking for an hour a day and maybe getting some help through a real trainer?

If I told you that by the time you are 50, you will be on eight different medications and the quality of your life will diminish, would you finally admit your lifestyle is killing you?

If you start now you might change everything.

When you can't pick up your granddaughter because you are too fat, but you are only 45, would you admit that saying an insanely stupid thing such as, "I don't need a professional coach. I burn the same calories avoiding fitness as I would going to a gym," is going to cost you the best years of your life?

Have an older friend or relative dying in the hospital? Ask what they would give for health, for one more day in love with their person? For one more Christmas with the family? Would you then finally admit you can control most of how you age and the quality of life you have through fitness?

If you stopped lying to yourself, would you admit you lie in bed at night crying because of how you look and feel...and because you already know how you live and the choice you make to ignore fitness is killing you?

If I told you there is life through fitness, and you can live to be wonderfully active, alive, healthy, and sexy until your final years, would you listen to me? Or is a life of inactivity, no energy, overweight, miserable, and where you merely watch others live while you watch—is this your dream?

If I told you every day you make a choice to live or you make a choice to hurt yourself through a lifestyle where there is a lesser future and no outcome but a walker, a wheelchair, and no quality of life, would you finally realize that what you are doing is not working?

What if I told you...?

FAILURE SHOULDN'T BOTHER YOU

You tried, and for whatever reason, just didn't have what it took that day.

Regret will slowly kill you. You will never know if you were good enough if you never reach to see how far you can take your life.

You should spend your life seeking failure, because you need to know the limits of your talents and abilities. Many are gifted in life; few ever test the limits in their universe.

Regret is sitting at a bar 20 years from now, staring into a glass, telling yourself you could have been someone if you had only tried. It is better to fail at a level others never dream of attempting, rather than regret that you never tried at all.

Failure—and ultimately success—is part of the growth of a human.

Regret is an emotion of a small person unwilling to risk being wrong or not good enough.

You will fail, and it will make you stronger.
Regret rots the soul and makes you a lesser person through the years.
Choose to try and to hell with the outcome.

THERE WILL NEVER BE A DAY IN YOUR LIFE
WITHOUT PROBLEMS

The day you wake up, the world loves you, everyone is happy, and there isn't a problem to be solved, is the day you realize you are dead. Only dead people don't have problems.

For the rest of us, problems are just another day of living.

How you handle those problems is what defines you as a person. You can fight back, moan, complain, blame others, and hate life, or you can quietly deal with every issue life throws at you and go about your business.

The difference between successful people in life and business and the losers who rail against the universe is that winners recognize that problems are simply tests of skill separating the pretenders from those who will one day rule the world.

The person who handles problems better than the next one is more successful. This person gets more done and eases the burden of an employer, lessens the burden of owning a business, and gets through another day of life with less stress and drama.

If you want to be good in any business, understand you are paid to handle the daily grind of a thousand complaints, issues, and screw-ups. That is what you do, why you are paid, and how you keep your job.

Handle that mass of daily quirks quickly, quietly, and without childish drama, and you will make more money.

Scream, "Why me? Will this shit never end? I didn't sign up for this crap!" and it will end as you lose your job, replaced by the quiet woman who accepts problems as her daily task and just gets things done.

There will always be problems in life.
Learn to handle those better than anyone else and you will be more successful.

Scream defiance in the face of the universe and you will fade away, vaguely remembered as the angry guy who could never get anything done—you know, the one who used to work here but was fired.

WHY IT IS EASIER TO LIKE YOUR DOG MORE THAN YOUR KIDS

Your dog never invited five Axe-soaked teenagers to sit in your living room with the music on, the television on, and all of them scrolling on their phones.

Your dog never borrowed your car and brought it back with just enough gas to get half-way to the gas station...filled with fast food bags, and smelling like overly cologned, testosterone-dripping young men.

The dog thinks you are cool no matter what tee shirt you are wearing. Your daughter takes one look at your classic rock tee shirt, rolls her eyes, and sits in the back seat even though she is the only other person in the car.

Your dog turns 12; she is a trusted old friend. Your daughter turns 12 and you threaten to send her to a convent until she is 30.

Your dog walks happily on a leash. Your son, sober no less, is driving by himself and flips the car while trying to text—a one-car wreck at midnight that even made the police laugh.

You see the dog's smiling face looking up at you every time you come home.
You have seen nothing but the tops of the kid's heads since you gave them their first phones.

It's weird when the teenage son drools watching a movie and the dog doesn't.

Toss a ball to the dog and he brings it back. Toss a $20 to the kid and she runs like an Olympic sprinter toward the front door, not to be seen again until the $20 is gone.

The dog thinks you are the best parent ever.
The kids think any other parent but you is the best parent ever.

I love my kids, I really do. But I wish they could be more like the dog.

PERSPECTIVE IS EVERYTHING

Saw this homeless guy sitting on the street on one of my latest trips. He was a little older, skinny as he could be and still sit up, wearing clothes that had felt the street for too many months. He just kind of looked up as people walked by, too beaten to even ask for money.

I stopped in a sandwich shop and got him a sub, milk, cookies, and a lot of other calories he probably needed, and then sat down next to him on the street while he ate.

He didn't say much, but was happy for the food.

Even though I was in nice clothes, as soon as I sat down, I became invisible. Most of the people looked the opposite way as they passed us leaning against the wall. Many looked down as they passed, doing anything to avoid eye contact. A few even mumbled the city should do something about these people.

I don't know what it takes to beat you down to the point where you sit on the street and stare. I hope to never find out how bad it has to get in my life to reach that point. But I do know if you slip a dollar to someone in need or buy a small meal that cost you little, you change a person's luck that day, and maybe a life tomorrow.

You sometimes take for granted your personal power, but today, go out and do everything you can to change at least one person's life with a small gesture of kindness.

I hope you will never know what it takes to be that man or learn how badly life has to beat you to lose all hope. But you can know what it feels like to help someone through a simple act of kindness, something that might be a small gesture to you, but might be life-changing for a lonely man on the street.

WHAT YOU THINK

What you think the clients care about when it comes to coaching:

Am I, their coach, in the best shape in the gym?

Is the workout a creation of a mad genius that took two hours at a desk
and three hours online to write?

No one can coach as well as you do, Mr. Gym Owner.
You are a training god,
and no one in the world can replace you for even one workout.

It is all about what you know—
and you know it all, as you constantly remind every client.

What the clients really care about:

Will this idiot actually show up on time today
or leave me standing here for 15 minutes with some bullshit excuse about traffic?

What part of "keep it simple" do you not understand? I am tired and beaten from
my job, and I am a middle-aged person thrilled to just get here two times per week. I
don't need the world's most complicated workout to finish my day.

I pay you $400 a month, and you dress in a cheap tee shirt, baggy shorts, and look like
you just rolled out of a crowded bed. How about a little respect for the person who
pays your bills, dude?

There are three different coaches in this gym, and all three corrected me differently
on how to swing a damn kettlebell. Who owns this place, and why can't all these people get on the same page? No wonder this business doesn't make much money. The
owner can't even control the product.

There is no excuse for a gym to be this cluttered and this dirty.

Let's see, the average age of all the clients is about 48, and the average age of the coaches is about 22. No, there couldn't be any disconnect at all between the client and the coach. You either train us too hard because you are young and stupid, or you train us too soft because you think we are too old.

Either way, how about hiring some adults in this place?

Coaching is a lot more than the workout.

It is not the coaching that builds a great business. It is how the coaching is delivered over time that keeps members staying and paying. Focus more on the coaching experience, and a lot less on the mechanics.

PERSONAL VALUES AREN'T WHAT YOU SAY

Personal values aren't the words you say; values are how you live.

We tell the world we treat everyone equally, yet in real life we treat those different than us as lesser people, whether by the color of the skin, or the status in life.

We tell the world we value family, but we spend all our free time sitting with friends in a bar, or losing an entire day to a race that doesn't matter to anyone but you.

We tell everyone who will listen that every opinion counts, and everyone has a right to their own views, but then we distance ourselves from anyone who disagrees with us.

We tell our spouses we are in this together forever, then we cheat and the world sees who we really are.

We run a charity event at the gym because we can get good publicity, then we walk past a homeless person who could use a dollar, with our eyes down and in fear of making eye contact.

We tell our kids we have to stand up for what we believe, then the kids watch us practice situational ethics where we are not willing to stand up for anything unless it is convenient and won't upset anyone.

We tell people they are loved, yet we ignore them. We tell friends we will always be there, and then we run when things get too tough. We promise our kids our love, yet we spend hours scrolling on a phone while asking them to be quiet.

We say the right things, but often live by doing anything but what we say we will do, and by letting our core values fade from disuse and peer pressure to be one of the many.

Values aren't the slick words we use to impress our friends about how worldly we are.
Values are how the world sees us live every day.
True values are how we live and treat people when no one is looking.

We do the right thing, because we know it is the right thing.

PEOPLE GIVE ALL KIND OF EXCUSES

People give all kinds of excuses for not working out and taking care of their health.

Hey, I am too busy, but not too busy to get fat; don't have the time, although the average TV is on seven-and-half hours a day in America, and perhaps the biggest self-lie ever, the classic: I can't afford it.

Look down and see if you have feet. Some of you will have to adjust excess baggage to check if the feet are there or may need to ask a friend to look for you. If you have feet, you can walk. Money issue solved, so we know that at some basic level we could all do better.

The next level is asking yourself this: How much money would you pay to be healthy the day your doctor told you it is cancer? What would you pay that day to regain your health and lose the death sentence?

My stepfather died of lung cancer. He would have given all he had, and much of what he didn't own, to be healthy just one more time. The bargaining didn't work, and he died the very painful death all smokers usually die.

We tell ourselves we can't afford a good coach, we can't afford to be healthy, or we can't afford to eat well...until the doctor tells us all that neglect now has a price, and that price is an early death.

Do you really have to be told you are dying before you are willing to spend a little money for years of good health and a full and rich life?

WHY THE TRAINING GYM
IS THE FUTURE OF FITNESS

A training gym isn't about price; it's about the results you get from being there.

Community is more important than the amenities few care about in any gym.

Too few chains do anything to improve the quality of their coaches.

The fashionistas, the smelly, the obnoxious, the gropers, and the gym fools are weeded out quickly in training gyms, and then end up in the cheap chains where they belong.

Failure is built in the mainstream land of do-it-yourself fitness,
but success for every client is part of the business plan in a training gym.

The cheap client who will join and fail goes to the low-priced cheap-ass gyms,
and the client who pays more and then stays and pays longer seeks out a training gym.

Awareness of personal health and fitness is rising, and a smarter,
better-educated client will always seek out professionals.

The mainstream world is now all about how cheap they can sell, while the training gyms are about how they can change lives. These are two different business plans, based on two very different price assumptions.

You can open a beautiful training gym and do over a million a year, with a big net for the owner, for a tenth of what it costs to build a mainstream box that nets seven percent if they are lucky.

Great people, delivering constantly good service, will beat the hell out of a too-young, too-dumb staff who won't be there next week.

Clients will stay because you are there, in the training gym doing your magic every day and changing the world around you...one satisfied client at a time.

It is evolve or die time for the mainstream world because, like it or not, a training gym is the business that will dominate fitness for the next several decades.

INDIAN RIVER, FLORIDA
Sunsets that heal the soul

IF THERE WAS EVER A TIME

IF THERE WAS EVER A TIME

If there was ever a time to take the china out of the cupboard, it would be now.

There is always truth in old sayings. The old adage above was a comment on people who kept their good china in the cupboard, waiting for a day important enough to use their best plates. That day never came, and the china remained unused until they died and all those beautiful pieces were passed on to the kids who didn't see a value in keeping something no one ever used.

We valued something so much, we never used it.

You do this today and in your own life as well. You have nice clothes you don't wear, waiting for the big date. You have good wine in the cooler waiting for that special day to break it out, but there is never a day special enough. You have things you value so much in life you never use them—just waiting for that special day, which you never let come.

Today is that day.
Every day you are alive is special.
Every day you get up in the morning and aren't dead is a day worth celebrating.

You are sitting with family or friends around a fire or on the beach,
and you think there will be better days in your life than those?

Your kids made you Christmas presents
and you think there will be better days than that special morning?

Your special person whispers, "I love you," for absolutely no reason
and you believe there are better days ahead?

Stop being greedy and understand every day is perfect; every day is worth a celebration.

Why believe a wedding or big anniversary is more important than a perfect day with your kids playing on the beach, or more important than a perfect night with friends lingering over a good meal, happenings that define your life?

The next time you are surrounded by friends or family, take out the china, drink the good stuff, wear the nice clothes, and understand that today might be the best day of your life and worth a celebration like no other.

FITNESS SHOULD BE MOVEMENT, BECAUSE MOVEMENT IS LIFE

Why is it people lift more, finally train upright and holistic, and now can't move?

We are training an entire generation of people who appear to be in great shape, but can't tie their shoes or pick up their underwear off the floor.

Saw a guy in workout clothes at the coffee shop who was about 55. One shoulder had tape running down the arm under the tee shirt. He appeared to be in good physical shape for his age and had strong muscle tone, but when he sat down, he looked like an 85-year-old man reaching for his walker. He had to reach down with one hand and steady the chair as he slowly lowered his butt.

He is in many ways a representation of so many of our clients these days. We train a guy to lift, be strong and look good, but what good does this do if he can't touch his toes?

Natural movement is the soul of the universe.
We have forgotten that natural movement is the very essence of life.

What is next in the fitness world?

What's next is the restoration of natural movement patterns.

Ask yourself this: Are your clients in shape, or are they in shape and they can move too?

THERE IS NO PERFECT,
BUT THERE CAN BE WONDERFUL

We often create this vision of a perfect we expect in others
that no human being ever has a chance of living up to in life.

You will fail yourself at times; you will fail others, and you will not always be able to live up to your own standards, let alone those set by someone else. You are not perfect.

But you can achieve wonderful.

Wonderful is the state that exists between two people, where each understands the strengths and weaknesses in the other, and accepts that person as who he is, not who he might be if everything was perfect.

You can be a mess and still be wonderful if you are willing to be who you are
and accept another person under the same conditions.

We can live wonderful every day. You should expect no less than love, support, caring, and nurturing from your chosen person and from close friends.

But perfect is a level you can never achieve,
so why hold others to an impossibly high standard no human has ever reached?

You may not be perfect, my friend, but you are certainly wonderful in my life.

IF I COULD TEACH YOU ANYTHING

If I could teach you anything, it would be to dream bigger, to linger more with the one you love, to slow down, be present, and savor the specials moments in your life that may never come again.

I would teach you to hug the kids longer, to sit quietly by yourself and read more often, to walk alone for an hour with your own thoughts, and to hold a hand that needs attention only you can give.

Stay up late with friends and drink the extra glass; forget being a purist for a day and eat the damn dessert. Give yourself permission to enjoy who you are, never listening to anyone who tells you that you are anything but special.

I also wish you would remember that on the worst day of your life as a professional coach, you probably change more lives than most people do in a full lifetime.

If I could teach you anything, it would be to remember that you are unique, and the world is a better place because you are in it.

SUCCESS IS NOT ALWAYS ABOUT THE MONEY

Success is not always about the money. In fact, your definition of success might be the very thing in life that keeps you from achieving it.

Success should never be about a big car, the monster house so big and expensive you cannot afford to leave for a night out. Success is not about the other trappings of wealth we buy to make sure the world knows we made a little money and are not afraid to flaunt it, even though the credit card bill paying for all of those trappings has not yet arrived.

When you start your career, everyone you know or meet will try to decide what success should mean to you. You will have parents trying to get you to live in their past. You will have friends, often those who have achieved nothing and never will, working diligently to keep you from ever living up to your own talent, which would then put pressure on them to do something with their own lives. You will have a spouse who will try to make sure you live her dreams of success and not yours. Finally, there will be those people wishing to sell you the "secrets" of their success, although all they have accomplished is creating a company selling the secrets and nothing more.

True success is freedom, and that usually does not require a lot of money. Get up today and work a job you love, live where you want, respect the person you are with in life, pet the kids and hug the dog, or the other way around, and maybe your life is already perfect and you are a greater success than you ever dreamed.

We often overthink the concept of what success really means to us due to other people attempting to dictate what success should mean.

Success is freedom to live life on your own terms.

Success is the ability to control your destiny and never be held hostage by a paycheck or a job you hate but have to keep to stay alive.

Success is the willingness to chase what you want in life,
never being held accountable for someone else's dreams.

Success is having the ability to define your own life, living it the way you want because you have made enough money or created work allowing you to have freedom of choice in everything you do.

You will see success defined on social media or in old-school motivational books as the mad chase for wealth, the biggest cars, and the oversized mansions of someone else's dreams, held out as shiny carrots if you only buy the secrets and commit to the plans.

None of those even vaguely compare in importance
to having the ability to live your life on your terms day after day.

If you want to chase lasting success—not something that makes you feel good for 15 minutes and then fades—chase a job or career you love, someone you love, and figure out how to make a living doing exactly what you want when you want. Those do not require vast wealth.

If you let go and think for even a few minutes, you might realize you are already the most successful person you know if you define success on your terms and no one else's.

Quietly, deep down, you might have already arrived at what is good and perfect in life, which is the ability to define your own life as you want to live it.

EVERY DAY OF YOUR LIFE IS YOURS ALONE

You are who you are because that is who you choose to be.

If you don't like who you are, make different decisions that move you forward.

Never blame anyone else for your problems.
Blame changes nothing.
Personal responsibility changes everything.

If you don't like the situation, change how you think about it.
The same old mindset guarantees the same old failure.

Every single person on the planet will screw something up so badly they can't breathe for a month. Get over those mistakes.

Getting your butt kicked is an honor, bestowed upon you from the universe that is trying to get you to grow up. Take the hint, learn, and move on.

If you can't manage your own life, why do you think you can carry others?

We are all different people, but we are all the same. We live, we try, we fail now and then, and at the end we are who we are because we chose a path that led to what we became in life.

If the path sucks, get the hell off it and try again.
There are lots of paths; choose the next one more wisely.

You might have exceptional talent—everyone has something special in life. Talent, strength, or attitude might make you more successful than some, but remember that the guy with millions buying coffee from a kid working his way through life is not a better human being.

Give back.
You were born to change lives.

No matter how little you have, someone else could use a little help and maybe that is why you are here...to change the world around you.

The day you discover it isn't all about you is your first day of freedom. At that point you stop giving a damn what anyone else thinks of you and that is truly being free.

PROMISE LITTLE,
BUT DO EVERYTHING YOU PROMISE

Very few people you meet in life will live by those words. In fact, most people live completely opposite, promising to do everything and be everywhere, but never living up to their words.

Promising little, but doing everything you promise applies to simple commitments to friends, but also to a much higher level of trust between two human beings.

Friends will come and go through your life, but each friend you have should be treated with value until that person is no longer your friend.

Giving your word by promising you will do something should never be given lightly.

If you promise to help a friend move and you commit to be there, someone is counting on you, and you should honor that commitment. If a friend asks for a ride and you promise, that promise becomes something you have committed to with someone who is important in your life, and you must do what you said you will do.

If you can't keep a commitment but promise just to make someone happy, never give that commitment because you will break the trust.

Promise only what you are willing to do, but never more.

This small thought also applies to life at a higher level.

If you are married, this rule applies.
If you are preparing to promise to be there for someone by committing to be partners for life, never enter into that relationship without thinking about what you are truly promising.

Only promise what you know you can do.

Someday you will start a career and this rule represents the bond of trust between someone who hires you and what you bring to that job.

Any job is important because you have the privilege to work;
there are no small jobs in life.

If you are hired to do something, you are making a commitment to the person who hired you.

If the employer turns out to be horrible, and the job is not what you want, leave. But while you are there, keep your commitment by being the best you can be.

Live with respect for yourself, respect for your friends, and respect for those who give you an opportunity.

Never compromise your personal integrity by refusing to live up to your commitments.

SIGNS THE WORLD IS ENDING

Signs the world as we know it is ending in death by phone:

- Text fights where two people bloody each other by vicious thumb typing because each interpreted the words differently, rather than calling and working it out

- Two people sitting at dinner who never talk because they are face down on their phones. The harsh reality hits you when you realize you are not nearly as interesting as the one on the other end of your friend's constant need to text and ignore you

- People who ignore and even snap at their children because they can't bear the thought of turning off the phone for even an hour—how dare those kids interrupt their scrolling

- The mistaken belief instant communication is more effective than a well thought–out response 20 minutes later

- The feeling you are so important and necessary in life, you have loud conversations standing two feet away from 30 people in an airport

- The hollow feeling when you have dinner with someone and their phone is right at hand in case somebody more important than you might post on Facebook about a cute pot belly pig and a dog

- The blatant stupidity of a guy sitting on the toilet in an airport carrying on a work conversation, or worse, standing at a urinal with the phone pressed between his shoulder and ear—drop it...please drop it

Try to understand—try to regain the perspective—that the more time you spend on the phone, the less effective you become as a human being, let alone becoming the world's most boring friend ever.

No one, not even you, is so vital to the functioning of the world that you can't shut the phone down for a few hours and actually attempt to live again.

SOMETIMES, THE BEST THING TO DO IS TO DO NOTHING

Sometimes, the best thing to do is to do nothing but slow down and breathe.

We often put pressure on ourselves, as do our friends and family, to figure out our lives now, today, and to start living as an "adult."

Sometimes this works. But usually pressure to move forward, when your spirit is screaming "I am not ready," destroys your confidence and sets you down a path you had no business being on, and possibly a path where there is no return.

If you aren't sure about what you think you should be doing, don't do it.

If you are making a major decision in life to please others, stop and walk away.

If you are thinking about committing your life and soul
because the world says everyone needs to grow up, run away and never look back.

There is a time for everything in life, and sometimes that time isn't today. If you are mentally beaten up because of the pressure to make a decision your soul is yelling don't do, value your own life and soul over the appearance of making someone else happy.

There are guides in life, but there is no one who should tell you what to do but you, and only when you are ready to listen.

Sometimes, the best thing you can do is smile, walk away, and keep doing what you are doing until you, and only you, make the decision to change.

Until then, smile, breathe, and live...the world will let you know when you are ready.

WORK ETHIC IS AN OLD-SCHOOL LIE

The modern truth is, can you get things done?

We talk about outworking every other human. We talk about work ethic and a willingness to work yourself to death to get what you want. We talk about your unique ability to sleep four hours a night and work until you collapse, and then doing it all over again tomorrow.

To me, none of that matters.
I will bet every time on the person who can simply get things done.

It doesn't matter how many hours you put into a job. Working until you drop is a badge of honor from your grandfather's day. What does matter is what you get done in the hours you do work.

You want to brag?
Brag about your effectiveness under fire.
Brag about your ability to hire a good team that gets it done every day.
Brag about your ability to take a few days off, but still master a great business.

Stop telling the world you have to do all the work because no one can do it like you can. Others can do what you do, and often better.

The skill set you need to kick it in life is the ability to attract and manage others who can be effective in your business.

Hard work is hard work and nothing more, and is no indication of success.
The only thing that matters is effectiveness.

There are a lot of people working 70 hours a week in a gym who are still poor.

If there is a secret in this business, it is do what you promise, get the work done on time, and use your time efficiently and effectively day after day, and most importantly, learn that all work isn't created equal.

Be effective at choosing what will make you money and let go of the busy work that drains your life but matters little to your future.

Busy is busy, but effective is what determines long-term success in life.

WINNERS ARE WILLING TO DO
WHAT LOSERS REFUSE TO DO

The sentence that makes up the title was written in an old notebook of mine dating back years ago, but it has been a guiding principle in my life for most of my career.

This idea means to stay and make one more call, get up a little earlier than other people, help one more person before going home, and turn off that phone and read one more story to the kids at night.

Being successful is not a huge secret process that just happens one day. Being successful, both personally and financially, is nothing more than a series of small actions we do that lazy-ass, unsuccessful people refuse to do.

Any time I get tired and get lazy, I always remember this old saying and realize the difference between success in my life and failure in someone else's is just a willingness to suck it up, do a little extra work, and get it done.

Somewhere, someone wasn't willing to do the work it takes to be somebody and quit too soon.

It won't be you today;
promise yourself you will never let it happen in your life or career.

HARD WORK WILL BEAT TALENTED AND LAZY 90% OF THE TIME

Hardworking average guys make money.
Talented, lazy people make excuses and fail.

HWG gets it done today.
LG talks about getting it perfect tomorrow.

HWG stays until the job is done.
LG forgets he owns the place and goes home early to have a beer.

If times are tough, HWG works even harder and saves the business.
If times are tough, LG falls apart because he never learned to do enough work to save the business.

HWG leads from the front, doing the jobs that make the business money.
LG delegates everything and then blames his team
because they can't do the work he has never done.

HWG could make it in any business because he will outwork anyone in his way.
LG always believes he is smarter and could go out tomorrow and get any job he wants, which he always fails at because he still won't do the work.

The hardworking guy always finds a way and just gets better with age.
The lazy guy reaches a point, usually in his 40s, where he either changes or is doomed to be that guy forever, dreaming about the next big idea, but never amounting to anything because change might actually take work.

The world belongs to those select few who chose to get things done each day, even though they have to step over the lazy failures lying face down on the road who die broke, still believing they are smarter than anyone else.

WHILE YOU OVERTHINK, OTHERS DO

While you worry, others commit and go.

While you make excuses, the dedicated few take personal responsibility and change the world.

Achieving in life is as simple as moving forward.

The worst workout you ever had was still better than the guy who didn't do it at all.

The biggest failure you will ever have is far more life shaping than not trying.

Making a decision and going for it is most of what success is and even the simple act of trying sets you far ahead of the dreamers, the talkers, and the failures to launch.

Trying, failing, adjusting, learning, and trying again is what life is about.
Failure to try, to show up, to risk is what regret is about.

No one on a deathbed regrets trying even if what they attempted resulted in a global ass kicking.

Everyone, at any age, if honest to themselves and with enough alcohol for true confession, regrets not going for their dreams.

You didn't try and you will never know if you had what it takes.

Failure will shape you; failure to try will haunt your soul until you die...
and maybe beyond.

WHY?

You are piled on the couch on a Saturday with your child on your lap and your spouse cuddled close and you are going for "parent of the year," watching yet another stupid kid movie for the 12th time.

The kid is safe, insanely happy, and content.

The spouse is napping and just happy to be next to you.

Why do you have your phone in your hand?

Who in your life is more important than that child or the one you love most in life?

What is there that could possibly be happening in your life at that moment that would take precedence over a lovingly lost hour with your kid and spouse?

Why?

You are out to dinner with the love of your life.

Both of you are face down on your phones.

Who is more important than an hour together just talking with the one person you swore you would love forever?

We trade time with the ones we love to text people we barely know.

We lose precious moments that shape our lives to scroll on a phone, watching others often pretending to live their own lives.

We give up most everything important in life to stay connected to people we hardly know.

Why?

WHEN YOU FIND YOURSELF

When you find yourself trapped and overwhelmed by the burdens of others in your life, breathe deeply, and repeat this slowly over and over again: not my zoo, not my monkeys.

Come on, one more time: not my zoo, not my monkeys.

It is fun to visit the zoo and hang out at the monkey house. Some zoos even let you feed the monkeys. But at day's end, you go home, and the monkeys have to live their own monkey lives.

If you tried to take care of every monkey in your life who needs help, you would end up with your own zoo and little time for your life, family, and business.

No matter how much attention and help you are willing to give, this sacrifice on your part will never be enough for some people.

For too many people, the entire goal in life is to drain others of their lives.

Feed the occasional monkey, but never become trapped by their needs and wants.

If you take care of yourself, you can carry a lot of other people,
but just a few needy monkeys can drain your life away from you.

Smile, walk away, and say it again, "Not my zoo, not my monkeys."

WHEN YOU ARE IN YOUR TWENTIES

When you are in your 20s, you should explore the world, try on new jobs and relationships, and experience everything a vast and fascinating world has to offer.

When you are in your 30s, it's time to commit. You find work that becomes yours. You might find the person you want to spend time with in life. You find a peace that comes from understanding what you want to do with your life.

When you are in your 40s, you master your work. You become a master coach, lecturer, or confident person who changes mindsets. Your years spent doing the craft results in a mastery of what you know and how you do it.

When you are in your late 40s and 50s, you reap the rewards of all that work. Your skill set and mastery should translate to dollars, books, personal achievements, and a life built on the work you have done earlier.

In your late 50s and 60s, you give back. You help people on their way up, you share your wealth, you share your knowledge to help others, and most importantly, you find a peace from a career that meant something.

In your 70s, you change careers and start again.
No one dies anymore; you just find new and interesting work and keep going.

We often rush life and miss our 20s by being too serious, where we commit too young to a career or to a person forever. We never have a youth, a chance to explore life, a chance to experience what it means to be 20 and just beginning a long and wonderful journey.

Working for a living is not the same as committing to a meaningful career.

You might change careers, you might change jobs, but you should always think of life as a journey spread out over a long and productive life, not as a "live by the moment" mentality that leads to years lost and talent wasted.

Where are you on this path? Does your life reflect a journey of thought and planning, or is being you a day-by-day existence leading nowhere?

Your life—your journey—begins with self-awareness of where you are in time.

WHEN DID YOU BECOME SO ANGRY OVER POLITICS?

When did you become so angry over politics that you are willing to lose friends? Politicians are cheap and can be replaced; good friends are much harder to find.

When did you become so pure about what you do that you drive people away because they are tired of the lecture? So this purist approach to life gets you an extra 10 years. It won't be any fun living those extra 10, because you won't have a single friend left who cares about you.

When did you decide money is more important than your family? Working yourself to death will leave your kids a huge inheritance, but they will just blow it on wild women or chasing crazy men, trips to places you only dreamed of visiting, good wine, and enjoying every day of their lives. You should have done this with your own money. Why work yourself to death to give money to people who would rather have your time?

At what age did you realize that being right about something is far less important than getting it right? Why do you think your way is the only way? Would you really rather fail at what you are doing your way than ask for help and maybe save your business or relationship?

Idiot!

At what age did it finally dawn on you that you are doing nothing but living to make someone else's dream come true, and that you have never, ever lived a day following your own dreams?

You will find people who will manipulate you until you only do what they think you should be doing.

Run, boy, run! Run, girl, run!

When did you finally realize being perfect, living perfect, and trying to make everyone around you perfect is the least perfect way to live?

Let up on yourself, family, friends, and especially clients.

There is no perfect, but there are good days being the best you can be with the flaws, missed workouts, and a glass of wine that tasted good and miraculously didn't kill you instantly as expected.

When did you realize being broke is a choice in life...and a bad choice at that? Money isn't the problem; you and money together is the issue, but you can learn and you can change.

And when did you learn that people who scream they can't live without you can live without you if you stop carrying them on your back every day?

Take care of yourself first.
If that works, take care of your family.
If you can't carry your own butt, you can't carry anyone else's.

If that works, take on a few project people, but remember there are people who live to drain the life out of others. There is nothing you can give that will ever change them.

At what age did you stop arguing, listen if someone tries to help you, and graciously say thank you? Maybe there are people who can help you solve the problems of business and life, but that only works if you are willing to listen.

If not now, when?

When did you realize that if your life is a success, it is your own damn fault, but if your life is a mess, it is your own damn fault?

Your life, your responsibility.

Blame anyone or anything you want if it makes you feel better, but in the end, you are who you are because that's who you want to be.

Nothing in life changes until you do.

THE 17 IMMUTABLE LAWS OF MONEY AND COACHING

Number One—Never fail to charge what you are worth.

You cannot be the cheapest coach in town and expect to be perceived as the best.

Successful coaches learn to charge what their talent, education, and experience is worth to the client. Many new coaches believe charging less than their competitors gives them an edge in the market. These coaches believe if they charge less than other coaches, they will take everyone else's clients, because being viewed as cheaper and therefore a better deal is what the client is looking for in a coach.

This strategy fails every single time.

The client simply doesn't believe the cheapest of anything can be the best of anything. Our clients make their decisions to choose a coach on whether they believe the coach can get the results they desire. In this client's world, price is secondary, behind the anticipated ability to get the results they are paying for over time. Price is also a perception of quality and if you are a money person, which our clients usually are, the more you charge, the better you are valued by them as buyers.

If one trainer charges $50 per hour and the other $100, who is going to be the best trainer in the eyes of most of our clients? These clients believe the expensive trainer is usually the best trainer. The higher-priced coach, in their eyes, must have the experience and education to charge this amount and must also have enough clients to validate that others paid this amount.

One of the biggest mistakes coaches make is undercharging for what they do. Your price sets an expectation of quality; the cheapest is never the best.

Number Two—Never tie yourself to a single methodology.

Single-methodology coaches fail over time. Single-methodology people are like a carpenter who is really good using a special hammer and then believes the magic hammer is the only tool needed to build a house. This would be a great theory until you need a drill or saw, and then the one-tool wonder falls apart.

Single-methodology coaches suffer the same fate. People become married to a tool, such as a kettlebell, barbell, yoga mat, or suspension trainer, or go so far as to build an entire gym around a single-methodology system. Then they try to force every client into this single-tool approach. I am a hammer and you are going to be a nail whether you like it or not.

Master coaches move beyond tools and think more as an architect working with a master builder to create a beautiful house. The architect can design an expected outcome and the master builder, with a vast array of tools, can build it efficiently. The master coach has to play both of these roles to get the most out of any client. You must see what can be created, but you also must have all the tools in the bag to be able to get the job done. Every client is different and every client might need a unique application of tools to get it done over time.

Single-methodology people limit their businesses to the client who can benefit from that exact process. Master coaches spend careers mastering many different tools to always have the right tool for the right client at the right time.

Number Three—If it hurts you, why do you think it won't hurt them?

If you are hurt and beat up from your own workouts, what are you doing to your clients? There is nothing more pathetic than a coach who is constantly in pain and beaten up from workouts applying this same brilliant approach to clients.

Many young coaches believe that constantly being dinged in that six-Advil-a-day pain range and held together with tape is a status thing: "Yeah, been pushing it hard lately and going for another PR this week." This is nothing to brag about, but rather is a negative statement on your IQ and mental stability.

If your approach to fitness is keeping you constantly fighting pain, what do you think you are doing to your clients, who believe every word you utter but who have much less base conditioning, technique, and experience?

Maybe you are the problem, not the solution you believe yourself to be. Maybe your technique, choice of exercises, ability to push through pain, and overall willingness to destroy your body in the name of fitness is a wrong approach that is killing you and hurting the very people who trusted you with their fitness.

Number Four—Never lose your integrity.

It takes a lifetime to create an image of integrity, but only a few brief moments to kill it.

Integrity is who you believe yourself to be. You create your own code based on your personal values, and then live by that code. Coaches need to be honest to the extent of obsession, respectful of others, including yourself, your family, and especially those who pay you for your help and guidance. They are willing to help when others can't or won't, and especially are willing to never do anything to a client for the mere sake of trying to make a little money selling something they don't need and only bought because you told them to buy it.

You can never be a master coach without integrity, nor can you ever be a good human being without integrity. Integrity is a bond of trust stating you will do what you promised and that the other person will not get hurt in the process. This applies to clients, of course, but also to your life in general. Do what you say you will do, when you promise to do it, and make sure you do no harm in the process, and you are on your way to discovering the integrity within your soul.

Number Five—Professionalism is the separator between the good and the great.

Everything matters. How you dress, how you speak, what time you show up, how prepared you are for a client, how you follow up, how you do not ever talk about other clients, how you shake hands, how you charge, how you protect yourself by never making a deal with a client you wouldn't give every client, and how you value your team are just a few small parts of what it takes to be a true professional.

There is usually an aura around those you respect, those from whom you want to learn and emulate in life. The aura you sense is a shield of professionalism that is never compromised or let down. If you are a professional coach, you live it every day.

Being the best-dressed coach in the room, the best spoken, the most prepared, and the one who is the most put-together compared against every other coach is a huge edge as you build your career. You can be the most educated person in the room and be neglected, or you can be the one who is educated wrapped in professionalism and be a guru to others in your field.

Number Six—I would rather go broke and die on the street than scam a client.

There is a time in the career of every coach when you will consider taking advantage of a client, even if it is only for a few seconds. You could be broke, desperate for money, or simply be with a guy who spends more than you make and find yourself looking for the easy money.

You tell yourself, "Hey, just once, and besides, this client has so much money, who will care?" Once you have talked yourself out of your integrity, you now find yourself trying to do some outrageous cash deal with a client to pay your rent. Worse, you enter the world of multi-level marketing and are now advocating products your clients don't need and you don't even believe in, all because you can see yourself making some easy money.

When you cross that line, it is nearly impossible to come back to the light. Once integrity is sold, there is almost no way to buy it back. If you want to make a living as a professional coach, swear to yourself that you would rather go broke and die on the street than ever scam a client.

Number Seven—You are not a role model; you are a professional coach.

Your physical perfection is not why the client comes, and is definitely not why the client might stay with you. The client trusts you because he believes you are the one who can get the desired results.

Wait, you say, the client trusted me in the beginning because he thought my almost-naked selfies and videos lifting heavy stuff with my exertion face proved I am a stud. The client knew if I can get myself into this kind of shape, just think what I can do for him.

If you ever said this to yourself, and you actually believe your own bullshit here, you are too stupid to be a professional coach and should move back to your mother's basement and go back to being the biggest stud who ever worked for Starbucks, because this is not why 99 percent of your clients chose you.

Professional coaches are chosen because they have the skill set, reputation, and experience to get results. Any drunken monkey with a one-day certification can take 20 people through a workout and only kill two or three, but it takes a professional coach with years of experience to get the maximum results from the maximum number of clients over time.

Getting this done is not about how you look, but what you know. Despite the misguided belief that every coach has to be a specimen suited for framing at a local art gallery, coaches come in all shapes and sizes, and yes, many of these fine coaches are considered works in progress, chasing their fitness goals and wrestling with their own fitness demons.

All of your ego-induced social media posts might actually be the very things keeping serious adult clients out of your gym. Your need to be in every ad without a shirt, every video in a workout bra, and every group shot flexed might be more of a personal issue you need to deal with, rather than ways to help you create a financially successful training business.

None of this will last. You will not be perfect forever, and if you base your business on a perfect day on your 30th birthday, what do you do for a living when you are 40 and not so perfect? Being a perfect specimen doesn't last, but being a professional coach can feed you until you die.

Replace "you" in all of your social media with clients who have succeeded because of your caring and helpful guidance. Your potential clients care much more about how you can help them meet their goals than they ever do about how you look without a shirt.

Number Eight—It is never about you; it is always about them.

You push clients too hard and for too long, because you apply your personal standard of fitness to them. Your goals and vision for your clients may be the thing that will drive them out of your gym, and maybe hurt them as well.

This is not about you and what you want. Professional coaching is about them and what they need to be successful. Your clients might only want to move and feel better and not give a damn about their weight, although you know that is what is hurting them. You can guide and suggest, but when you push, you lose them forever. They are moving; they are happy dropping in once or twice a week and that is enough.

The side note here is that as purists, you drive your clients crazy, and probably your family too. There is nothing worse in life than a Paleo freak at a holiday dinner yelling at poor Aunt Edna because she stuffed a giant biscuit covered in butter in her mouth and washed it down with beer.

Living pure is your choice. Expecting your clients to live up to your idea of a perfect fitness life will not work very well in the business world. Yes, there will always be a posse who will follow you because of your intensity and purism, especially for those who own single-methodology businesses. But will 25 hardcore clients be enough to support your career over time?

Your clients have different goals, lives, and time commitments. While you could create the perfect fitness life for them if they would only listen, most just want to slowly venture down the fitness path of life, maybe stop and drink a beer along the way, and occasionally stop for a biscuit. They don't have the same deep belief you do...and all of that is okay, because at least they are with you and moving forward and that is enough.

Number Nine—One-dimensional coaches fail over time.

Coaching isn't enough. If you want to be successful, you have to force yourself to be good at all aspects of professional coaching.

- Have you mastered marketing and branding?

- Can you handle your own social media, and then teach someone else how to do it for you? "Successful" is defined as social media that brings in enough new clients every month to create a financially successful business.

- Do you understand money? Do you save and invest? Can you run the financial side of a growing business?

- Do you understand staffing and can you hire and create a team to grow your business?

- Have you learned to present your ideas in public or speak in front of groups to grow your business?

- Have you ever had anyone look at your professional image and help package you as a professional?

- Have you learned about negotiating professional contracts that might affect the jobs or endorsement opportunities you may have in the future?

- Have you learned to network and surround yourself with a team who can help you and your career grow over time?

Being a professional coach isn't just about learning to train people. Being a professional coach is about becoming a well-rounded person, able to create and manage a career that could span your entire life.

Number Ten—You can help more people with a million dollars in the bank than $12.92.

It is never about the money...until it is. It is easy to say you are not in it for the money and be that reverse snob where your poverty is a badge of honor, but then a kid gets sick, you get married and look for a house, or your parents age and need some help. Then it is about the money and what little you earned or saved.

Money only has one purpose and that is freedom. Money lets you work where you want to work, leave when you don't want to be there any longer, live where you are happy, help people who need your help, and allows you to live your life on your own terms without being held hostage by someone who controls your cash flow.

Chasing money is not important, but the process of chasing money is important in life. The difference is, you will build a more successful career, a more financially successful business, and enjoy a sense of freedom and peace missing in coaches who live check to check. Make creating money part of your life's work.

We create money to take care of our families. We create money to allow us to say no to stupidity that makes us unhappy. Most importantly, making money validates your talent in many ways, because making money proves you were right: You are a professional coach and people are willing to pay you for your help and guidance.

You can be happy and poor, and you can be a simple monk and change the world. However, most people who desire to live as a professional coach will find they can help a lot more people with a few dollars in the bank than they can while broke and barely surviving to the next payday.

There will also be a day when you might not be able to do what you do any longer. You might become injured, burned out, or simply have had enough and want to move on in life. Money is your way out. Money is your way to turn 50 and say, "I have had enough of this and want to go back to college and maybe teach for a few years."

The hardest conversation in the consulting life is telling a person over 50 that the few thousand dollars he has saved isn't enough and that he will have to work every day until he dies. Money isn't made as a status; the biggest houses, newest cars, and most gadgets isn't what you are chasing. You are pursuing the freedom that only comes from having enough money to live life on your terms.

Number Eleven—You did not get to be you without a hand up from somebody.

You are you because somewhere, at some time in your life, somebody gave you a hand up. There are no self-made people, only those who have forgotten where they came from and who helped them in life.

Remember who helped you and say thanks. Make sure to help others who are further down the ladder than you are. You are who you are because someone cared…and now it is your turn to care for others.

Number Twelve—Hire someone to coach you to break out of your comfort zone.

You have been training for 20 years and think you know it all? Hire a coach you respect and get coached for a week. You need to force yourself out of your comfort zone, but most importantly, you need to be reminded there are other ways to get results. What you know is not what everyone else knows and maybe, just maybe, you might learn something new.

The same thing is true in life. When you think you know it all is the day you should hire someone to ask the hard questions in life, everything from money and family to personal goals and retirement. Often asking for help when we think we have it all figured out gets us to the point where we remember we don't even know all the questions. Fresh eyes can help us leap years ahead of our slow and self-dictated pace.

Number Thirteen—Knowing when to say "no" is the sign of coaching maturity.

One of the best days you will ever have as a professional coach is when you look at a client and say, "I don't think I can help you, but I can refer you to someone who can."

That is the day you have arrived as a professional coach, because that is the day you stopped faking it and finally stopped forcing a client into what you know. You admitted there are clients who don't fit your skill set and the best answer is, "No, I am not the one for this job."

Young coaches too often force every client into a box, even if the client doesn't fit their training model, or worse, has medical concerns they shouldn't even touch. "Hey, this is what I know and if I throw you into the box I will force something to fit you somehow." This approach is sort of like a guy buying a shirt and the clerk says, "It looks fine; we can make it work. You look amazing," when the shirt is a 3XL and the guy wears a medium. I have the shirt for sale and it is the only one I have, and you will buy it now.

Knowing when to walk away is a sign of maturity. Knowing who to refer out to is a sign of a professional coach. You do not need to be right every time, nor do you need to know how to train every client. A professional coach needs to know who can get it done; sometimes the best advice you can give a client is to go somewhere else.

Number Fourteen—How are you different than every other coach?

Generalists eat last; specialists own the future.

The future of coaching belongs to specialists who focus on narrower populations and then master that area. For example, you might focus on:

- Fitness after 50

- Women after 40

- Severely obese

- Junior golfers

- Stressed-out female executives

- Guys over 50 with fitness and hormonal issues

- Movement analysis and correction at a corporate facility

- Male executives who are in the 40s and later

This is a partial list of specializations a coach could make a living and a career mastering. There is truth in many of the old adages, such as *Find something you love and learn more about it than any other person and you will always make a lot of money.*

The age of the generalist coach is fading and the one-size-fits-all approach that worked so well 20 years ago is dead today. People want to work with coaches who understand them physically, but also mentally as well. Someone specializing in stressed-out female executives would not only have to know how to train those women, but know what they think, understand what are they going through at this age, know their special nutritional issues, how they learn, and what they really want in life and from their fitness.

Generalists eat last for a reason these days: The specialists in coaching have driven them away from the table.

Number Fifteen—You have to earn the right to be called a master coach.

There is nothing funnier than a coach with two years of experience. He has an entry-level certification, 12 clients, a one-day wonder certification stating "You are now the man," and who is still working for $10 an hour at a mainstream fitness chain and calling himself a master coach.

You have to earn being a master coach. You have to pay your dues over time. You have to take the beating through the years that molds you into a coach who has seen it all and who has practiced the craft with discipline through those long years.

What does it take to be a true master coach?

- You have to have done at least 10,000 hours of sessions with every type of conceivable client.

- You have to have a strong entry-level certification, a movement-based certification, and advanced nutritional certifications and training. Couple these with a never-ending string of new skill certs, such as kettlebells, the Olympic lifts, or sandbags that are added every year as new tools are introduced into the market.

- At least 30 hours of education a year should be garnered through attendance at major coaching events, such as the Perform Better Summits.

- The willingness to at least once every two years admit that everything you learned until then might be out of date and that you need to reinvent yourself one more time.

There is no certification for a master coach, but there is that moment when your peers come to you for help and guidance. Then you will know you have arrived at the point when what you know and who you are is respected by others in the industry. Until then, keep your head down and just keep working.

The driving force behind all of this, of course, is the premise that if you do not grow each year, you will wither and die early in your career.

Coaching is not only about making change; coaching is about accepting change and knowing what you knew even a few years ago might be considered out of date and something the industry has moved past.

Grow or die should be your motto if you want a career that lasts and is respected by others. If you put in the years, one by one, one day you might become the master coach the two-year wonder child already thinks he is.

Number Sixteen—You will not be successful until you know what it means to be you.

What do you want from your experience of being a professional coach? Ten years from now, what will you answer if you are sitting in a bar and someone asks you, "So you have been a professional coach your entire life. What did it mean to be you?"

You can't reach the upper levels of success if you don't know what you are trying to accomplish in your career. Ask yourself these questions:

What professional mileposts have you set for yourself? Speak at a major conference? Own a training gym that does a million dollars a year? Get an advanced degree? Create an online training empire?

The problem isn't that you don't know what you are trying to accomplish, the problem is that you don't dream big enough. Create a list of milestones that stretch out for years and dream big. Give yourself permission to chase your real dreams, not those watered-down statements you share with your drunken friends over too many beers.

There are other questions that will also matter when you come to the end of your career. Did you make a difference in the fitness world? Did you leave the field a better place because you were in it? Did you help others and help get a generation of young coaches on the right path because you gave a damn?

What will it have meant to have been you?

Every coach who ever amounted to anything could answer this question.

Number Seventeen—You change lives.

If you want to be a respected coach, remember this: You exist to change lives!

Changing lives is your purpose in life. If you are a true professional, this is why you were born—to make a difference and to change the lives around you.

If changing lives isn't your thing, you will have a difficult time reaching an upper level of coaching.

All the great ones make the world around them a better place every single day they are alive. If you think everything written in these last few sentences is something found steaming in a pile under a bull, you will not make it as a master-level professional coach.

Changing lives is what you do. Changing lives is what professional coaching is all about. You are either in or you are out. If you aren't driven to change the world, it will be a very short and boring career before you leave to find work that might be important, but that will seldom have the impact on as many people as being a professional coach.

NAPA VALLEY
Sunrise balloon ride following in the chase balloon

THERE WILL BE A DAY

THERE WILL BE A DAY

There will be a day when you reach your personal peak physically. That single day, you will be the best you ever were and, most distressingly, the best you will ever be.

After that, many of you will waste your lives trying to recapture that brief moment, where for a short period, you had it all.

One of the big mistakes people make is training clients compared with who they used to be instead of dealing with their current reality.

Think of the 40-year-old woman who used to be the athlete—an attractive woman, physically gifted, and who is now aging gracefully by our standards. In her personal dreams, she is always frustrated and struggling, because no matter how hard she works, starves, overtrains, and complains to her coach, there is nothing you can do to turn back time.

The same is true, and maybe more so, with the man in his 30s or 40s who used to be an athlete. He will never be satisfied with his training or with his coach because he is constantly competing against a younger self, a battle he cannot win.

How many injuries happen when a guy in his 50s pushes his body to keep up with a group of people in their 20s and 30s? How many people quit trying or blame their coaches for a failure that never had a chance to be a success, because who they were is who they will never be again.

The greatest gift you can give your clients is to help them accept who they are today, and to train them to the highest level of success their current bodies can achieve. To do this, you have to be wise enough to understand that the standards they are secretly holding themselves to—as well as holding you to and that you aren't even aware of—are standards impossible for any coach without a time machine to achieve.

You will never know when "the day" was until you get years beyond it, but chasing your past is like chasing shadows in a dream.

We all used to be somebody, but it is more important to be the best version of who we are today and let the past stay in those sweet remembrances of the day we had it all.

THERE IS NO SKILL SET IN DYING

In fact, we are all not just good at dying, we are perfect at it in the end.

What so few of us master is the art of living.

Living life with intensity every single day.
Living life, doing only the things we love and value. Changing the world around us and leaving our small bit of the world a better place for having been there.

This is the art in life, and where the hard work of living gets done.

According to surveys, fewer than five percent of the people in the United States do work they love.

The rest go through the motions and waste life, quietly frustrated and fading away every day.

Most of you reading this have discovered the rare art of living fully in your own lives, and chase your dreams each day with a smile on your faces.

If you aren't busy living hard, you might be part of the endless line passing through quietly and who leave without a sound.

THERE ARE A LOT OF THINGS I CARE FOR IN LIFE

There are a lot of things I care for in life, but what you think of me isn't one of them.

Hard enough to live my own life without also caring about what others think I should do or how I should feel about something.

I do care about doing the right thing,
and maybe making the world around me a little better each day.

I don't give a damn about mean, petty people, the takers in life,
who spend their lives living off others.

I do care about giving a hand up to those who have the talent and ability to rise above others, and the courage to realize that living up to their talents can be a lonely but fulfilling path.

I don't care about anyone who doesn't try. Regret that you could have been someone if you would have only tried is a personal collapse and should be suffered alone. Those who try and fail at levels above where others refuse to even attempt earn my respect.

I care about people who chase a healthy life, even when they stumble and remain forever a work in progress. I have no respect for anyone who by choice gives up on health, the most precious gift in a life well lived.

I do care about those in the coaching profession. I respect that what you do appears so simple from the outside, yet is so difficult a way to make a living once you cross the line to the inside.

I can't stand anyone who criticizes a young coach, who while maybe not yet making a lot of money, is willing to dedicate a career to changing the lives of others. The person who criticizes has probably never attempted to chase his dreams, but is now willing to kill yours.

There isn't a lot I worry about in life, but the one thing I wish you would learn is that your life is your journey. You should never spend even a second worrying about what anyone thinks of who you are, how you live, and who you want to be in life.

Care about what is important in life— your family, friends, your dreams—but the rest can head off to hell in a little red wagon, because there isn't much else that is important.

THE PROFESSIONAL COACHES'
CODE OF RESPONSIBILITY

Number One—Always the professional in dress, respect for my clients and fellow coaches, and in my preparation for my clients. I will never bad mouth or talk about any client or coach. I will show respect, even if I don't agree with a position or beliefs.

Number Two—Never on time, always early. I will respect my client's time and commitment to me by always being there early and ready to go.

Number Three—I understand the client had a choice and could have picked another coach. I am grateful and respectful of every dollar paid by every client.

Number Four—I will remember it is about the client and what is needed, and not about me and what I want. The client's goals and standards of success may not be mine, but I will always honor the path.

Number Five—I will work the client to a challenge, but never to failure or pain. I must keep every client safe and healthy.

Number Six—I will never discriminate by race, age, sexual orientation, or weight. Every client deserves the best I have every day.

Number Seven—My most important goal is to increase the client's quality of life and movement.

Number Eight—It is my responsibility, and mine alone, to stay current in my field and to annually update my skills.

Number Nine—I must retain a professional relationship with all clients at all times. I will always ask myself if this is good for my client, or am I doing this because it is good for me?

Number Ten—Charging what I am worth is a direct reflection of who I am and the professionalism I bring to this relationship.

Number Eleven—I understand coaches exist for only one purpose: We are here to change lives.

Number Twelve—My goal today, and every day as long as I am in this career, is to become the top coach at what I do.

I will do the work necessary to reach that goal.

MAYBE YOU SHOULDN'T OWN YOUR OWN BUSINESS

Do you have the killer instinct, the ability to drive a business to success?

Do you know how to make money when others can't?

Can you set goals and then make them happen, even in the toughest months?

Are you coachable?

Are you afraid of money?

Are you willing to charge what you are worth in your market?

Do you have a good work ethic?

Are you willing to work 60 hours or more a week doing what is necessary to make sure your business stays alive?

Are you willing to master all the components of the business beyond merely training?

Do you understand you can't just hire people to do the work and believe you are in business?

Can you sell, ask for money, follow up, and add new business every month?

Are you willing to do the work and master all the jobs in your business, and then lead and teach others to do those tasks?

Do you believe no one can do it better than you and you have to do it all, or can you build a team who follow what you believe, allowing you to run your business instead of being trapped in it?

Do you ask questions and learn from people who have gone before you doing the same thing, and then actually do what you learn, or are you the type of person who has to do it your own way although you have never made a dollar?

Do you believe business is a series of processes and systems that take hard work to implement, or do you believe if you waste enough money listening to everyone in a dozen different mentorships, somewhere someone will teach you the special "magic" that is the secret to making money without working?

Do you work like an owner, or do you still act and think like an employee in your own company?

Most small business people, especially in the gym world, end up buying themselves miserable, low-paying jobs in their own businesses. They refuse to learn how to make money; they never lose the employee mindset.

I AM TIRED OF PERFECT PEOPLE

I am weary of friends who suffer because they could never live up to their loved one's perfect ideals, people who themselves are as flawed and damaged as the rest of us.

I am angry at the parents who ruin sports for children because they expect a 10-year-old kid to be perfect every game, every time, pushing the child to achieve something the parent never came close to achieving.

I am done with coaches who are genetic freaks, who open gyms and try to convince their clients that their methodology is for anyone, and then hurting almost everyone they touch.

I am sad when I sit with someone who cries because she feels like a failure who could never live up to her own standard of perfection, nor could anyone else in her life.

I border on hate for people who impose perfection on their spouses, their children, their parents, and friends, yet live life as a mediocre failure at everything they do.

I preach against women who fail in the gym trying to be 21 at age 44, chasing an impossible standard of fitness perfection few ever achieve once in life, let alone as a mother, a wife, a career-driven woman, and someone who has a life that matters.

I wonder at careers lost because of athletes who drive themselves to a level of perfection that requires the total destruction of their bodies.

I work every single day to help people understand that they will fail, they will succeed, they will struggle, and there will be days when they absolutely screw up so badly the world is amazed. All of that is part of being human—get over it.

There is no perfection in life.
There is no perfect you.

There is only a wonderful human being who is flawed like the rest of us.

You can benefit from understanding that being the best you can be is all there is; there is no perfect in any of us, no matter what anyone else tells you.

Taking life as far as you can go is all that matters.

The only standard of excellence you should ever listen to is the one you set for yourself.

WIMBLEDON, COURT ONE
Roger winning yet again